# Farewell Fugley Island

Changing my life on Britain's most
inaccessible inhabited island

# Farewell Fugley Island

First published by The Shetland Times Ltd., 2022.
ISBN 978-1-910997-50-5

A catalogue record for this book is available from the British Library.
British Library Cataloguing-in-Publication Data

Printed and published by
The Shetland Times Ltd.,
Gremista, Lerwick,
Shetland ZE1 0PX.

# Contents

# Prologue

Simon and I were fortunate to be living in Foula (pronounced Foola) when we were able to experience the last vestiges of the traditional culture on Britain's most inaccessibly inhabited island. Its unique situation and the inhabitants' outlook were to influence my future, changing the path of my life as I enjoyed, and adapted to its physical constraints.

Born in the 1890s, the oldest inhabitants could remember their parents' struggle and stories from the generation before them. They had experienced the population diminish from 260 to only 28, and witnessed the remnants of an inherently dangerous and unique way of life.

Everything was impressive on this magnificent 3½-miles long by 2½-miles wide island with the second-highest vertical sea cliff in Britain, where the rocky ledges provided homes to hundreds of thousands of birds. The islanders traditionally relied on the birds for part of their survival, climbing the sheer rock faces to obtain eggs and fowls to eat and sell. It was said of the Foula men in the 1800s that: 'his grandfather went before, then his father went before, and he must expect to go over the cliffs where he would fall to his death as so many Foula men had before him.'

In previous centuries they had experienced difficult times providing food for themselves; on occasions requiring special help when the weather prevented their boat from bringing in stores, but they had always managed. As the population shrank the agricultural work became more challenging, and with a rapidly declining fishing industry, the already limited opportunities on the island diminished. By the time we arrived it had faced a spiral of decline, projects requiring co-operation no longer had the numbers, there was no adequate shelter for boats, and the lack of young people made even crewing small boats difficult.

The ability to survive now required a multitude of different jobs, some depending on the vagaries of the weather. But even with an improved mailboat service and the construction of a gravel airstrip, the limited access to and from the island remained a significant factor for any type of employment or small business, as well as threatening the viability of the small school, and health service.

The younger generation was changing, often struggling to find time among their work to look after their own parents, let alone other elderly islanders who no longer had close relations on the island. Unable to survive the way their forebears had, and with the four children at primary school inter-related, there was concern about the future as the islanders could no longer take a partner from within the island.

They rarely complained about the housing standards that were well below those experienced on the mainland; no mains water, electricity or sewage – factors that would handicap future generations in attracting partners from elsewhere. As if that was not enough, a few months before we arrived two marriages had broken, causing turbulence, the departure of two people, and a third unsure of where his future lay.

I was lucky to make my living by diving. That had taken me and my working partner, Simon, to 11 other islands and numerous shipwrecks. Simon, aged 27, had trained as a journalist before becoming a diver, and I, now 25, had studied agriculture before training as a commercial diver. We had both been diving for only three years and had chosen islands for their inaccessibility to most divers, leaving us numerous untouched wrecks.

Islands near shipping routes had attracted wrecks over the centuries. Fair Isle, where we had been working before Foula, had over 80 known shipwrecks on an island that was only three miles long by 1½ miles wide.

We also became involved in unpaid work on archaeological wrecks such as the *Adelaar* on the isle of Barra – a Dutch East India ship of 1728 that had been carrying bullion – and the *El Gran Griffon*, an Armada ship that had been wrecked on Fair Isle. At times we also dived for the pleasure of it on ships like the *Politician* that the *Whisky Galore* film was based on. Like the islanders, we also recovered whisky from her.

When based in Fair Isle we learned of the wreck of the *Oceanic*. At one time the largest ship in the world, she had sailed the Atlantic as a luxurious passenger ship before being commandeered at the start of the First World War only to run onto a submerged reef off the island of Foula while patrolling the wild waters to the north of Scotland.

Our work in Fair Isle had been carried out by the two of us diving from a 13½-foot rubber inflatable to explore and recover parts of heavily corroded ships that had already been broken up by the heavy seas that continually pounded them against the rocky seabed. When we became successful in Foula we purchased a fishing boat to increase our capability and transport our stores and equipment to the island, and an islander became part of our team. The work could be dangerous; I was flown out twice by air ambulance for life-threatening injuries but after I returned to the island to recover it gave me new opportunities to explore and enjoy the community.

Islands and their inhabitants had already influenced my life, but living in Foula I could feel my life being absorbed into the island as I watched the gradual loss of traditional livelihoods with irreversible changes to the island culture, often to the anguish of those who wished to remain. The time lag between Foula and the rest of the country was beginning to widen but everyone hoped the island would retain its unique flavour due to its spectacular wild life, although its remoteness continued to make it inaccessible for weeks or months during winter storms. I had never lived in or visited a place as impressive and interesting as the island of Foula.

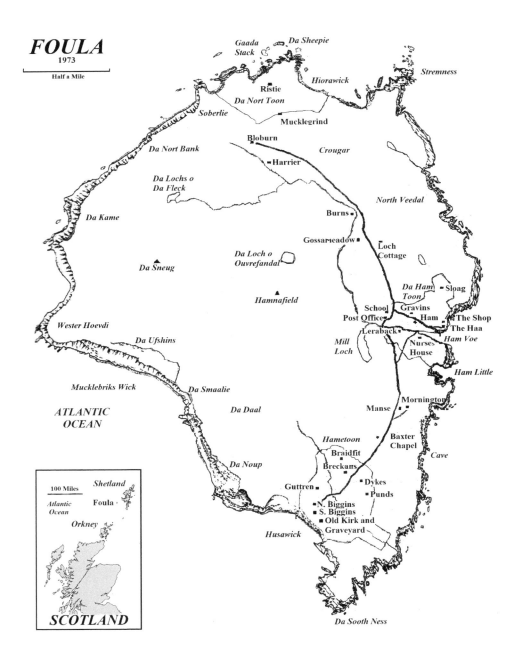

Map of Foula by Alec Crawford

# Chapter 1
# Our Home at the Haa

Although our personal possessions could be fitted into a couple of kitbags, the equipment for our work made it sensible to charter the Fair Isle mailboat, *Good Shepherd III*, to take us to Foula. The six-hour trip passed quickly on a calm sea and I became excited and slightly nervous as we approached the island. A few weeks earlier I had been on a brief recce to find accommodation, and was now concerned that Simon, my business partner, might be unhappy with my decision, although with only one available house it was *Hobson's choice*. On approaching the entrance to Ham Voe, a small inlet where the pier lay, I nervously pointed out the building.

'What d'you think? It's called the Haa.' My heart beat faster with the excitement of seeing it again – I liked it.

'Not what I expected,' he replied, 'but it looks OK.'

'It's the best I could get.' I had only been on the island for a few hours, and not being aware of anything else I had taken an immediate affection to the Haa, but was unable to see inside other than through the windows; there could be a surprise for me as well. It was important that Simon would be happy working here, as he'd originally taken some persuading to come to Foula, although was now enthusiastic.

'I'm sure it'll be alright,' he reassured me.

The *Good Shepherd* cautiously nosed its way into the entrance of the voe. Everyone stared at the house – a square block, possibly the start of a tower, had been built on the east side of the original building in the place for a porch – it looked baronial and unfinished, like a house with an identity confusion, seeking grandness but ending up looking odd. I wondered if this reflected the people living on the island. I knew little about them. They would soon see we were wanderers searching for our fortune, but this island living was not new to us.

I had always felt happy to put my roots down in every place I had been, and we had only moved on because our work in Fair Isle had run out. I loved the

Approaching Foula                                                                 *Lesley Timings*

excitement of landing and working on another island, always looking forward to walking round, meeting the inhabitants and, on many occasions, envying their way of life.

When we tied up at the pier Elizabeth was there to meet us. She had arranged with the landlord for us to rent the house. 'I've lit the fire boys,' she said. 'Come on up when you're ready an' I'll show you round.'

'Thanks,' I replied, from the deck of the boat.

She picked up one of our small bags that had been thrown onto the pier, taking it up to the house with her. I could see Simon's eyes following her, then he lifted his head to get a better look at the house. Other islanders stood on the pier asking if they could help.

After all our equipment was deposited on the pier we walked up the mailboat slipway towards the Haa, passing a small, concrete winch shed, before I sensed the magical reek of peat, and looked up to see the smoke weaving its way out of a chimney pot. Happy memories of working in the Outer Hebrides flooded back. I felt myself smile, and any doubts about being in Foula vanished with the smoke.

**The Haa is the nearest house to the pier** *Lesley Timings*

Elizabeth met us at the door. 'Come away in boys, come away in,' she repeated, as we followed her into the back porch. A damp, unlived-in smell pervaded the dark, flag-stoned passage leading to the living room. It was not unpleasant but typical of an uninhabited building, and I was sure it would disappear after a few days, but it reinforced my feelings of entering an old, interesting property.

Casually glancing back at Simon, I remained concerned about his reaction. Had I made the wrong decision? But I could see he was relaxed, unfazed by anything, as he concentrated on using the bottom of his jersey to clean his spectacles – the lenses were so scratched he often referred to them as being like "lavatory windows".

We passed the bottom of the stairs before turning right and entering a large sitting room that looked as though it had come from the previous century.

'Well, there you are boys,' Elizabeth said, moving to one side to let us pass as she ushered us in. I could sense that she hoped we'd be pleased. With only two small windows to let the light in, the peat fire threw moving shadows in the darkness behind the furniture, obscuring the walls until my eyes adjusted after the brightness outside.

Closing the panelled door to keep the heat in, I instinctively reached for the light switch only to remember the house had no electricity. Realising I had not over-egged the pudding when describing the Haa to Simon, I relaxed as I saw his happy look of unconcern. I loved the house, its age, its position, the ancient feel of it; we were incredibly lucky to have such a convenient place to stay. The old furniture matched the room's aura, and the fire threw out warmth with its burst of light lending it real character, just like the island. Already it felt like a home.

As my eyes acclimatised I noticed the dark varnish on the wood-panelled ceiling, and similar woodwork reached half-way up the wall where it was topped by a dado rail. Above it was a canvas-type material, bulging in places where the plaster behind it had crumbled. Painted with old-fashioned white wash – a mixture of salt and hydrated lime – it looked yellow in places where it was dulled by years of damp and peat smoke.

From the east window the sea melted into the horizon, above which, like a faint pencil sketch, was the rugged mainland of Shetland about 27 miles away.

Turning back to the room, I walked across to the window on the south side to stand beside Simon. This window was set into a three-foot thick gable-end; larger than the other it faced towards the pier. The small panes of glass were set in a fussy frame that restricted the light. I could imagine a child curled up on the window ledge, comfortable and warm while reading a book on a wet and windy day.

Next to the window was the open fire, the scorched stone at either side having been eroded by years of use. Above the fireplace was an oil painting, blackened by smoke. I moved towards it to see if I could make it out.

'It's the nort o' the island,' Elizabeth said. I thought I could make out the coast line.

From above the fire gas pipes led to an old, mantled lamp on the ceiling. I reached up to the low, dark ceiling and ran my fingers along the pipes; they felt loose to touch, the mantle damaged and unusable. Elizabeth watched my movements. 'You'll need to use a Tilley lamp. It should be in the kitchen. Mind, if it's not there, I can lend thee one o' mine.'

'Thanks, but we've brought one,' replied Simon, as he bent down and felt the seat of the mock-leather settee on which patches had been glued.

I looked at the woollen carpet that covered much of the floor. Small holes, tears and damp patches were obvious, but the chair and matching settee had been deliberately placed to obscure the worst of them. The wood floor visible around the extremities of the carpet looked solid, but was stained with the occasional white mark of damp. In the centre of the room was a table with several wheel-back chairs and a book case and chest of drawers lay against one wall. In the darkest corner was a small table with three drawers.

'Are there many of the laird's bits in the house?' I asked.

'Na, a few books and the like, anything else would be ruined wi' the damp. I'll show thee the kitchen,' Elizabeth turned to go out.

The kitchen had a concrete floor and the bare stone walls felt cold to touch. A substantial wooden table dominated the centre of the room that also had an old gas stove near the sink that lay beneath a window. Simon tried one of the taps but no water came out.

'The water comes off the roof, but the outside tank's rusted through. It'll maybe fix but I've plenty water if you need it.'

Simon looked at an old container of Ajax; the perforated metal top was covered with a thin film of rust. 'Is there a shop on the island?' he asked.

'Na, it's closing, there's little in it. You'd be better to order frae Walls (pronounced Waas) on the Shetland mainland. They'll send a cardboard box with your messages (groceries) on the mailboat.'

'The house is fine,' said Simon, as if to reassure her, or perhaps me, as we walked out into the sunlight.

'Mind, if you're needin' anything, come up to my croft at Ham, you know where it is,' was her parting comment as she directed a nod towards me.

We returned to the sitting room. Simon moved towards the fire and sat on the settee trying it out for comfort. 'You've done well, Alec. It's ideal and being so close to the pier it's handy.'

'It feels a bit damp, but a few days with the peat fire and I'm sure it'll dry out,' I said.

Considering we had been living in a single room in a wooden hut in Fair Isle this was a big change, but the hut did have running water and an electric light,

The *Oceanic* built in 1899 as the largest ship in the world was lost two and a half miles east of the island.

although only for a few hours each evening.

'Is there much peat available?' asked Simon.

'There's some in the old stone shed outside. If we're here for long we'll have to find out how to get some more, or order coal from the mainland. I'm sure Elizabeth will help us arrange anything we need.'

'Has she a husband?' queried Simon.

'I don't think so. There's an old lady called Joann (pronounced Joanne) who lives with her.'

'It would be useful to know something about our landlords, don't suppose anyone's said anything?'

'No, just what I've told you, but that's hearsay. We'll ask Elizabeth when we get the chance.'

Like Simon, I was curious about the concept of one person owning an island, it made me think of a would-be-politician who amused me when he asked the question, 'Why was there only one Monopolies Commission?' Fair Isle was owned by the National Trust, which seemed simple, but we were both

**Simon and Alec working on the diving compressor.** *Alison McLeay*

curious about islands, how ownership affected the islanders, if at all, and how it might affect us. Could they throw us off if they didn't want us here? I had been reluctant to ask Elizabeth for more details when I first met her, and now we had been helped by the owners in getting the use of the Haa it seemed ungrateful and intrusive to enquire too deeply about them – at this stage.

Taking our bags up the wooden stairs we looked at the bedrooms. All the walls and ceilings were lined with bare, unpainted wood; there were a few signs of previous leaks from the roof in the form of white, gritty marks between the wall and the ceiling where salt brought in with the rain had crystallised. I hoped they'd been repaired. Simon took the bedroom on the south side, above the sitting room; I settled for the one at the other end of the house, its single window looking out to sea. Between our bedrooms was a smaller room with two beds, ideal for anyone who wanted to come and stay.

When we returned to the sitting room I looked around and thought, 'This is to be my home, whether for weeks or years I don't know but, right now, I hope it's for a long time.'

Simon went over and rummaged in a drawer, shifting its contents to the one

Elizabeth.                                                                                              *Simon Martin*

below to clear it out before putting his camera and film in it. He found a small, black purse with a hand-written note inside; it read, *This is the purse I had with me when the Lusitania sank.*

'Typical Holbourn,' Simon said, 'he'd not leave his purse behind,' – it was well known the landowner's family were cautious with their money.

When we later asked Elizabeth about the purse, she explained Professor Holbourn had been on the *Lusitania* when the liner was on her way from New York to Liverpool in 1915. She had sunk after being torpedoed off the south coast of Ireland, resulting in a loss of 1,198 people. Only 761 had survived, including a 12-year-old girl called Avis, whom he had saved. She had been sitting down to lunch when the torpedo struck and the *Lusitania* suddenly listed. The professor, at a table 20 feet from Avis, put on her lifebelt and placed her in one of the boats but, as it was being lowered, two men attempted to jump into it from the deck and the boat capsized. Avis swam clear towards a raft where she was pulled aboard, before she was rescued by another boat and taken to land. On the way to England the professor took care of Avis until they

From the right, Ham croft, Gravins, the schoolhouse and Mogul with the post office and telephone box.

met with his wife, Marion, who accompanied her to Avis's grandparents in Worcester. They remained in contact throughout their lives and Avis was still alive when we moved into the Haa; her eerie, smoke-darkened portrait hanging on one of the sitting room walls.

After we had carried the rest of our gear into the house, Simon walked up to Elizabeth's croft – called Ham – with a water container, while I traced the pipe back from the tap to find where it went through the wall and connected to the corroded tank outside. That would be our first job; we needed a water supply, even if it came off the roof. On Simon's return we perched our cast-iron kettle on the open fire, sitting in silence, enjoying the heat and light from the flames of the burning peat as we waited for the water to boil.

Filling up our Tilley lamp with paraffin, I fitted a new silk mantle. Pumping up the pressure, I lit the methylated spirit to heat the vaporiser and opened the valve, allowing the pressurised paraffin to cough and splutter from its narrow orifice before it settled to a steady, hissing flame as the paraffin vapour burnt on the mantle. (Although we had a wick lamp as backup, it was rarely used. The light it gave was poor in comparison, only sufficient for one person to work, whereas the glow from the Tilley would light the whole room and we found it was the light of choice among the islanders.)

Simon chose some canned food for a meal and opened a tin of steak and kidney pie before placing it in the oven. We would follow it with creamed rice, custard and fruit. It was a lazy way to eat but with neither fridge nor freezer we were content to live like this until we could better organise ourselves. We were both full of energy, and there was no way the challenge of living on an island would hinder us; in fact the reverse – it spurred us on, but I was not sure what to make of it all, other than being happy. Our move had happened so quickly and easily – it was difficult to believe we were in Foula, this mystical island that the rest of the world knew so little about.

We were kept busy by our diving when the weather was good and soon found the remains of the *Oceanic*, but the stories we had heard about it being undiveable were partly true as the tide ran like a river, severely limiting the times we could work on the wreck site. But the broken up remains contained hundreds of thousands of pounds in value of copper and brass, much of it already broken free and ready for lifting. We quickly realised this was going to be at least two years' work and started to plan accordingly.

Our rent had been arranged on the basis of repairs to the house to be undertaken. This was in our mutual interest and, apart from the work required, it would make the house more comfortable. But before replacing our leaking water tank we asked Elizabeth if she knew where the original Haa well had been, just in case it was easier to pump water from an existing water supply. (Most of the crofts had their own well, some fed the houses by gravity and others still required the water to be hauled up in a bucket.) When we searched, we found a wet hole mostly covered by sphagnum moss; the surface of the water was rust coloured, giving it an oil-like taint that we assumed leached out from iron in the rocks. It was an easy decision not to use it, deciding instead to fit a larger tank on the gable end after temporarily patching the old tank.

We would use the water sparingly, even though Foula soon proved it had no shortage of rain, but we became surprised by how much water we used, particularly if we had people staying, and even with extra tanks fitted the water had to be reserved in the summer for personal washing, dish washing, and cooking. Although the tanks held the heaviest of rain without overflowing they would empty if they were used to wash and rinse clothes during a dry spell. We thought this might make life difficult, but the lack of plentiful running water and electricity had little impact on us, other than not washing our clothes so often, which was more related to our reluctance to do it.

If a visitor asked for water we would tell them it came from the roof, and we only ever had one complaint, made by a camper. When offering him a cup of tea after he had seen the long, white streaks left by the gulls when they perched on our chimney pots, he asked, 'How can you possibly drink that water, the birds make messes all over the slates?'

'It's been boiled,' I replied.

'Where d'you get your water?' Simon asked.

'From the burn below Ham,' he answered. 'It's nice, clean, fresh water coming down from the hills. It's a pleasure to scoop it up in my hands and drink it.'

Simon replied, with a deadpan expression, 'And you don't mind that there's a dead sheep lying next to the burn further up by Mogul?' – which was accurate, as we'd seen it the week before but, wading into the bog, we were unable to move the sodden, partly-submerged carcase.

We were never quite sure how to repay Elizabeth for her help in arranging the Haa, lighting a fire, giving us eggs and generally being kind to us. It was a situation where you feel money is not right except to pay direct costs, like the times we used her phone. A visitor to Foula in 1899 had remarked that, 'If a neighbour needs help in his work on the field, or with the peats, the neighbours come to his assistance, work the whole day without any reward than their food. We are all members of a single family.'[1] Simon and I felt it had not changed.

We offered to help Elizabeth on the croft but I felt she did not trust our ability enough to let us do any work unsupervised. Why should she, as she knew nothing about us. But the opportunity came when walking towards her croft a few weeks after we arrived. Blocking our way was her old, grey Ferguson tractor carrying a heaped load of peats in a trailer. Johnnie, Elizabeth's brother, who was on the island for a few days, was trying unsuccessfully to reverse it into the yard. Simon egged me on to take over – he knew I had been brought up on a farm – but I was reluctant in case I upstaged and embarrassed Johnnie, or made a fool of myself. After watching numerous attempts and realising he was never going to manage, I offered my help. He could not get off the tractor fast enough. I jumped on, first going forward to straighten the tractor and trailer before backing them through the Ham gate and along the track where Elizabeth, who had been watching with eagle eyes, raised her hand as the trailer drew level with the depleted peat stack. Turning, she looked up at me, her glasses first coming into sight, followed by a mischievous smile creeping over her face. I could see Simon grinning behind her; he claimed it was at that moment she realised we could be useful. The gleam in her eyes, he said, was the same as if she had won the jackpot. But that was Simon, always stirring and making a bit of fun. I put it down to him originally training as a journalist as he always enjoyed the tittle-tattle with Elizabeth; he was an expert at it and so, it appeared, was Elizabeth.

After that episode we were trusted to mend fences, catch sheep and undertake mechanical repair work and, as word spread round, we no longer restricted our help to Elizabeth but also to others, although it was generally only required by those that had no fit person to assist. It became an enjoyable distraction, as well as being a useful way to repay people for their help. We never asked for anything in return but Elizabeth often gave us a leg of lamb, eggs, or simply took phone messages for us; a relationship that worked well.

When visiting Elizabeth at Ham I would give Joann, aged 81, the occasional smile as she rarely joined in with the banter. Her voice was frail and Elizabeth had a habit of putting her down if she disagreed with what Joann said. At 54, Elizabeth had seen her much younger husband leave earlier in the summer and, apart from the additional work that had fallen on her shoulders, it was obvious she missed the company. We realised that Elizabeth enjoyed our company, perhaps as much as the help we gave her. She became relaxed with us, smiling when we met her and, as time passed, she became more familiar, asking, 'How are *my* divers today?'

Foula is larger than Fair Isle and Hirta (the main island of the St Kilda group, which lost its 36 inhabitants when it was evacuated in 1930). The island has one of the highest hills in Shetland – the Sneug at 1,372 feet – its summit lying close to where the high cliffs run along the west side, making the island look unforgiving both for livestock and people. The bulk of the island is heather-covered hills with boggy ground in low-lying hollows, and maritime grasses on the lower, flatter land near the coast. But it does have three arable areas on the lower ground on the east side – Da Hametoon, Da Hamtoon and Da Nort Toon – along with a strip along the higher reaches of the Ham Burn where habitable crofts remained on land that had been drained, manured and cultivated over the centuries. A "toon" was defined as an area of arable land with associated common grazing rights in the scattald (hill land), and occupied by a number of tenants. The severe winds and rain had hastened the destruction of the uninhabited crofts, but there were still sufficient remains to allow a glimpse of how 260 people lived on the island a hundred years before.

Apart from the land for keeping livestock there was a vast quantity of good-quality peat that supplied the fuel for heating and cooking. This was a major factor for the survival of the population over centuries, and Simon and I had eyed the peat banks with the hope that we could be allocated one.

I was sure the ownership of the island might go part of the way to explain its present circumstances, but this rarely came up in conversation. Only basic information slipped out, and that varied, depending on the people we spoke to. There was an ambivalence about the nature of the ownership, whether good or bad, shrouding much of the island history in mystery. Relatives of the owning trust had married into the island and that could make any perceived criticism of the ownership discourteous – but not for Elizabeth.

When the opportunity was right I asked Elizabeth, 'Who owned the island before Holbourn?'

'They say Scott of Melby,' she replied.

We later found out there had been an advertisement in *The Scotsman* in 1889 advertising the island for sale:

FOULA, MAGNIFICENT ISLAND
Of about Five Thousand Acres, best Wild Bird Habitat in United
Kingdom. Price Two Thousand Guineas.[2]

The island was sold and passed into the hands of William Gilmour of Glencassley[3] before Holbourn acquired it.

When I asked her why the professor bought the island, she went through to the ben end (the best room) and came back with a book, *The Isle of Foula*, by Ian B. Stoughton Holbourn.[4] It was published in 1938 by his wife Marion, three years after her husband's death, but using manuscripts written by him during his lifetime. Dust fell off the book as I quickly flicked through the pages. I held up a blocking hand to Simon who was itching to get a look at it, although we had previously seen a copy in Fair Isle where we had looked through one chapter to find out about a shipwreck. This mention of a wreck was the reason we had come to Foula.

'It's got all the folklore as well,' I said, as I looked at a chapter titled 'Superstitions and Fairy Tales.'

'Mind, some of it's nonsense, and it's not just me that says so, most on the isle say it's a lot o' rubbish.' As Elizabeth repeated herself I noticed old Joann nodding her head in agreement.

The present ownership stemmed from John Bernard Holbourn, whose first glimpse of Foula occurred when he was on board a ship travelling to Iceland.

After that brief sighting he had been determined to own it. There was little family money available as his father had been a Congregational minister, but after considerable haggling with the owner and a mortgage of £1,000 from a wealthy and generous cousin he managed to buy it. There appeared no economic motive to his purchase, only his emotions as he had romantically fallen for the physical beauty and ruggedness of the island, perhaps not surprising with his main interests being Greek archaeology, the philosophy of art, and poetry. The isolation of this community must also have captivated him, as I had felt the same intrigue when I first saw the island appear on the horizon.

After purchasing Foula in 1901, when he was only 28 years old, he changed his name to Ian B. Stoughton Holbourn – Ian being the Scottish term for John, and Stoughton was his mother's maiden name. His intention of being "the Laird" was emphasised by creating a Holbourn tartan, which he wore when staying in Foula, presumably unaware that Shetland culture was completely different from the clans of mainland Scotland.

Foula originally came under udal law – Tait from Orkney states, 'Orcadians and Shetlanders like to think that the classless society of today derives from the udal tradition, where every man is equal, but also every man has an equal duty to society.'

The islanders were made up of a mixture of Norse, Scots and others, and very independent by nature.

Holbourn's wife describes her first time on the island: 'Some of the women addressed me as "Lady", others as "peerie jewel". Most of them louted, or curtsied, while the men stood bear-headed while they spoke to us, or even when they sighted us on the road.'

The islanders obviously knew how to "play the game" and Ian Holbourn, in return, was always well-mannered. With 240 people living on the island at the time of purchase, he had ample people to ask about, and record, the folklore from their past.

He continued his academic career and became a professor at two American universities, while spending most of his time on lecture tours. His ownership of this inaccessible and primitive island would be used to add interest to his talks. His main residence was near Edinburgh in a house called Fountainhall, which he renamed Penkaet Castle.

Each of the professor's three sons was given a Greek name, a Highland name, and a family name, and they all spent time in Foula during their holidays. Hylas, the eldest, died in the sixties, leaving four children: two boys and two girls. The girls, after obtaining university degrees, settled permanently on the island, marrying islanders and falling into the old way of crofting with little new enterprise to boost the flagging island economy. But it was fortunate for the survival of the population; they were unrelated to anyone and brought their new blood which was badly needed as most of the existing young islanders were related.

Hylas's two boys, John and Rob, also lived and married in the island: John, who was full of ambition, married Elizabeth; and Rob married a girl who came to the island. Of my generation, there was only one island marriage that survived over time. In these complicated and unhappy events it is difficult, if not impossible, to determine if the cause was partly related to decisions having been made because they loved the island so much and marriage offered the means to stay there.

It would be surprising if the island made Holbourn any money at all. It seemed clear throughout the professor's life that he had no vision for the island, other than trying to keep it in the past. He undoubtedly stretched his resources, and may not have been able to afford any improvements to the island, even if he had wanted to. He was not like an industrialist, farmer or fisherman who might be interested in improving the standard of living; in fact it was the opposite, as he states: 'In 1914 a grandmotherly and extravagant government provided a pier when a simple landing place would have been cheaper and more satisfactory. It ends in a jagged sunken skerry as a trap for unwary vessels. The romantic approach is completely spoiled, but this is what we call progress.'

The rents were not high: the Crofters Commission Inquiry on Foula in 1883 stated the annual rents ranged from £2 to £5 per croft.[5, 6] Most of this may have been paid in barter by the supply of a cow or some other produce. The only mention of cash being collected is at the beginning of the First World War when the professor and others had been considering a way of buying extra provisions of flour and meal, because the island was never self-sufficient in grain for the winter.[6] He mentions collecting 20 pounds in rent, and offering to lend it.[4]

Apart from starting, but not finishing, a Scottish baronial-style extension on the front of the Haa, there is no evidence that he spent any substantial sums of money on the island. A "new" manse, the nurse's house, a low-cost school extension and upgrading the road looked to be the only noticeable capital improvements carried out within the last 50 years, and it was likely the council and the church paid for most of them. He appeared to be a benign landlord, and gives the impression that he was happy that the island and its people were locked in time with Foula remaining as a romantic island where the professor could enjoy the concept of a fairy tale existence on his visits.

He died in 1935, leaving his widow the use of the estate. Now aged 88, her youngest son Phil (short for Philistos), appeared to be acting as the head trustee, although he lived and worked in Wales and his time on the island was limited to holidays.

We felt the general ethos of the past generation of ownership was reflected in a small cardboard box we found in a drawer in the Haa. I lifted it out and opened it. Inside were small bits of string, slight twists on them as if they had been cut from knots. There was a note in the box – it said, "Bits of string too small to be of any use."

Perhaps the island was like a myth to the owners, drifting through time with no real meaning, purpose or use, other than just being there. But for us, it was a wonderful place to live.

# Chapter 2
# Friends and Neighbours

The small size and remoteness of Foula made it difficult to attract a permanent nurse and school teacher, the positions often requiring to be re-advertised every few years. Even doctors were reluctant to be flown in to reassess long-term patients in case they become trapped on the island if the wind freshened or the fog came down.

The character of "outsiders" varied with their past and the nature of their present occupation. Simon and I had worked on islands ranging from the Hebrides to Shetland and met different outsiders, from doctors, nurses, teachers, priests and ministers to artists, croft entrants, potters, and even an ex-military man who had a croft on his own tiny island that was only accessible by a vehicle at low water. It takes a brave person to cope with the adventure of starting again, or taking a job on an island, as most come from the safety of a more settled lifestyle. Foula also had its limitations, particularly for young children who were keen on sport or other organised activities as there were no large indoor facilities, and only four children as playmates.

Maggie, the nurse, was popular and lived with her husband Dal, but Simon had a theory that if you have a female nurse on an island you can guarantee her husband will be quite a character. Dal did give the impression he was looking for things to do, and this was, according to Simon, 'part of the role he envisaged as a male, and an attempt to overcome the male gender stereotyping – common on islands – of being known as "the nurse's husband".'

Creating a role on a small island was difficult and probably unnecessary, but in doing so the nurse's husband usually turned out to be a talked-about character. This, Simon thought, was therapeutic to the island, detracting from the more serious island issues, and with such a small, isolated population, the behaviour was like a large family where gossip on petty differences could grow legs. Although it is tempting to think of the islanders and their different ways as something unusual, in reality it was us outsiders who were the quirky ones. We were the minority, the incomers, with our normal expectation of running water, electricity, plumbing, and our wish for consumer goods, pubs and restaurants that were unavailable.

Maggie and her husband appeared settled. They had arrived on the island several months before us and gave every indication that they were here for a few years. She was considered an excellent nurse, giving up a good job in Edinburgh to come to the island where she quickly blended with the population as her job involved seeing everyone. Dal was a people-person, he would have suited work behind a bar, organising events or entertaining people. Unfortunately, these jobs were not required in Foula and he therefore threw himself into the only tasks available, although they were often completely foreign to him but gave purpose to his life. Some were essential work – like cutting peats, in which he became proficient – but others, involving mechanical or electrical work, quickly confirmed that his enthusiasm far outweighed his ability.

The nurse's house was provided by the council and built in the thirties. It lay on the opposite side of the voe from Elizabeth at Ham and a small, pedestrian bridge crossed over the steep-sided burn to connect them. This closeness tended to encourage Elizabeth and Maggie to play light-hearted tricks on each other. They reminded me of a pragmatic phrase written in 1797: 'For what do we live, but to make sport for our neighbours, and laugh at them in our turn.'[7]

Dal, in particular, had time on his hands to entertain or embarrass us all with many of his ploys. My first brush with his abilities occurred when I was fed up digging the drains around the Haa and was relieved to see him approaching as it would give me an opportunity for a break.

'Do you think you could bring your electric meter and have a look at my generator, Alec? It's stopped and I can't get it going.'

'Why'd it stop?' I asked.

'It wasn't running well and I gave it a service, but that doesn't seem to have worked.'

The nurse's house was a five-minute walk and the generator shed was at the bottom of the garden, a sufficient distance to make the noise from the engine less obtrusive in the house. Inside the concrete-block shed was a Lister engine driving an alternator, and lying beside it were a used air filter and some access panels that Dal had removed when he "serviced" the engine. After tidying it up I completed the simple job of cleaning and replacing fuel filters, and draining some water from the bottom of the fuel tank. Water in fuel was a common problem on the islands where fuel was transported in barrels and cans, allowing condensation and sometimes rain or salt water into the old containers. After a quick wipe with a rag the engine leapt into life when the starter was pressed.

The next time I was called out it was not so simple. It was around midnight when Dal shouted up our stairs, 'Alec, are you awake, can I borrow your meter?'

Can I borrow your meter was a way of asking me to go with him – male ego being what it is.

'Coming,' I shouted, as I emerged from my bed feeling for a torch while pulling on a pair of trousers.

'What's the problem?' I asked.

'Our generator's been off too long; the deep freeze is starting to thaw and Maggie's got drugs in the fridge. I can't find the problem.'

'I'll come across with you,' I replied, as I saw Simon appear in his dressing gown and bobble hat at the top of the stairs. He looked upset at having his sleep disturbed as we'd be working early the next day. 'It's okay, Sy. It's only Dal's generator, I'll be back when it's fixed.'

I walked beside Dal in the dark, trying to draw out an explanation of the problem, but he had no idea other than it had stopped every time the power was switched on. We passed the front of his house where I noticed he had extended the chicken run for his hens.

'Are you getting more hens, Dal?' I asked, having heard that some had blown away in a recent gale.

'Just a few, but I'm giving them more space,' he replied. 'I won't have to let them out the run in bad weather.'

As he opened the shed door he said, 'I've changed the filters, tightened the engine bed, checked the fuel, but it just stops.' He lifted his arms and gave a shrug before starting it. Sure enough, as soon as the power was turned on it stopped. I was surprised the fuse didn't blow until I looked at the size of it. When the generator was disconnected it ran normally, but when it was connected to the house it blew the replacement fuse instantly. It became obvious to both of us that there was a fault in the cable leading to the house.

'Have you done anything in the control box?' I questioned.

'No, just the fuel filters as you explained last time.'

'Are those new fence posts you've put in for the hen run?' I asked

'Yes, I shifted it to line up with the house. It looks good doesn't it?'

From the door of the generator shed I could see the new chicken run was in an exact line to meet the edge of the house. He had made a neat job with the chicken wire that was nailed to high posts and its position allowed the house and engine shed to act as barriers either end to keep the hens in, and give them shelter.

'Have you had the generator running since you finished the run?' I asked.

'No,' he replied. 'It was off when I made the run because of the noise. Now it won't work.'

I had some spare lengths of power cable from our work and nipped back to the Haa to get them. We laid them on top of the ground to bypass the existing cable. I started the engine and switched the power on. It was back to normal; the house lit up like a Christmas tree.

'It looks like the cable's faulty,' he said.

'Dal,' I said, 'you've driven one or all of your posts through the power cable. They're in an exact line with where the original cable runs.'

'You'd better not tell Maggie,' he said. 'She's a bit upset about the generator being off.'

Declining the coffee offered by Dal – because the lights going on were bound to wake Maggie – I was quietly sneaking away when I heard Maggie's raised voice coming from the house. It was definitely not praising her husband's skill in fixing the generator.

Foula's physical inaccessibility was only part of the problem, but one that could be improved. They also had the continual problem of not having sufficient funds to store enough non-perishable food like grain over the long, winter months when the weather prevented any services to the island. Other Scottish islands where the population had declined in the past had also found life hard; the islands of St Kilda, Mingulay, Stroma and Swona had all lost the battle for varying reasons and were now uninhabited. As an outsider, I saw potential in Foula, maybe through my ignorance. But I found the harshness and remoteness an attraction rather than deterrent, and was sure I was not alone in thinking it, although Simon and I had been lucky.

We had found the wreck of the liner *Oceanic*. She had been built in 1899 as the largest ship in the world, a predecessor of the *Titanic*. She lay 2½ miles off the island in currents of up to nine knots, where a heavy Atlantic swell rolled over the site most days. Filled with valuable metals it gave us the opportunity to set ourselves up for life if we recovered them at a reasonable cost. Being based in the island was the only way we could achieve this.

After the first year we purchased a salvage boat called *Trygg* that was considerably larger than the mailboat and could be used to bring people or equipment in or out of the island.

The gales during the summer could keep us off the wreck for two-week periods, giving us plenty time to enjoy the island. When the weather permitted we were only able to work as the tide eased, sometimes for as little as 20 minutes and up to a maximum of two hours, and this only twice or three times a day. Working in the winter months was impossible, but at times the wind and rain became our friends when we were exhausted and just wanted to relax, reading books or repairing something small. The Haa had regular visits from the few islanders of our age who came down to the voe where the convenient position of the house made it a good stopping point. Often with time to help, we found it an enjoyable way to repay their kindness.

The Isbister family rarely needed to come to the pier unless the mailboat came in, but they were known for their hospitality and island knowledge and we were encouraged to set off on the one-and-three-quarter-mile walk to their house at the Hametoon. There was a shortcut across the burn and past the nurse's house, but we often took the longer route past Elizabeth's Ham croft, and Gravins – old Tom's croft – before meeting the main track running north and south.

Turning south, we passed the neatly-built schoolhouse which looked the best two-storey house on the island. Mima – mother of Jim, the mailboat skipper – stayed in it with her unmarried sister, Mary. She cooked for the school children attending the classroom that was an extension built onto the side of the house, with an outside toilet block behind it. Past the school was the telephone box and then Mogul, in which Harry lived and ran the post office from a small porch. Inside the porch was a counter which he had to climb over, and at 59 he claimed he would retire when he was no longer able do so. In a field behind Mogul I noticed the rust ravaged remains of a 1930's Morris 8.

The track ran down to a vehicle bridge over the Ham burn, its sides thick with wild flag irises, the yellow flowers standing out in the summer like streaks from a paintbrush on either side of the meandering burn. Following the track up a hill we passed Leraback croft on our left, and the ruins of the Mill Croft on the right. It was here at the side of the road we noticed the remains of two motorbikes lying randomly as if, after failing to make the hill, they had been abandoned. It was not uncommon on islands to have the remains of pieces of machinery left lying around for use as spare parts. As a last resort they would adapt anything to make a repair for a tractor, boat, or house.

'It's not very tidy,' said Simon, as he bent over to look at the carcase of one of them.

'Harry said they'd been left when they broke down.' I'd had a look at them previously, but they were not old enough to be interesting.

'Thank God they didn't have horses!' replied Simon.

At the top of the hill we stopped beside the microwave antenna that pointed directly at its mate on the Shetland mainland, allowing the ten Foula telephones to link with the rest of the world. We looked back over the 'toon o Ham', seeing how it nestled around the small inlet; beyond it, in the distance to the north, were only three inhabited crofts.

The next cottage was the manse. Built in 1938 it still had a new look about it, but perhaps that was in comparison to the other crofts, and it was unusual in that most manses were quite grand houses and beautifully built, reflecting the status of the church, but this was Shetland which rarely went in for pretentious behaviour of any sort. The school teacher, who also acted as the 'missionary', inhabited the manse that at present looked void of life, although it was obviously lived in as beside it lay a tidy vegetable patch. The area around the house was low-lying and boggy, with soft rush growing, its tubular stems sticking up amongst the heather; its internal green pith had at one time been used as lamp wicks to suck up animal fat or fish oil. Long disused peat-cuttings

**Eric and Bobby Isbister.** *Alison McLeay*

lay at either side of the road on the slightly higher ground, each one neatly cut to follow the curved contours of the land, making them look like unhealed scars where the soil had eroded from the base of the old banks.

We then passed what at first appeared to be a well-kept cottage sitting on its own, set back from the gravel track, but it was a church, with plain glass windows and a slate roof. It was different from a croft in that it had no chimneys in the gable ends, just one in the small vestry attached to it. There was no graveyard beside it, and the unbroken rising ridge of ground behind looked appropriately like a stairway to heaven as it climbed in a gentle slope all the way to the summit of Hamnafield at 1,126 feet. Not a regular church goer, I gave little thought to it with never the slightest hint in my mind that I would be married in it three years later.

To the east we looked down on the recently improved gravel airstrip that ended abruptly at the cliffs on the east side, where Shetland lay in the distance. Now close to Hametoon we passed a fertile area where history has it the Norsemen took up residence after they conquered Foula in around 800AD,

The gravel track through Hametoon with Niggards Croft on the left and Breckans on the right.

and gave Foula a Norse heritage rather than Scots. The Norse left many names throughout the island which are still used.

From here it was a quarter-mile walk to South Biggins croft, passing the Hametoon grind (gate) to enter a walled-in area containing about 100 acres of croft land. On our right were the remains of the last inhabited black-house in Shetland, where Robbie of Breckans had died in 1964. It was not the case that he put up with it because he had not experienced any other way of life; he had spent his younger days at sea travelling around the world, happy to return to the island and live in the same conditions as the generations before him – but I suspect he could not have lived like that, or would have wanted to, in a more populated place.

Across the other side of the bridge over the Daal burn stood a roofless church adjoining a walled graveyard, and to the right of it at the end of the road we could see the white-painted South Biggins with its gaily-painted door and windows. Behind it were sea cliffs which led to Da Noup at 803 feet high. Smoke rose from the Isbisters' chimney, bringing with it that irresistible smell of burning peat. Bobby and Eric came out to meet us in front of their small porch, and welcomed us in to their beautifully-kept home that Bobby's father had built during the early 1900s. During these initial days we were wary of visiting people as we did not wish to intrude, but Elizabeth had almost certainly seen us go south and probably phoned ahead to alert them, and mention we had no flu or colds. Illnesses made the islanders uneasy because of their limited resistance resulting from lack of exposure, making them feel vulnerable to infection.

When I first met the Isbisters on my exploratory day trip to the island I had been expecting folklore myths that you often hear from retired people in remote communities, but Bobby lacked the eagerness of the Hebrideans to talk about religious tales and superstitions from the past. Simon and I were happy to leave mythology for another time as Bobby, born in 1899, was more interested in the real than the imaginative. He had been at sea and seen the world, and was now enjoying an active retirement. His personal stories related to his own experience with a larger island population that had worked together at planting, harvesting and caring for stock, where many hands had made light work. He mourned the loss of cultivated land, pointing out the neglected drains resulting in the good grazing turning to rushes. He talked about islanders scaling the cliffs for wild birds' eggs, their times out fishing, stories which reflected the hard work and risk the previous generations had endured, alongside the comradeship they enjoyed. But with the reduced numbers none of it had survived.

I soon became aware that the family were like guardians of the island traditions, knowledgeable on every aspect, but at 74, Bobby felt his time had passed. 'It's the young folk that'll have to do something about it,' he said, while looking at his son Eric, aged 31, who shuffled his feet and twisted his body nervously as if he was being asked a difficult question. Perhaps he was, but otherwise he seemed happy and comfortable in his home.

I wondered if Eric dreamed of a different future. Since being born on the Shetland mainland he had never been off the island. I wondered if he was content to let life pass, comfortable and relaxed within a world of little change. If I'd had the courage I should have asked him, but I felt it was a very personal question and might be taken as rude or prying, until I knew him better. Simon enjoyed discussing people on an individual basis whereas I was normally more interested in their involvement with agriculture, the sea or other physical

**The white painted South Biggins with the ruins of the old kirk in the foreground.** *Simon Martin*

aspects of the island. The topics bounced back and forward with Eric getting quite excited and vocal at times on aspects of the island that interested him, like Norwegian fishing boats that he had painted as they passed close to the island, or unusual birds he had seen, particularly Manx shearwaters that nested below ground behind his home.

I thought Bobby's lack of religion made him more of a realist. I had noticed that Shetlanders, as a cultural group, were always forward looking, their thoughts going into the improvement of their lives rather than indulging in the past. The population on the Shetland mainland appeared youthful with the older generation encouraging the young to build their own future. But it was not the same in Foula which had an elderly population; it was as though their quest for survival had made it too risky to try new ideas.

We asked about the numerous ruins, and in particular the black-house where Robbie had lived amongst the peat smoke from the fire in the centre of his house to over 80 years old. Bobby described the old cottages saying they mostly consisted of two rooms, a "but" and a "ben". The but end was the kitchen which was about 20 feet long and 10 or 11 feet wide. In it were the beds, chests for clothes, meal and items of everyday use. Two resting chairs sat at either side of the fire and in the middle was a huge hearth-stone over which hung a chain with a hook, called a crook, in which the large pot or "muckle kettle" hung when the family dinner was cooking. The only light entered by holes in the roof which let out the smoke. They slept in box beds, entering by opening doors at the side, these protected them from the winter snow and wind which would blow through the cracks between the stones of the old drystone cottages. Instead of a blanket they used a "taated rug" to cover themselves; it was a coarse, hairy rug that had to be made in two halves and then sown together because the looms were so narrow.[8, 9]

Bobby's cottage was very different; it was warm and cosy, had a battery-powered record player, and a number of records were stacked on a shelf next to books on ships, with any surplus space filled with maritime magazines. I imagined they threw little away, always making the most use of what they had; no rampant consumerism here or products bought through vanity.

'Some tea and a buttered scone?' asked Aggie-Jean, making Bobby pause from his descriptions as she passed the plates.

I wondered why I was so interested in the past. It seemed that most lives had been spent just trying to survive, with little time for big improvements or free time as we saw it today. Perhaps it was my admiration for how they had persevered in such difficult circumstances, but now in vivid contrast to the south their progress had ground to a halt.

Bobby's family had run the island shop for many years before passing it on to another family in the hope new blood might somehow make it work. Like many island jobs, there would be little profit from the shop with so few people, but I was realising that any additional income at all, when combined with the croft, fishing, knitting and other work, was essential to survive. Unfortunately, the dynamic woman Isobel, who had been running the shop, was one of those who left a few months before we arrived.

The Isbisters worked their crofts using traditional methods, all three of them digging the vegetable patch with Shetland spades. The physical work required would limit the land they could cultivate, but hay was cut with a scythe from the permanent grassland to provide additional fodder for the milk cow and sheep. It appeared a simple way of life; it gave the feeling of self-employment and independence, and they supplemented it by having a small boat – a yoal – in which they went out fishing in good weather to catch something for themselves and Edith. She was Aggie-Jean's younger sister who lived across the burn in a croft called Dykes. We rarely met her except when we were visiting the Isbisters but she was a truly "bonnie lass", short and slightly overweight but with a happy, smiling, rosy face, and always laughing. She disliked goats' milk and after the Isbisters obtained a goat to replace the traditional cow, she would bring a small jug with her own milk to put in her tea. Always well dressed and full of fun, she joked with Simon about the Foula ways, and how we would eventually get used to the delays that occurred, and settle into the island routine. She had upgraded her neat cottage with a bathroom, and both croft and house were always immaculate with a well-kept garden supplying many of her needs.

Edith was one of the few islanders who seriously knitted Shetland jerseys to generate an income. Traditionally, the women's special work had been carding, spinning and knitting to make hosiery. The Foula women had never made the fine lace Shetland shawls as for many years their wool was unsuitable, but they produced the less showy hosiery that was known to be cosy and comfortable, and at the Highlands and Islands agricultural society in 1892 the first and second prizes for spinning were won by Foula girls.[10]

I imagined the rent for South Biggins croft would be minimal, in tens of pounds rather than hundreds, and there was sheep subsidy, and Bobby and possibly Aggie-Jean would be on a pension. Heating costs would be zero as the island was plentiful with peat; there was no electricity, just the price of paraffin for Tilley or oil lamps; and water was drawn from a well, with the barn at the back providing a suitable toilet. They kept a small and very basic rough-terrain vehicle driven by a petrol engine, with a bench seat and a platform on the back for carrying peats. Manufactured for farmers by a small company in the Scottish borders, it was called a Limpet and seemed ideal for the island as it was light enough not to sink in the soft ground and simple enough to repair.

When it came to political news or world events they appeared of little interest to them, probably because they had minimal relevance to their way of life. They did not covet wealth, and their chosen way of life was close to the mythical "good life" of self-sufficiency dreamt of by many people who wish to escape the rat race. In contrast, Simon and I had seen some of our friends jump eagerly onto the treadmill of good earnings where their compensation would be a prosperous future, but not necessarily a happy one; my mother used to say that 'you are better being rich and miserable than poor and miserable'.

Foula was like no other place I had ever been. It had this real past, more interesting than the superstitions and myths recorded by Professor Holbourn. Where I came from in Fife the mythical stories tended to be founded on buildings, often similar tales to other areas – a face appearing on a wall, haunted houses, a poltergeist that burnt the curtains and dropped furniture through the floor – whereas islands were more likely to base the tales on some romantic landscape feature that made them suitable for religious sects, bards, hermits or mystical creatures.

Foula was so visually stimulating it could make anyone's imagination run riot. The Sneck of the Smaalie was known as a home for trolls. It was a geological feature that fitted the stories like a glove. I certainly did not require any additional influence to discover my own preconceptions when I saw it, and Simon, who jokingly used to say that myths were the provinces of the "arty-farty", was only happy to take on a mythical dream when he could make some fun out of it.

Bobby played the fiddle, the Shetland fiddle tunes often conjuring up something physical like *Ronas Voe*, or the *Shaalds of Foula* that represented the waves breaking over a reef lying off the island and used for a dance of the same name. But there was a change coming as many of the young, like Eric, were moving away from the fiddle to a guitar or similar instrument where they could sing as well.

When walking back to the Haa, content after our evening with the Isbisters, Simon remarked, 'I'm surprised they don't get together to organise an electricity and a water supply, there must be a grant available.'

'If they can live without them and keep their independence, perhaps that's all they want.'

'Have they really got independence? What about education and health?' asked Simon.

'Yes,' I thought – money again – 'but there's a lot to be happy about in the present. The island works, isn't that the important aspect?'

'But what about the next generation?'

# Chapter 3
# Weather Permitting

Like everything we found in Foula, from our own experience and as Edith had told us, it always seemed to take a long time for anything to happen. The island ferry, referred to as "the mailboat", was no different. As well as carrying all the stores it provided a focus for the community every time it returned. The sharing of work when unloading created a social event.

The islanders held a contract with the Post Office to deliver the mail on one round trip every week in the summer and once a fortnight in the winter, but the contract only paid a miserly amount as there had been no rise in payment for 25 years. Other revenue came from the council, and parcels and goods were charged, but as the population dwindled it bore little resemblance to real costs, leaving the mailboat owners no financial means of upgrading the vessel. The one-way trip to Walls took about 3½ hours and, although a schedule of leaving times was published, being weather-dependent the boat rarely sailed at the allotted times, or even on the allotted days. Foula's Achilles heel was its inaccessibility, but this was also its blessing as it gave the island its character and the islanders their peace.

By the time we arrived in Foula what had once been a new engine in the mailboat had became an old engine that was no longer reliable, with Jim, the skipper, undertaking all its maintenance and repair work using the limited tools and parts available. As the boat was so close to the Haa he would often look in when he had finished work in the evenings. Tall, good-looking and as strong as an ox, Jim was solid in body and action, like an anchor. He always wore a "skipper's hat" and could speak perfect English or broad Foula-Shetland depending who he was speaking to. His nephews called him Uncle Jim, and Simon thought this appropriate as he behaved like a wise sage, so we often referred to him as "Uncle Jim". He had one of the few, if not the only marriage among his generation that was solid. His wife, Sheila, loved the island and was

Rob steadies the mail boat as it is lifted ashore onto its cradle

an unbelievably hard worker, looking after their three children and carrying out much of the croft work.

Jim, with Rob the crew, was always cautious about the weather conditions in which the boat could safely make the trip to Walls and back as they might be storm-bound for days or weeks in Walls. They only left Foula when the forecast predicted the good weather would last long enough to ensure their return home. But if they could not manage the round trip there was a wooden shed – called the "Foula Hut" – with bunks and a stove at Walls where they stayed. Jim was not an early starter. After he was up he would phone to get the latest weather reports before coming down to the boat where Rob was preparing it for launching. Rob was a bright young man with a degree in naval architecture. He had wanted to join the merchant navy but was colour blind; an automatic reason for failing the medical. Initially shy until he got to know us, he regularly looked into the Haa, always having a cup of very strong coffee while he waited to sail, and often leaving after 10am which was later than the time on the schedule for leaving Walls on the return journey.

Once lowered into the water the ever-present swell caused the boat to range

**Harry.** *Simon Martin*

backwards and forwards, even when tightly secured by mooring ropes. Jim would have to jump aboard, remove the shackles to detach the boat from the crane, and then his large six-foot-five-inch body would disappear under the cowl into the cramped space of the engine room. The Perkins engine required warm air to be sucked into the air intake before it had any chance of starting. This was carried out by either a small gas blowtorch or, if the gas had run out which was often the case, old newspapers and magazines were burned next to the inlet manifold allowing warm air to be drawn in. There was a happy sigh of relief from us all when black smoke poured out from the exhaust, indicating the engine had started. As the smoke declined and the engine sounded a steadier beat, the goods bound for the mainland were lifted aboard. Not much was exported from the island, but empty barrels and cans to be filled with paraffin for lighting or diesel for tractors were hurriedly put on deck. After they were loaded Harry, who ran the post office, would hand down the mail bags while Jim secured them forward under the whaleback, one of the few dry spaces.

The boat carefully edged its way around the pier, the helpers watching and hoping she would make a safe trip. After she faded into the distance, Harry would always comment, 'Boy, boy, I'd better get back to the post office.' But he usually stopped off at Elizabeth's for a chat on the way.

At Walls, the boat tied up alongside the "Foula pier" to pick up the smaller items from the shop and close by the Foula hut stored small parcels. But for larger items the boat crossed to the steamer's pier where there was a modern shed that usually contained sacks of feed and larger items delivered by a carrier.

After loading, Jim would phone Foula from a phone box to give Harry a time to expect them back. Due to the late start, the boat would usually arrive in the evening. When news of the arrival time spread round the island people would start gathering at the pier, often an hour before the boat was expected. This was a social occasion where people met and chatted happily as they looked forward to their food supplies and post arriving. The young would join us in the Haa, drinking tea and coffee while eating whatever biscuits remained, and bask in the warmth of the peat fire that was burning to its extreme. We kept a casual lookout through the Haa window hoping to sight a light from the boat; Jim would usually flash a torch when approaching as his navigation lights rarely worked. If it was a particularly dark night, with bad weather looming, we would place the Tilley lamp in the window where we hoped Jim would see it. If we missed seeing the boat first, Elizabeth would come in the back door and shout, 'Harry can see the lights of the boat.'

'Thanks, Elizabeth, we'll be down,' someone would answer back, and then add, 'are you coming in for a minute?'

'Na, na, I'm doon to the pier.' Elizabeth rarely entered the Haa further than the sitting room door.

Once the boat was near the voe, Harry would flash his torch to light up the end of the pier and, during these final moments, we all stood on the raised ledge at the bottom of the concrete parapet, talking in hushed tones as we looked out into the dark attempting to glimpse a light swaying with the roll of the boat. As she came closer, if the moon was out the white bow wave reflected the moonlight and we could be sure it was the mailboat and not a fishing boat. A wave of relief would flow over the onlookers; we became relaxed, and happy at their safe return, with everyone talking normally while moving into position to take the ropes and help unload.

As she rounded the end of the pier we could catch a glimpse of the size of cargo she had on deck, most secured beneath a heavy tarpaulin to keep it dry. Being young bachelors Simon and I would keep an eye out to see if any young passengers arrived, but it rarely happened between September and May. Even in the summer the birdwatching fraternity seemed weighted to be middle-aged and mostly male, but any young people arriving gave us a lift. We found it refreshing to see a new face, particularly female, and looked forward hopefully to a visit from them in the Haa. Eric, as the youngest unattached islander, would suffer from gentle teasing as various women were hinted on and verbally guided in his direction if they were deemed to be suitable partners. But Eric was far too particular, causing a bit of banter whatever age of woman arrived.

'She'll do thee fine boy, thee will get no better,' someone would say.

Eric, slightly nervous, would never give a vague reason for a refusal, but always a definite point. 'Nae, nae, I think her a-a-ankles are too thick,' he'd reply, with a stutter and embarrassed smile, while quickly attempting to change the subject, 'I expect the h-h-hen food's arrived this trip.'

After the boat was secure, Jim would stop the engine and help Rob pass up the boxes to willing hands ashore. This was followed by the 45-gallon drums of paraffin which were parbuckled up the face of the pier using two ropes, before rolling them a safe distance from the sea for collecting the following day. Sometimes the cardboard boxes had become wet and any heavy contents were taken out to be passed up separately.

Elizabeth had a habit of continually "mithering" people, reminding them to be careful. 'Mind, mind,' she would say, 'that's too heavy, you'll hurt thee self.' Or, 'Mind thee, mind thee, yon'll break.' But she was mostly ignored, as you can only cry wolf a few times.

Harry would take the mailbags and walk up to the post office. Depending on how late in the night the mailboat returned, he would either come back with our letters or deliver them the next morning. In the winter he knew there was no urgency as it would be at least two weeks before the boat would go out again with the mail.

After unloading, the boat was craned out and hauled up the slipway well clear of any waves which might go over the pier. Everything was tidied away or secured before we took our "Walls boxes" up to the Haa, opening them on the kitchen table to see if any of the treats we had ordered had been available. Sometimes some of the islanders would come with us, helping to carry boxes, and stay for a cup of coffee or tea before making their way home. If packets of chocolate digestives or caramel wafers had arrived they were opened and shared; it gave us an excuse to enjoy them, often fooling ourselves that they were better eaten as they might not keep in the damp house.

Everyone complained about the infrequent mailboat service in muted terms as they knew how essential it was, but the crossing was known to be dangerous; not only could the weather be particularly bad but there was a strong current running between the island and the mainland. In 1834 a traveller described the situation on the 23rd of June during the height of summer: 'The dreadful howling of the storm this morning intimated to us too plainly we could not proceed to Foulah. A boat and crew of five men belonging to that island have been detained here since Friday last, and the poor fellows are sadly anxious to get home to their families. They have agreed to transport us to the island for twelve shillings, bag and baggage. The distance is eighteen miles across a stormy ocean … Using both sail and at times oars it had taken about nine hours but is often accomplished in three hours if there is a fair wind.'[11]

The first mail contract had been issued in 1879. Formerly, Foula had been looked upon as nearly inaccessible as St Kilda, but after the contract it was said that with wind and weather permitting, a regular fortnightly mail service was to be made by Messrs. Garriock and Co.'s smacks from Reawick.[12] But the service remained irregular and in 1879 Robert Cowie, a Shetland medical practitioner, had written: 'Three months have, however, frequently elapsed without a mail, and a gentleman resident at Walls, only twenty miles off, used to remark that he had, at the time, a correspondent in Foula and one in China, and that he could often get an answer sooner from the latter than the former.'[13]

The Foula men were upset that they had not benefitted from the original contract and came to the end of their tether in 1888, claiming their mail service would never be satisfactory until the contract was given to a Foula boat, which it eventually was.[14, 15] By 1912 the mailboat was fitted with an engine which made for a safer crossing but it still had to be dragged up the beach after each trip to keep it clear of bad weather, a job requiring both strength and numbers of people.

To make life easier a new pier had been brought to the attention of the home secretary in 1885 by the Crofters Commission, but Foula found their financial conditions impossible to meet, stating that the people were only able to provide a small proportion of the cost as they were in a place where many of the population were depending on public charity – it was said 'the Government must either give Foula all or nothing.'[16, 17] The Pier Committee convened by islander Robert Gear raised some funds and attempted to obtain money from Professor Holbourn, but he claimed that he had spent valuable time and money in surveying the voe and left the raising of the additional money to those who had a direct interest in it.[18]

It was not until 1913-14 that the pier was built. It was 75 feet long, and included a five-foot high wall, or parapet, on the seaward side, all constructed using mass concrete. The new pier did little to slow down the loss of inhabitants, and it was not until 1948 that their open mailboat was replaced with one having a deck.

The new boat was designed and built by Howarth's,[19] a boatyard at Scalloway, and called the *Island Lass*. She was fitted with a 15-horse-power Kelvin engine, and built to the order of the five crew of the previous boat.[20] To accommodate the new boat the pier was extended by 15 feet between 1946 and 1949, over the worst of the rocks, making it possible for small fishing boats to lie there in good weather. A slipway was added with davits for lifting the new boat out, but this remained difficult in bad weather as first they had to lighten her by passing the boat's ballast onto the pier before connecting hand tackles to do the actual lift. Harry told me it could take an hour before she was finally winched up the slipway by hand, and it was an exhausting job, particularly in bad weather when she had to be lifted out of the water as quickly as possible, requiring a number of people to take turns.

Unfortunately, the *Island Lass* was lost in March 1962 when the engine failed on a crossing to the island during bad weather. The crew were taken off by a Scottish trawler. Although no one was lost or injured it was a blow to the island.

Since that loss a big improvement had been made to the pier by replacing the davits with a crane, and it was now a relatively quick and easy job lifting out the present mailboat, *Westering Homewards*. Originally a Liverpool Class RNLI lifeboat, 35½ feet long, the design ensured it was almost unsinkable, but the numerous bulkheads restricted the quantity of stores and equipment it could carry. To meet safety requirements they had replaced the original petrol engine with a Perkins diesel. Most of the cargo was stored on the exposed deck, which made both the boat and its cargo vulnerable to damage in heavy weather. The crew's limited shelter was behind an open cowl that gave access to the engine room through a watertight door, and the sole method of navigating the boat was a compass as she carried no radio for communication or radar for fog.

Our preparations for Foula had started as if we were working in any remote area, and assuming we were embarking on at least a two-year project, possibly longer. As a standby we always took a stock of catering-size tins of food with us just in case we were unable to get supplies during the first week or two. Feeding ourselves was always an issue, but it had evolved and I usually continued working outside while Simon knocked up a meal. This was never negotiated, but when two people know each other's strong points and weaknesses the separate tasks just fall into place, each doing what they are best at. It was just like our diving where Simon was always best at searching for wrecks or wreckage and I handled most of the dismantling.

Food was prepared on the basis of ease and speed. If we had bread from a recent mailboat trip, we would make sandwiches by cutting thick slices off our catering-sized blocks of cheese or use jam or marmalade from large catering tins. Normal-sized jars would be quickly emptied and were too fragile to carry with us. Simple cheese omelettes always provided a quick meal but in the evening, if we had time, we might treat ourselves to a big meal. For vegetables we used powdered potatoes, tinned carrots and peas, as well as a small supply of freeze-dried, unless we could get something local. Occasionally, as a treat, we would open a tin of Carnation milk for our coffee or tea, otherwise it was cartons of long-life milk or, in extreme circumstances, made-up powdered milk that neither of us liked. As we became established our planning improved, and if the mailboat had been out we could order fresh meat, vegetables and bread from the Shetland mainland. When the weather was too bad to work, Simon often made spaghetti Bolognese, "spag bog", as he referred to it, and other more exotic meals. My timing on cooking was never as good as Simon's, the individual items rarely being ready at the same time.

Never sure when supplies could be replenished, little food was wasted; rather than dump the mouldy bread I would scrape off the mould and make bread and butter pudding. If the bananas were over ripe, as they usually were by the time they had reached the final destination of Foula, I would make banana bread. For daily use most of the islanders made soda bread and had no reliance on imported loaves, although Maggie, the nurse, was the exception and made bread with yeast. She gave me lessons in baking until I had grasped the basics, but I was not the quickest of learners and I am sure I tried her patience. The Haa kitchen was on the north side and was always cool, making it ideal for kneading the dough, but finding somewhere warm and draught-free to allow it to rise evenly was a problem. After a few tries Maggie suggested placing the bowl of dough in a plastic bucket with a towel over it in front of the peat fire. It worked, and the freshly-baked loaf was sliced and liberally coated with butter, jam or marmalade before being eaten. It rarely lasted more than an hour with Simon and I picking at it, enticed by its irresistible smell, and if we had visitors it instantly disappeared. Our only problem was obtaining live yeast, until we found we could buy it in slabs from the baker in Scalloway on the Shetland mainland. If we ran out, a fishing boat outward-bound for the island grounds might kindly drop some off at the pier. But cooking when working still lacked enthusiasm from both of us, normal meal times bearing no relation to the times we ate as our meals had to be based around our diving times. We hoped we could find another person to deal with this side of our life.

The Foula shop had been through difficult times, the final straw being the loss of the person who ran it just before we arrived on the island, and Harry, being Harry, the kind person he was, had been helping out until all the stock had been sold. Harry was tall and strong, had obviously been a good-looking young man, and now his weather-beaten face gave him a unique island appearance that actors would die for. Still fit, he never stooped, and had retained his strength, lifting drums and cargo off the mailboat with ease.

We arranged to meet him at the shop as it had no specific opening times and we wanted to see the remaining stock. It was close to the Haa and the stone building looked to be in desperate need of repair. The rain was pouring down as we cautiously pushed our way in through the door of the wooden porch to find

The shop is on the right of the Haa with ponds cut in rock in the foreground for washing fish. Hamnafield is in the background.

buckets and plastic containers strategically placed around the floor to catch the leaks. Harry stood behind the shop counter with his oilskins on.

'The roof looks as though it needs attention,' said Simon.

'Boy, it's a while since anything's been done to it, it's bound to be needin' a bit of work,' replied Harry, shaking his head in agreement.

'When was it slated?'

'I'll not know, but the Haa roof was slated in 1874, the year my mother was born.'

'Has it ever been renailed?'

'Oh, I don't mind of that,' said Harry.

'It explains why we were losing slates in the gales,' I said. 'We've had to hook them back with wire; if we replace the nail, we disturb other slates and they all come loose.'

'There's a fair bit of work needin' done on these old buildings,' replied Harry, as he shook his head again as if in exasperation, knowing it would never be done.

Cardboard boxes of tinned food had been stacked in dry areas; the boxes looked damp but the tins appeared free of rust, and those in plastic wrapping were like new. I expected they were normally sold by the case, as few had been unwrapped. In better days the shop would have opened when the mailboat returned; I'd seen a photograph of the Isbisters with a Shetland pony and cart and assumed they used it to carry the stock up from the pier.

Simon and I looked at the labels; the remaining selection was poor. Carnation milk, spam and corned beef would have been consumed regularly by us, but there was none. We bought a few cases of beans and some tinned fruit, more from goodwill than immediate necessity. We started chatting to Harry about our work as he had taken an interest in us since we arrived, and being concerned for our safety, he had mounted a heavy wartime naval gunsight on top of a fence post to keep an eye on us when we were at sea.

I paid him for the tins, and waited while he rummaged through a wad of notes to give us change. The notes were a strange colour and unrecognisable to me.

'They look like old notes, Harry,' I remarked, as I flicked through them, not to count them but to examine them.

'Boy, boy, I'll sort newer ones for thee,' he said.

'No, they're okay, I like them,' I smiled, as I put the change in my pocket and Simon and I lifted three cases each off the counter.

'I'll bring the other two cases once I've closed the shop,' said Harry.

Outside the rain was moderating and the sun was coming through. I looked back into the dank building where Harry was sorting his bundle of cash and placing the change in a drawer.

After we dumped the boxes on our kitchen table, I took the notes out of my pocket. There were four; I passed two to Simon and examined the others.

'It's a 1933 Commercial Bank of Scotland £1 note, the other's a British Linen banknote,' I told him.

'I've got a '37 Commercial Bank and a Union Bank of Scotland note,' he replied.

'Do you think they're worth anything?'

'I don't suppose so, they're not in very good condition, they've been handled too many times.'

I bent back the dog ears to see if that improved them. It didn't. 'They'll never look like new, Sy.'

'The only banks in Foula are peat banks,' he replied light-heartedly as he began taking tins out of their cases to place on our shelves. 'There must be stacks of old notes here.'

'They'll quickly lose them when the shop closes. I wonder if they're legal tender?' I put them in the tin beside the petty-cash book, opening it up to enter the amount.

It became obvious why the notes were so old. Nearly all financial transactions were carried out through Harry's post office. The pensions paid out were spent in the shop and then banked at the post office; as long as more money came into the island than went out, the same notes circulated perpetually. The old notes seemed so typical of Foula, where money appeared to play such a small part in their lives. There were few consumer goods and many people were pensioners, the others surviving with work on their crofts and small fishing boats. It was a case of make do and mend; a way of life that bred very practical people. If they were unable to do a repair themselves there was nearly always another islander who had the necessary skill.

It was sad that the shop had to close as it was another symbol of the island's decline. The Foula shop was described in 1834 as the residence of Mr Scott's factor, Mr Peterson, where he kept a small store of tobacco, spirits and fishing lines. The lower rooms were occupied by the family, and the upstairs rooms could be let to visitors, 'the stairs being broken or rotted away, but the roof was in most places intact, and he [the visitor] felt it was no small comfort in this rainy island.'[11]

Over the centuries Foula had issues with destitution and funds had to be raised to support the island, but the root of the problem was the boat service. The island was not self-sufficient and regularly required meal and other foods from the mainland as they were unable to afford to buy sufficient quantities to last the whole winter. As the population declined, by the 1930s the shop was temporarily closed and everyone started running short of meal, tea, sugar, paraffin and other necessities. The situation became serious and two letters were written in 1931 to Zetland County Council. This was the year after St Kilda was evacuated, and the letter alleged that: 'the natives, about 140 in number, are starving for lack of the necessities of life.' One of the letters went so far as to state that the people were on the point of starvation with the recent mailboat delayed for a month.[21] A suggestion was even made that Foula should be evacuated.

After our first few weeks on the island we considered the pier as the social centre. Apart from the mailboat, several small island boats were moored in the voe using the shelter it offered and, as our work was based at the pier, with our house overlooking it, we quickly noticed any activity. If we were not working we'd wander down to chat or offer our help if they needed a hand; they in turn would offer their assistance if we required it. This usually ended in the younger generation coming up to the Haa if they had the time.

Nearly every day we saw old Tom. If we had been out working early he would be waiting for us on our return, his pipe unlit but firmly clenched between his teeth, glancing around as if looking out to sea but all the time watching what we were doing. From a family of blacksmiths and crofters he, surprisingly, had no interest in our equipment and kept well clear of anything on the pier including the mailboat when it was being manoeuvred on land.

At 70 years old, he had never been married but lived with his sister until she died. Now, an air of neglect and dereliction hung over both his frail body and his poorly maintained croft, called Gravins. He was slightly built with receding grey hair and coarse grey stubble on his chin, wearing clothes ingrained and smelling of peat smoke. His black, rotten teeth had been worn down to his gums, where they held his rarely-lit pipe; whether it was the cost of tobacco or that he just liked the pleasure of having the pipe between his teeth I never knew. He always wore a fisherman's grey-and-white-flecked polo-neck jersey over dark woollen trousers that probably came from the police. His traditional cap was a tight fit to secure it from blowing away in the strong winds, and it had distinctive marks where his grimy fingers had held it on the rare occasions when he took it off. An old pair of black, laced leather boots kept his unsteady feet dry when he walked on the gravel road, rarely stepping off it, not willing or possibly not able, to risk venturing onto rougher ground. Unfit for any work, he would slowly shuffle down to the pier on dry days or between rain showers to see what was going on.

Tom's croft lay alongside the road a few hundred yards further on from Elizabeth's. His house had been built onto the front of an older house that in turn had been built in front of the original turfed-roofed dwelling that had

**Old Tom.** *Alison McLeay*

probably stood for several hundred years. The three separate gable ends were clearly visible with a noticeable change in stone quality from the original uncut and drystone (un-cemented) rounded stones of the old buildings to the newer, partly-cut stones with the gaps sealed with cement that were used to build his existing home. The tar from his bituminous felt roof had run down the front wall leaving black streaks like Dracula's teeth. Two unpainted windows with net curtains drawn were positioned either side of a central door that was always locked, the steel face-plate worn smooth from use. He had no running water, electricity or toilet; the inside of the croft would undoubtedly give a glimpse into another time, probably packed with old and unusual items that should have been discarded years ago, but now would be well placed in a museum. To the east of his house lay another small but neat stone building that contained an original blacksmith's forge, complete with all the tools used by him and his family before him.

We were told he never invited anyone in, and even when we carried peats from his peat bank to the back of his house and offered to take them in he said he would manage, although it appeared a slow task as he could only carry one peat at a time. Whenever we passed the cottage and saw the smoke curl out of his chimney, we felt assured he would be warm and could enjoy his life in a cosy room, probably listening to Radio 4 on a battery-powered radio.

His main purpose in life seemed to be an attempt to capture people with conversation, and then he would bend the conversation towards the weather, news or old stories. He never approached us when we were working but waited until we moved clear of the equipment before he headed unstoppably towards us, removing his pipe with the obvious intention of speaking.

'Man, I'll tell thee, man, I'll tell thee,' he repeated several times as he approached.

'Hello, Tom, how're you today?' one of us would ask, and we reduced our pace as a matter of courtesy, but he would quicken his in an attempt to move in front of us.

'Man, I'll tell thee,' he continued, as he looked up towards the clouds, the pipe now held by the bowl in his right hand with the stem pointing upwards in line with his eyes as if he was about to make some great revelation.

'The wind, she'll be strong, force six frae the west.' He'd then recite his prediction of the day's weather that was identical to the shipping forecast we had heard at 6am that morning on Radio 4. There was hardly a dry day he didn't search us out on the road or the pier, but occasionally the stories would be interesting, like telling us that due to the high cliffs and hills on the island, they caused a peculiarly turbulent wind condition called a "flan". During a storm you could light a pipe in one place and ten feet away a flan of wind would pick you up or blow you over. Like being told a ghost story, I was not quite sure whether to believe him until we heard the same reports from several others and then experienced it ourselves, finding both the wind strength in places and the quietness in others like nothing we had ever experienced. It was frightening at times, making us glad to retreat to the safety of the Haa.

The wind could be dangerous and in February 1903 there was a report about a storm in Foula when Mr Henderson, the teacher, was outside and had his right arm severely injured, besides suffering other injuries after being lifted and thrown to the ground. Parts of the garden walls round the school house and other crofts were blown over, and cottages and byres lost their roofs. Two men had a narrow escape when the roof of a recently-made porch was carried bodily over the dwelling-house and deposited several fields away, and the zinc off the porch roof of an inshore house was found on the seashore at Liorafield (old name for the Haa).[22]

The year before we arrived a tractor and trailer were blown onto their sides, and it was said the exposed nature of the island and the effect of its hills combined to create some of the worst winds in Shetland. I asked a Shetland fisherman what he thought of the weather on the island. He described it as 'eight months of winter followed by four months of bad weather'.

'Is it a good place for anything?' I jested.

'Aye, it's a fine place to get the boat the hell oot of,' he smiled.

We learned from repeated experience that Tom would stick to us like a limpet. He never paused from talking, rarely asked a question, or listened to anything we said.

'Thanks, Tom.' I would reply, as we attempted to escape, but he took no hint. Eventually we would walk away while he was talking, gradually increasing our pace to reach the banking at the side of the mailboat slip, knowing it was too steep for him to climb. Standing at the bottom he continued to talk until we were out of his hearing range, when we would see him stop, slip the pipe back between his teeth and look around, presumably seeking another victim.

On one occasion when we were cold, wet, fed up and desperate to get into the warmth of the Haa, with our manners and tolerance worn to a thin veneer, Simon tried a new tack.

'Tom!' Simon shouted, as he pointed towards the Haa. 'Our house is on fire, we'll have to run.' He hardly paused as we ran off to the diminishing sounds of 'Man, I'll tell thee,' but I'm sure I saw a wry smile coming from that well-weathered face. Perhaps we should have been more considerate. I can see now he was just a lonely person desperately seeking some company.

# Chapter 4
# The Island Dilemma

Going out on a small lobster boat with an islander was always enjoyable; it was the anticipation when hauling a creel and whether there would be anything in it, usually some crabs, possibly a lobster, and occasionally a large conger eel. The simple process involved emptying the creel, baiting and then relaying, often working among the dangerous rocky areas close in to the shore that the islanders knew well – or I hoped they did. Lobster fishing did not require regular trips to the market as the lobsters could be stored live in keep pots for weeks. It was also seasonal fishing that was more suited to the island way of life.

The Foula boats never worked with the same energy as the three larger lobster boats from the mainland that fished many of the same grounds. Starting in the spring, as soon as the weather allowed, the Shetland fishermen would live on their boats for the week, lying at the Foula pier in good weather or anchor off, ready to start work at daylight and continue until late evening. Even in thick fog they would be working; we could hear the engines sounding mysterious and eerie, as if from another world, as they passed close but unseen, making good use of their radar. Their frequent visits were often used to bring fresh food and other requests to the island, particularly for nurse Maggie and her husband Dal who liked a bit more than Foula could provide. When the catches fell and the lobster females spawned, the boats returned to the mainland to make their living by traditional fishing methods such as trawling, seine netting, dredging for scallops or other types of fishing in Shetland waters.

The four island yoals kept in the voe were between 15 and 22 feet long with a beam of up to 5½ feet and were primarily built for rowing by three men, and sailing with a square sail, but in Foula they used an inboard or outboard engine. These yoals belonged to the Isbisters, Jock Ratter, Jim Gear and Ken Gear and, apart from lobsters, they were used for catching mackerel, sillocks, piltocks, ling and cod. Jim's boat, the *Happy Voyager*, was built in the traditional yoal style but with the addition of higher planking and a small increase in length, making it safer and roomier for lobster creels. The lobster bait consisted of undersize fish from the whitefish boats if they were fishing nearby, or piltocks and sillocks as a last resort as they were never considered good bait, but if they caught a quantity of mackerel it was salted and stored as the preferred lure for lobsters. The fishing was a part-time occupation for all the islanders, Jim taking it most seriously, but he had other work running the mailboat and helping with the ponies on his croft. Jock and the Isbisters fished for the pot but Ken, Jim's brother, would fish until he had a good haul of lobsters before going to the mainland to cash in his earnings and then might not return for several weeks as he was often bored on the island.

To access the moored boats the islanders had "flatties" – small dinghies – with a flat bottom that were light enough to carry ashore, their size being restricted to conveying one person at a time. When Jim went out in his flattie the water was almost coming over the edge because it was so small and he was so big. Simon, in his usual fashion, would shout out some remark: 'What have you been eating for dinner, Jim, a whole cow?' Jim would give a wide grin, frightened to laugh in case the water came over the edge of the boat, which would have delighted Simon. When ashore the flatties were turned upside down and heaped with stones to prevent them being blown away. The beginning of September was considered the latest time they could leave their small boats safely on moorings.

One of the few things all the islanders agreed on was the need for a better pier and the construction of a breakwater to create a harbour. We had seen up to eight large foreign factory ships and trawlers anchoring or dodging on the sheltered east side of the island during stormy weather. Not that a new harbour would be suitable for them, but it showed how the island acted as a large breakwater against the Atlantic waves. It would be possible to improve the existing pier for the smaller boats used by the islanders but, in most other islands we had worked, and in remote communities, the larger fishing boats were nearly always based at the nearest harbour accessible to the markets.

One hundred years before, when sailing boats turned to steam and later diesel, the large southern ports expanded as these trawlers took the opportunity to land their fish wherever they could get the best price, often the closest seaport

The island yoals pulled up on the Ham beach. The Haa and shop can be seen in the background. *Lesley Timings*

to highly-populated areas or close to a railway line that led to a city. In Shetland, both Scalloway on the west side and Lerwick on the east side had fish markets with processing factories and good access to the main markets in the south via the ferries. Engineering firms and ship-repair yards were established, allowing the fishermen to safely leave their boats to be fuelled, stored, repaired, and finally to have ice put aboard to make them ready for the next trip, while the crew took time off.

In the island of Barra the larger fishing boats, the *Venture* and *St Clair*, used to land their fish at Mallaig, carry out repairs and buy anything they required, including ice, before returning to a sheltered mooring at the island to give themselves a break with their families before returning to the local fishing grounds. Unfortunately this was not possible in Foula, and never likely to be due to its lack of a good place for shelter, otherwise it might have been a very different island. Foula was never likely to be anything other than a small outlying harbour only able to provide limited shelter in moderate weather conditions.

The Ham pier provided a platform to land goods such as tractors, gravel or stock, and of course included the facilities to lift out the mailboat. But it was still a poor place to run a consistent mailboat service. The cost of an upgraded harbour would run into several millions, a near impossible decision for the council to make, particularly with little help coming from the island and no guarantee that it would ever get increased usage by the islanders to create enough revenue to help pay for its maintenance.

On the occasions Simon and I had to go to the Shetland mainland our only way to guarantee a speedy return before we had our salvage boat was to take our 13½-foot inflatable to Walls, about an hour's journey from pier to pier. We would then get a bus, if available, or a taxi into Lerwick, a distance of 26 miles that could take over 40 minutes on the narrow, twisted but attractive road. The trips to the mainland in the early days were always exciting; seeing new people and old friends, going to shops and a pub. On our return to Walls, if we had equipment with us we would hope to load it and, if possible, our inflatable aboard the Foula mailboat for a more comfortable journey back.

On one trip our holiday feeling deserted us when we came back to Walls in the evening to find the mailboat was not leaving until the next day, and we had to share the only remaining bunk in the Foula hut as Jock and Rob were also waiting and were sleeping in the other bunks. The following morning Rob contacted Jim to find out that he would have to wait for a day as Jim was bringing some ponies through from Lerwick. Rob had no choice but to stay as he was the mailboat crew, but Jock surprised us by asking if he could come across in the inflatable. Jock Ratter was in his late fifties and gave the impression of being unyielding, with a subtle and slightly black sense of humour. A thickset man with large hands and a rugged, weather-beaten face, they said he'd had a tough time as a young man when he was a Japanese prisoner of war on a cargo ship in Singapore. He lived at the south end of the island in North Biggins with his wife Jessie, in the next croft to the Isbisters. He rarely smiled, but when he did he would push his cap back on his head and give a great beam that completely changed the shape of his face.

The Ratters were one of the older island families. In 1832 Lawrence Ratter, who was the skipper of the Foula boat, had his home at Gittorm (Guthren) at the south end and was described by a visitor … 'We entered, of course, in the Norse fashion through the offices, or rather the "outhouses", and from thence passed through one door after another to the chamber of dais, where I found seated his wife and children. Everything bore witness of a superior style to most of the cottages I had seen in Shetland. The whole wall was panelled in woodwork as clean as in Switzerland, and numerous cupboards of good workmanship were arranged, and well filled to all appearances with good warm clothing of wadmead, and with carpenter's tools and fishing apparatus. It was indeed a remarkable fact to meet with so clean a house amidst the poor inhabitants of Foulah.'[11]

The Ratters had been a large Foula family, a mainstay of the island, but they were now down to Jock and his son John-Andrew, Jock's brother Peter having left for Scalloway with his family several years before we arrived.

Jock regularly drove down to the pier on an old, khaki-coloured army motorbike, often with a gun slung over his shoulder, making him look like a wartime dispatch rider as he checked his 60-year-old Shetland yoal. He fished, and often shot seabirds for the pot, adding to his natural food supply to make him almost self-sufficient in much that he ate. We thought he lived like the Foula folk of the past and, after telling him we had lost two diving knives, we discovered that he was a good blacksmith. He asked to be shown a knife and was given an explanation of how it could be made better. Two days later he gave us two improved knives, hammered out from old car springs using his blacksmith's forge. He refused payment so we offered him copper recovered from the wreck. This he transformed into "ram's head" letter openers and small kollies (lamps) that he sold on the mainland.

When Simon and I required tuskers – a traditional Shetland tool for cutting peat – he also made them for us. It was never a chore for him to make tools, and these were one of his specialities. He had even made a stainless steel tusker from a landing strut off a wartime aircraft that had crashed on the island, and Simon and I had watched him beat out the red-hot steel from his peat-fuelled forge. The peat was extracted from the deepest peat bank, it was hard and looked blue, as if it were turning into a coal-like substance, and gave out a tremendous heat. The red-hot metal slowly formed into the correct shapes as he beat it out on his anvil, and we could see the obvious pleasure reflecting in his face. He was carrying on a long tradition of making items. Foula Islanders had made their own turning lathes, looms, spinning wheels, cloth, clothes, boots, shoes, clogs, furniture of all sorts, boats, spades, mills and wheelbarrows, in fact everything they needed.[23] That explained why three blacksmith families remained on the island.

Jock's typical dry sense of humour was seen when Elizabeth had accidently let a bottle of Robinson's concentrated orange juice fall out of her "Walls box" as it was passed up from the mailboat. It plunged into the sea and was broken between the boat and the pier.

'What's become of it?' she asked, staring down before she saw the contents start to discolour the sea. 'Yon's a tragedy,' she repeated a few times while shaking her head, before Jock replied in his matter-of-fact way of speaking, 'Woman, woman, never bother theeself – it'll no' damage the sea.'

I was surprised Jock chose to come in the inflatable. When we asked him if he had any luggage, he appeared with a wooden sea chest the size of a small trunk and, passing it down to the inflatable, I secured it in the centre with ropes. The weather was good, with a long, slow swell and no wind, allowing Jock to sit comfortably on his sea chest for the entire trip. We could see he was enjoying the new experience, declaring that he felt like a "mally" (fulmar) gliding over the waves. After he said it, he pushed his cap back on his head and smiled, and it was then I knew we had the real Jock Ratter aboard.

Approaching Foula we could see in the distance the mast and derrick of a boat sticking up above the pier. She was not a fishing boat, which made me give Simon a questioning look as we were always worried about competition.

'It's the *Shetlander*!' Jock shouted above the noise of the outboard, as he pushed his cap back and smiled.

I returned the smile and nodded, knowing the boat by reputation. The Shetland Islands Council ran this ancient, 70-foot converted fishing boat. It was used as a "flit boat" – a small cargo vessel that was able to get into the more remote piers in the islands with bulk cargoes of sand, stone chips, cement, timber, sheep and cattle, basically anything the mailboats were unable to manage. She returned to the mainland with products or animals to be sold. Although certificated as seaworthy, the *Shetlander* gave the appearance of being close to the conclusion of her working life.

Lying across the end of the pier, we had to duck under her stern mooring rope as we motored around her to get to the steps.

'I'll see what's aboard,' said Simon, as he jumped ashore and looked in the hold.

'Gravel,' he shouted back. 'It'll be for the road.'

The sound of our boat had alerted the crew and a head appeared out of the wheelhouse window. 'Are you coming aboard, boys?' queried Robbie, the larger-than-life skipper who had a Whalsay accent, which at times was indecipherable to us.

'We'll be down when we've changed,' Simon shouted back, as he pulled back the hood of his oilskin jacket.

'Let's get some food first, they're not going anywhere,' I said.

The *Shetlander* and her crew brought "Para Handy", the fictional puffer skipper to mind. There were similarities in the traditional way the boat was operated. It was not powered by steam, but a Kelvin engine that required attention, and she spent her whole time going into small piers and harbours where the crew were not averse to a drink when they tied up. We knew she was soon to be replaced by another boat, the *Spes Clara* (meaning hope and brightness), but Robbie would continue as skipper.

After a quick meal, Simon and I wandered down to the boat. With the

*Shetlander* unloaded, Robbie and the crew were relaxing, but we left after a beer to walk up to Ham to see Elizabeth. When we arrived we found her pacing up and down inside the house, going from checking the kettle to spreading butter on soda bread before returning to recheck the kettle. She appeared upset, as if bursting to tell us some news and yet not wanting to say the words. I was hoping it was not something terrible.

'Boys, boys, some of my kye (cattle) are ga'ing the morn,' she said, the words tumbling out of her as if she couldn't hold them back any longer. She had been talking about selling the cows since we had been on the island, as she was no longer able to grow enough hay for their winter feed and it was too costly to buy in animal feed from the mainland. Her only option was to sell the last of her beasts, although she was already missing the supply of fresh milk and butter as her milk cow had been taken out the month before by the fishing boat *Spray*. Now, with Robbie's arrival, she had the opportunity to dispose of the last cattle in Foula, an island that must have had stock for centuries. But it wasn't the loss of their meat or milk that was bothering her, she was unhappy because she was fond of them; they were like pets.

'It's for the better, Elizabeth, your life'll be easier,' Simon said, as he tucked into his warm, buttered soda bread.

'I don't know. I've always had kye and the poor beasts are to be loaded into yon hold of Robbie's boat.'

'He'll have special slings for loading them,' I said, 'and the forecast's good, so they'll have an easy crossing.'

'They'll bring in some money,' Simon ventured, with a smile.

'Aye, there's that,' Elizabeth cheered up. It wasn't to be such a black day after all.

The following day Simon and I went down to the pier to see if we could help the *Shetlander* as she prepared to load the cows, but Jim, Ken and Rob had returned earlier that morning with the mailboat and they were experienced in this type of work.

'Mind, mind my kye,' repeated Elizabeth several times as they started to place lifting slings on the first beast. 'I canna watch,' she repeated, as she walked further away up the pier, much to the relief of the people loading the boat. But they had everything under control, handling the docile cattle with ease, checking the slings and signalling Robbie to start the lift. Robbie stood at the winch completely relaxed while keeping an eye on the process as if it were an everyday occurrence. Each unhappy beast dangled helplessly in the rope slings on the end of the winch wire, a rope attached to the horns being held by Jim to prevent it swinging and to keep the beast's head clear of any obstruction as the derrick slewed from the pier to the hatch. Down the animals went, disappearing from view as they landed in the bottom of the hold where they were pushed against the forward bulkhead with gates; this would stop them falling when the boat was at sea. The hatch boards were replaced and the canvas cover fitted, leaving a gap above the cattle to allow the air in.

The *Shetlander* backed off the pier, slipping neatly out of the voe on her way to the Shetland mainland. Disheartened islanders watched from the pier, the shop had closed, two islanders had recently left, and now the cattle were gone. What would happen next?

There were two island events that involved co-operation: the first was peat-cutting for the elderly, and the second was the collecting of sheep from the scattald (communal grazing on the hill). This occurred in late summer or

Ken and Jim guide the last cows into the hold of the *Shetlander*.

autumn, and was referred to as a "cruie", taking its name from the drystone walls forming a curved V-shape used to trap the sheep into a flock for rooing (removing the wool). The estimated 2,000 sheep on the island required the scattald to be divided into multiple areas, a separate day being required to drive sheep in each area, providing some of the most energetic days in island life.

Although rumours spread about the dates for the cruies, Simon and I were normally asked the day before whether we would be free, as all able-bodied adults and children were required. The intention was always to start first thing in the morning, but it almost took a separate cruie to gather the islanders. Between 15 and 20 adults and children eventually assembled, along with several excited dogs. Most of us, particularly the elderly and children, would ride on Jim's tractor and trailer, taking them as near as possible to one of the V-shaped dry-stone walls; the actual "cru". It normally lay close to accessible in-by land, but there were some in remoter areas well beyond the worked land, making it an arduous trip to carry or drive tethered and hobbled sheep back to the nearest place the tractor could reach without the risk of it ending up stuck in a bog, or overturning on steep land.

The elderly and children checked the cru making sure it had no obvious gaps for the sheep to get through, as the stones and wire netting often became displaced, and at times the wind would demolish sections of the dry-stone walls. The remaining herders were sent by roundabout routes to positions behind the sheep with every effort being made not to disturb them. Simon and I being young and fit were sent up to the highest area. Jim, the person in charge, would initiate the progress of the line by signalling with his arm, this would be passed on by each herder who had to remain within signalling or shouting distance of each other. There were always large gaps between individuals because of the expanse of hill, the small number of people and a lack of good dogs. Even at this stage some of the dogs would be out of control running wildly about, chasing small groups or individual sheep; at times it was luck that drove them in the right direction. Kimmy, an island dog, was a particular culprit. As the line advanced and we closed in, the sheep became wily, taking any opportunity to run back towards us, even straight at an individual if they expected a trap. Although the herding principle was simple, Foula sheep were reluctant to gather into a flock; they had instincts like their owners, desperately trying to remain independent. The hills were too steep in places for humans, but not the sheep, although eventually most of them succumbed and moved in the same direction, if not the right direction. When they gathered speed, we had to run over the rough ground, jumping over rocks and mounds of heather in an attempt to cut them off from escaping to the side, and at the same time trying, often unsuccessfully, not to frighten them into running faster. John-Andrew and his father Jock thought nothing of chasing after them on the steeply sloping grounds; it seemed crazy to me as many of these steep banks terminated in vertical cliffs. We kept to the safer ground, trying to ignore the dogs beside us that barked and ran, becoming more excited the faster the sheep moved. Sometimes the dogs assisted as the sheep were frightened of them, but the odd dog having returned from one foray would end up pursuing a single sheep into the far distance, with an angry owner shouting and cursing while chasing after the dog with little hope of its return until it had run itself into the ground.

'Kimmy, Kimmy, come here you!' was a much repeated phrase floating over the island until the sound was gradually absorbed by the hills, along with the dog.

At the north of the island we drove about 200 sheep down towards Harrier on one occasion, and Mucklegrind on another. The old and young helped to guide them the final stretch towards the cru, where they were eventually penned, but that was just the start. Where the dry-stone wall was too low or damaged, Rylock netting had been placed on top, but the sheep remained undeterred. These wild animals would climb on top of each other to make an attempt at jumping out. Some were fearless, charging straight at us or the dogs until they had tested every weak point; it was only then, after accepting defeat, that they started to settle down.

Each island family had their individual mark on their ewes and also on some lambs that had been caught during the lambing season. The remainder required sorting, with an attempt at finding their mother to give them the correct mark. It usually ended in guess work with an eye to be fair as, in many cases, unless the lamb or owner recognised the mother there was no way of apportioning them. The men manhandled the sheep, giving them to the women to be roo'ed. The wool on the Foula sheep breaks naturally when the new growth starts in the spring, allowing the fleece to be pulled off. Starting at the middle of the back and working down either side, it comes off in various parts; this is unlike most Scottish sheep that require to be sheared with clippers as the new growth is unbroken from the old wool. The women excelled at this job and, as I had learned to hand-shear as a boy, I was given those that were difficult to roo or required tidying up around the tail, before treating them for general health care, including keds, fly strike, foot rot or any of the numerous ailments to which the sheep are prone.

After the tractor disappeared with the elderly and first load of lambs to distribute them to the appropriate crofts, we would bundle all the wool, release the breeding ewes back on to the hill, and continue to sort the lambs, hoggs, and ewes unsuitable for breeding. By the time all the sheep had been sorted the soft, dim light of the Shetland night had crept in. Feeling an ache in my back when I stood up straight I looked to the north, hoping to enjoy the northern lights dancing over the sea. During the summer the midnight sun is often too bright but later, after September, it became a beautiful sight, encouraging us when we had to drive the lambs and carry the wool, often over boggy land, shallow burns and steep ridges, to the nearest place the tractor and trailer could reach. The lambs still required continual attention to stop them escaping, even though the worst offenders were hobbled by tying a piece of rope from a rear leg to the opposite fore leg. When the final load of sheep and wool were on the trailer, we made our way back. If there was space we would sit on the edge of the trailer, if not we staggered along the track, gradually falling back to become a trail of exhausted and silent people; all our remaining thoughts concentrating on getting us home.

As Simon and I passed Ham, Elizabeth, who must have been watching for us, called us in to have a meal. She was fair delighted that she had some wool and lambs to sell, and we were pleased to sit down at her table and not have to cook for ourselves.

Back at the Haa, the Tilley was lit and the slow process of taking clothes off began as we looked for keds – brown, hairy, wingless flies about a quarter-of-an-inch long that behave like ticks and live their entire lives feeding off sheep's blood. After handling the sheep, I always found a few round my waist. The most I ever counted was 40. We soaked our discarded clothes in a strong industrial detergent in the hope it would kill anything that had been missed. For the next few days every itch or scratch was given a good looking to, in case it was a creature that had escaped our search.

I had enjoyed all the islands I worked on, but somehow Foula was different, it was like falling in love; there was a magic, an unknown combination of the physical attraction of the island and the character of the people. I knew Simon was happy, even though for him it was not a preferred choice. He was a social person, enjoying an organised life with plenty of people where he could indulge in gossip, banter and interaction, whereas I preferred person to person, or small groups, and liked to be involved with all the practicalities of life. I always looked forward to every day as I could feel my time enhanced by the experience of our life on the island as well as the diving, but by the end of our first November we had no option but to go to Edinburgh to sort out the legal aspects of our wreck. Word had spread about the value of the wreck and we were required to defend our rights to work it.

Having worked closely with Simon for 18 months, we had begun to know each other so well that we were beginning to sense what the other wanted to do, even sharing one suit between us, known as "the company suit".

**Edith starting to roo a sheep.**

The arrangement worked well as we rarely went to anything smart, and if we did it was not at the same time. This good relationship made our lives easy and non-confrontational. I dealt with the engineering options and Simon handled most of the dealings with people, resolving a multitude of living decisions that made our life easier. In Fife we'd go out to the pub together, make up foursomes and had many of the same friends. Simon was always popular; he had a good sense of humour and a knack of making up nicknames for objects as well as people that were so appropriate they tended to stick.

Our work together was likely to end when this project was completed as Simon declared he would get "a proper job", returning to journalism, the public relations industry or even running a pub. Whatever happened, I knew how different my life would be, but it was impossible to ignore the experience I was gaining here, and there were times I seriously considered the option of staying on the island. Perhaps it was the contrast with Fife that enhanced both places, seeing one without the other would have lacked something, like scenery painted in one colour. Unfortunately, I knew there could be no compromise in the future, there could be no half measures. It would have to be a decision to live in Foula, or somewhere else.

After a week south, we agreed that Simon would stay and sort out the remaining legal business that had turned into a court case, while I returned to the island to look after our work and continue making improvements to the house.

# Chapter 5
# Alone at the Haa

Taking the ferry from Aberdeen to Shetland, I used the first short break in the bad weather to cross to Foula in our inflatable. Arriving just before the wind and rain reappeared, I was met by Rob at the pier who helped me lift the boat ashore. Running up to the Haa I opened the door to see Elizabeth had lit the fire for me and, after removing my oilskins, I sat in my usual chair when I was startled by a sudden rush of air that made the flames surge up the chimney. I thought the back door had blown open and cursed myself for not shutting it properly. Reluctantly, I moved from my chair, pausing as I heard the door close. John-Andrew Ratter appeared in the doorway. At 19 he was the youngest adult on the island, and with a wild bushy beard had all the good looks expected of a fictional island character. He was dynamic, always busy, exceptionally good with his hands at carpentry or mechanical work, but less patient with crofting. Married to Francie, he lived at Punds, a croft in Hametoon at the south end where he was determined to try and carve out a future on the island.

He sat on the settee in front of the fire, water dripping off the oilskin jacket he carried. He had his waterproof trousers pulled down below his knees, a trick we all used if we were to sit down for a brief visit; the effort involved in removing boots to get the trousers off was just too much and often messy if there was mud on the oilskins. We both looked up when we heard a loud howl from the wind outside, expecting to see some debris fly past the window; how different this was to Fife.

John-Andrew had brought me a shag he had shot. I went to the kitchen to fetch a bowl for the edible parts, along with a packet of digestive biscuits, while he started skinning the bird on a newspaper on the table. By the time I returned he was able to place the two breasts in the bowl; the meat looked dark and oily, not at all like I imagined the flesh of a bird. The inedible parts he wrapped in the newspaper for disposal in the sea or burning. I picked them up to throw in the back of the fire when I was again distracted by the Tilley lamp starting to pulse, the light fading and glowing in a rhythmic fashion as the pressure varied. He glanced at me as if asking approval to work the pump, I nodded and wondered if there was a superstition about it.

'Cooker still working?' he enquired.

'Just,' I replied, 'it'll cook the bird.'

The Calor gas cooker was near the end of its life, the burner inside the oven so corroded that the flames were no longer level and if the gas was low the flames looked more like a row of badly-burning candles. Simon intended to bring a secondhand replacement when he came north but until then it had to do, there was no alternative.

John-Andrew had few opportunities on the island. Francie, his wife, worked hard on the croft, providing vegetables and fresh mutton, as well as bringing in a small income from selling lambs and claiming the sheep subsidy. He brought home wild birds' eggs at spring time and fowls all year round. It was always an easy conversation with him as we had a lot in common talking about boats, animals and the work that had to be done on the island. I rarely asked personal questions as I might in Fife where I had friends I had known since childhood, but when Simon was here he liked to push the conversation in that direction. He had the ability to ask the questions without sounding as if he was prying into their lives – which was exactly what he was doing.

John-Andrew explained how during the summer he had been going out with Jim on his lobster boat, but it was not regular work and they were unable to carry enough creels to make a living for both of them. He followed this by saying he would have to leave next summer unless he could get work on the island. I was shocked – the island could not afford to lose another of its young. Typical of a talented lad, he was struggling to make a living with the limited opportunities available, although 27 miles away on the Shetland mainland there were numerous jobs available in the boatyards, crews for fishing boats, oil related work, and building sites that had become busy due to the oil industry. There would not be a better place in the country to offer such good openings for someone with his talents.

He stood up to leave, pulling his oilskin trousers up and lifting the wide braces over each shoulder. His words had made me question whether "just surviving" was a sufficient reason for staying on the island, but the island had been home to generations of Ratters, and both John-Andrew's parents were still alive. He had a home and it was unlikely he would want to leave. Even I felt a bond to the island after only being here for a short time, but I also understood the necessity to earn a living and knew that many of John-Andrew's ancestors would have left the island to find work. A compelling reason for this generation to stay had been brought on by the critically low level of able-bodied people to keep everyday life going. If any of the few young were to leave, they knew it could have a disastrous knock-on effect to the rest of the island. Fortunately for us, after we established ourselves on the wreck, he was able to join us.

After seeing John-Andrew to the door I found an old copy of my mother's Scottish Women's Rural Institute cook book. Tucked inside the cover were many of her handwritten recipes that were faded and stained with food. One recipe started with the instructions: 'Take your sheep's head, and using a blow torch first singe the hair …' I doubted if it had shag in it, but as it was my domestic instruction manual I required it for anything but the most basic cooking.

The dark colour and meaty texture of the cooked breasts did nothing to reduce the strong flavour of fish. It was certainly edible, and filled an empty stomach, but not an experience I would recommend. Leaving my plate on the table I filled two more hot-water bottles from the kettle before smothering the fire with the crumbles of broken peats to let it smoulder for the night. After a brief visit to Elizabeth, I climbed the wooden stairs to my room where I slipped into the damp bed with most of my clothes on and lay awake listening to the wind rattling the slates. Unable to sleep, I realised the advantages of an island house having either Orkney slate that was as thick as paving stones, or bituminous roofing felt – neither would rattle. Eventually, when the wind dropped there were still odd sounds that woke me, like a bird pecking at the window, but for a short period there was silence before the gales and horizontal rain returned with a vengeance.

With winter approaching, the weather in Foula became unpredictable, gales and heavy rain dominating the outlook. Working outside became a challenge

John-Andrew with a razorbill. *Lesley Timings*

and I often looked for an excuse to stop and walk up to the warmth and comfort of Ham under the pretext that I wished to know if Simon had phoned. Sitting next to Joann with a cup of coffee in my hand, we chatted about the island and I listened to any recent gossip Elizabeth had picked up – there was little news that escaped her.

On one of the few dry days, Elizabeth came to the Haa to ask me if I could cut a field of oats. Of course I agreed. I had seen the oats growing next to her walled yard that contained kale and tatties and often wondered what would happen to the weather-beaten crop as it should have been cut weeks ago; it was now the 17th of November. If it was left much longer the next gale and heavy rain would destroy it. She claimed this would be the last year she would grow oats because there was no one to help her, and with the cattle sold she would struggle to cope with all her sheep, let alone cultivate the ground for a crop of oats. They had been planted by her husband John, a dynamic man, much younger than her, who had also started to construct the foundations for a hostel next to Ham. They both loved the island, but when it came down to a very limited choice of partners, this marriage had unfortunately ended up as a bad decision for them both.

Finding a traditional, two-handled Scottish scythe hanging in the byre, I walked with her to the partially flattened crop that was drying quickly in the fresh wind. The oats cut easily; the swish, swish, swish of the scythe dominated the day as the crop fell cleanly off the sharp blade to lie in a row beside me. Elizabeth followed, her short, stout body having difficulty bending over as she gathered the crop into sheaves before binding them with twisted lengths of straw. At 3.30 in the afternoon, when the darkness began to creep over us, she returned to Ham to check on Joann and fetch a lamp. Occasionally we would stop and she would look at me with a tired but pleasant gaze before shining the lamp around to see how much more we had to harvest, but the cold quickly worked its way into our stationary bodies forcing us to continue. We hastily cut and bound in silence as both of us knew there might not be another dry day, and when the rain returned it would all be lost.

With the field finished we returned to Ham in the blackness of the night. I could see by Joann's face that she was relieved to see us and the three of us sat there like a family. There was something gratifying about it, something intangible, an affinity that had been brought on by the harvesting of a crop by hand. There was an undoubted bond when working the land that could not be replicated, and it was heightened by our small achievement through hard physical work. Elizabeth looked tired, and showed her age, but with a broad smile she put on a pot to boil up some salt fish and tatties before collapsing onto a chair. I became lost in my thoughts and fell asleep on the resting chair beside Joann, only waking when I was disturbed by her patting my hand. Glancing up I could see her looking at me with a deep, kind smile, pointing out a cup of coffee beside me. I must have been dreaming about the island as I wanted to ask Joann about her life; she was normally so quiet but now she had picked up and looked well and happy, but this was not the time. Tonight we would relax and enjoy the salt fish and tatties as we celebrated the harvesting of the crop.

I had mixed feelings about returning to Fife for Christmas and New Year as Foula was unique in holding Yule Day and Nuerday, as Christmas and New Year day were called, on the dates of the outdated Julian calendar. The rest of the country used the Gregorian calendar which was first introduced to the UK in 1752. Foula had been left behind by the 12 days difference, but time and dates only became important when you have interconnected transport systems and an organised society, a few days here and there were of no significance to the islanders. People marked their days by nature, the time to cultivate the ground, birds migrating, lambs being born and, as the weather improved, the small yoals being launched. Plants began to flower, the mackerel arrived, and the long, light summer nights were followed by the harvest. Then gathering the sheep, and finally the boats being taken ashore as the daylight gradually reduced and winter approached. It was a natural cycle that had continued over centuries, unbroken by man-made timetables. It was lived at a measured pace, requiring a different mentality – a life that followed the beat of nature's heart.

On Nuerday there would be quite a party and, as social gatherings were unusual, it was an experience I wished to be part of, but it was not to be as I had other, more serious commitments. Simon and I had business decisions to make and we were obliged to operate on a timetable when south – and I was looking forward to seeing Mary, a girl I had been going out with. It was times like this that I could understand how difficult it must be for young islanders to make the choice between living on the island or romance, particularly if no partners were available on the island. Nature would be vying with nurture.

The last time I had seen Mary was in Fair Isle. She and her friend Margo came for a week during their summer holidays. Simon and I had looked forward to seeing them; they had said they would come and they had kept their word, although it was a difficult place to get to. It was a treat to see them both arrive on the *Good Shepherd*. I always felt comfortable with Mary, never nervous. I don't know if it was the result of her being local and knowing her family, or that she knew most of my past; there was nothing to hide or mist over. She was a bright girl who, after university, had ventured abroad to undertake voluntary work in Thailand, Laos and Nepal, returning with a mature and experienced view of the world.

In Fair Isle, where we had no work pressure, our routine was pleasantly disrupted by their arrival. We took the week off to share the pleasures of living on an island, bringing them with us in the inflatable when we dived, or to admire the cliffs and geos (small inlets) and let them see the fantastic bird life. If the weather was too bad at sea there was always plenty to do on the island with lighthouses, visiting crofts, or just lying on top of the cliffs looking up at the sky or down at the birds and enjoying the tremendous feeling of freedom it conferred. I was on a high, enjoying the summer as we tried to make a living, my mind full of dreams of the future, but those dreams did not include a strong relationship and I was not sure that her dreams included one either. It was never discussed as I felt it might dampen our pleasure.

I was told by a diver friend, Peter, that: 'You rarely marry those you know well from a young age'. It was anecdotal, but he claimed that if you already knew each other's boundaries it reduced your expectations, whereas with a stranger there is all the "excitement of discovery". Peter had a failed marriage and I wondered if his wife was a childhood sweetheart and this was his excuse. It seemed such an odd comment at the time but it used to bounce around my brain, and when I looked at my friends, few had married those they knew well when they were young. Perhaps we were genetically programmed to marry a stranger, to spread the gene pool, or because the grass was always greener on the other side of the fence. I realised it wasn't just Foula that had people leaving their homes for better jobs; many of my friends had also moved, including Mary to work in England. But in Fife their leaving was always balanced by new families arriving; there were few ruins or empty homes, in fact the reverse as houses were being built or restored in every town and village, particularly nearby St Andrews, the home of Scotland's oldest University and golf.

Finding a partner was nature's high priority to most young people, including myself, and I could understand how difficult it could be where choice was limited and they might have to leave to marry the person they loved. I mentioned to Simon that leaving the island 'might be better than a failed marriage'. But Simon replied, 'Maybe not. Any children must be good for the island community.'

Arriving in Fife six days before Christmas my time seemed to fly as we also celebrated a successful battle in court that allowed us to continue our work on the wreck. I saw Mary, and I also became selfishly bound up in my work with Simon. When she left I longed to go back to the island, but I wasn't quite sure why. I was enjoying finding and ordering new bits of equipment and in the evenings we relaxed in our local bar. Simon was content to stay in Fife; we had won our court case and he could now sort out a more formal contractual agreement on the *Oceanic*. But he also accepted that it would be a good idea to maintain our presence in Foula to enforce a legal aspect regarding our hold on the wreck. This would allow me to continue repairing the house and prepare for the new season.

I boarded the steamer to Shetland during a spell of good weather and caught the first mailboat sailing to Foula since Christmas Eve, the island having sustained a period of over 40 days without any service as it was now the 4th of February. Immediately after the mailboat arrived the sky opened, the wind increased, and the boat was hurriedly unloaded and hauled up the slipway. Elizabeth welcomed me back and asked me to look in, before she rushed back with her Walls box to gain the shelter of Ham.

The damp had swollen the back door of the Haa, making it difficult to open or close, and with the house in darkness I felt my way along the passage before seeing the familiar wood-panelling of the sitting room. The light from the fire welcomed me as I rummaged in a drawer for a torch. The atmosphere was captivating. I smiled, it was just what I had been looking forward to seeing, and was enhanced by Elizabeth kindly lighting the fire. I hauled off my wet-weather gear and hung it on the rail below the mantelpiece then shifted the cast-iron kettle from the large brass nut to place it in the centre of the burning peats. The water was already warm, it would not be long before it boiled. I lit the Tilley lamp, my arms going automatically to the various pieces – the methylated spirit, matches, and paraffin

– as if I'd never left. Carrying it upstairs I entered my bedroom and immediately felt the warmth from the fire, but smoke lay in the room like mist. I poked the fire; it was poor at drawing, maybe the chimney was partially blocked. Placing my hand in the bed I could feel it was still damp, almost wet, and would require hot-water bottles to dry it. Leaving the fire in the bedroom to burn out, I hoped the smoke might at least kill any insects that had sneaked into the room since I left in December. After filling a hot-water bottle I bailed water into the kettle from the bucket we used to carry it from the kitchen, and put the kettle back on the peats to fill more of our large stock of hot-water bottles.

Settling back in the Haa I realised how island life had forced on me a degree of self-sufficiency that had strengthened my life, making me experience the actual labour of living. It added time to each day and was more challenging than south, but it was certainly no hardship at my age. Taking my new diary I laid it on the table where I knew I would carefully fill it in each day. Looking up from writing in it, my thoughts went to Simon. I could imagine him sitting in a warm pub in St Andrews, friends beside him, relaxed and easy as they discussed sport, girls or just general banter to fill their evening. Tonight I preferred the noise of the rain driving against the windows. I felt secure, comfortable and protected within this happy house and I was pleased to leave the rest of the world and all its problems. I liked being on my own. It was not that Simon was difficult to live with, in fact quite the opposite – he was easy-going and little bothered him – but we were often thankful to get a break from each other. We were so close at times, literally, our lives depending on each other when we were working underwater.

Each day I sat in front of the warming peat fire and ate a breakfast of porridge and fresh milk, until it ran out, when I reluctantly made up powdered milk. I started work at eight while it was still dark, and after bringing peats in I continued to dig out the main drains around the outside of the house. My pick penetrated deep into the ground above the old, stone-built drains, loosening the accumulation of earth and debris around them, and when the drain became exposed I broke up the packed material that had blocked it before carefully replacing the flat, stone covers. The exercise kept me warm, while the rain battered against my oilskins and drips ran down the back of my neck whenever I looked up to search for a glimpse of the sun, willing it to break through the dark, evil-looking sky. But it was not until ten o'clock that it gave me a few hours of daylight, and then the darkness returned by three; the daylight hours were short in winter at 60 degrees north, the same latitude as St Petersburg and southern Greenland.

I found these moments of simple but hard physical labour became thinking times, weighing choices about my future, my work, where I would live, the type of person I might aspire to marry. It all whirled round my head only to evolve in a different conclusion each time. But I knew that I must make some decisions; I wanted my life to be based on choice, rather than default.

Carting all the mud and silt from the drains up to the Haa yard, I spread it out in the hope we would make a vegetable garden, something that later proved easier to imagine than achieve. During the spreading I found short cuts of old 35mm film that must have been dumped by Michael Powell's film company in 1936 when they made the film *The Edge of the World*. The film portrayed the abandonment of the island in a romantic version of the real St Kilda evacuation of 1930. Powell had been allowed to use the Haa on the condition that he would undertake maintenance and improvements in lieu of rent – no signed papers or contract, it was by word of mouth with the owners – just like us. The entire film crew lived in wooden huts which were assembled in the Haa yard after the soil had been removed. Their own steam yacht, the *Vedra*, had been used as transport for all their needs but spent most of its time in Scalloway because of the weather. Many of the island population were employed as builders and general hands, as well as extras in the film in which John Laurie was one of the stars, later to become well-known playing the undertaker in the well-loved *Dad's Army* production.

When anyone appeared I took it as a good excuse to stop work and put the kettle on. Peter Gray, who was a fit, over-80 living in Burns croft, very tactfully advised me on rebuilding the open fire place. Although the fire remained usable the stones had collapsed at the sides and it was just a matter of time before the fire would be unsafe. Peter suggested I should purchase fire bricks and showed me the correct way to rebuild it, gently reminding me that the flames should not be able to touch the large, sandstone mantle, and it would be wise to build in a plate of iron beneath it to avoid the stone cracking if quickly heated by a sudden roaring fire. Instructed to do the job in such a well-worded, knowledgeable and delicate manner, I felt obliged to follow his method, thinking he might return to look at it when I had finished. I then began a hunt on the island for suitable materials and was lucky to find a plate of cast iron that had been used as ballast in an old boat, the *Edna*, that lay derelict at the side of the slip. I was allowed to take it and, at the same time, I asked for rails from a small, ruined slipway, originally built by Alasdair Holbourn – the middle son of the professor – for his yacht. The bolts holding the rails had rusted through, making them easy to remove before I dug holes for two of them in the Haa yard to act as poles for a washing line. I was realising that it was impossible to get anything completed without having the ability to make do and adapt materials that were available; ordering from the mainland might take weeks or months.

I often looked across the three miles of sea to the Shaalds – the shallow reef where the lobster boats worked in the summer and where our wreck lay. There was usually a maelstrom of white water as enormous waves tumbled over each other, tripped by the shallow rock several metres below, only to crash down before being flung up again when they collided with the following wave. I would shake my head, knowing it could be several weeks or months before we could get back to work.

Still being woken at night when an exceptional blast of wind shook the house, my tossing and turning caused my bed to collapse; the springs in the bottom had rusted through. I hauled the old, rust-stained, horse-hair mattress downstairs and set it on the floor in front of the fire. The following morning, to replace the springs I wove rope through the best of the wire netting that supported the mattress; it may not be so comfortable but it wouldn't give way again.

It was after this incident I began to feel unwell. Knowing the islanders had little immunity from infections, I shouted to Elizabeth from a distance outside her door in order that she could tell everybody to keep away in case it was something I had brought from the mainland. In the past, epidemics had spread through the island taking their toll on the population. It had been nearly wiped out in the early 1700s by smallpox, which repeated itself every 20 years until vaccinations eroded and eventually wiped out the virus. The lack of resistance to infections was emphasised by the war memorial – of the five people lost in the First World War, three of them had died of fever or pneumonia while on service. It was no wonder the Isbisters were wary of visitors with colds.

Settling into an isolation routine with the peat fire always lit, I was happy to lie on the settee and doze. Elizabeth banged on the door every day and I went to the window so that she could see me and shout any messages before going to the back door to pick up the occasional parcel of food she left; usually a few fresh eggs or some oatmeal. Never having spent so much time inside with little to do, I began, for the first time in my life, to really enjoy reading. From the bundle of books gathered from south I became fascinated by those of Aleksandr Solzhenitsyn. Reading to the small hours made the time pass quickly.

It was two weeks before I felt completely fit again but I waited before going to meet anyone, allaying any concern by the islanders of infection. When passing the schoolhouse Mima, Jim's mother, an elderly lady who was nearly always dressed in black, came out to see how I was and, as if making an apology for not looking in when I was ill, explained that there was a flu epidemic on the island when she was 14 that killed several people including her father.

My life soon developed a routine: repairing the house, helping with croft work – including burying Elizabeth's sheep that had not survived the hard winter – and a return to enjoying sociable evenings around the fire. The drains were finally finished, replacing the earth above them with gravel, barrowed up from the beach along with sand for making cement to point the lower walls of the house. Barrowing was a laborious and time-consuming task that usually involved Tom latching himself on to me. I never wanted to be rude, but it became difficult to get away from him to continue my work as all he wanted to do was speak. He occasionally blocked my way to ensure I was listening, but it came to an end after a radio broadcast warned of poisonous drums that had been washed off the deck of a ship near Foula – he turned back after I was 50 yards from Elizabeth's croft, not wanting to go any closer to the sea.

The stormy days were broken by unexpected arrivals as the weather improved. A fishing boat, the *Bairn's Pride*, came in carrying the furniture for the new school teacher/missionary. The young on the island helped the fishermen unload and move it all to the manse while speculating how long this teacher would last and what he or she would be like, along with their partner if they had one.

Not many islanders had telephones and I had no phone so planning was impossible and mostly unnecessary, but my evenings were rarely spent alone. Foula livened up in the evenings; Jim occasionally brought his fiddle, with Rob, John-Andrew and sometimes Harry joining in at the Haa. If the weather was not too wet and windy, I might have visitors during the day or I would go out to see someone, often the Isbisters at the south end, or cross the voe to visit the nurse and her husband, before ending up at Elizabeth's. The standard of living may not have been considered high, but they had freedom to choose their hours of work.

When a relation of one of the islanders returned on a visit I was asked to the "hamefarin" held in the school. It was an island party and I was pleased to be asked, although not sure of any formalities; it was not as if I could nip out and buy some cans of beer or a bottle of whisky. With no bath or shower in the Haa I did my best with boiled water from the kettle and a plastic basin on the sitting room floor before digging out the cleanest of my meagre collection of "not very clean" clothes. Most of the able-bodied islanders attended the party, which had a relatively slow start until the fiddlers, Harry and Jim, got going, and for the first time I saw the Foula reel being danced. The movements as the partners joined together and parted represented the motion of the waves passing over the Shaalds and, like most traditions in Foula, you could understand the origin – it was real. Between the dances, Bobby Isbister sang songs he had composed, accompanied by Eric on the guitar. It was six in the morning before I left with a happy heart, lightly tripping my way down the track in complete darkness to collapse into my bed with no intention of doing anything the following day.

I began to know Harry better when boxes of parts arrived for Elizabeth's generator as the alternator had burnt out and the engine required attention. With the bad weather this was the perfect time to rebuild it, not least because it was in a shed and would keep us out of the wind and rain.

After the work was started Harry frequently came by to help and perhaps keep an eye on me, but it gave me an ideal opportunity to find out about this quiet and gentle man.

'How'd you learn about engines?' I asked Harry.

'When the film crew were here they brought a small Morris car with them. I drove it and learned to maintain it,' he replied. Harry would have been 22 years old at that time.

'Is that the car lying near the Post Office?' I asked. I had seen an old Morris 8 lying derelict in the field outside his house.

'When they went I became the owner an' kept it going as long as I could.'

'Did the film have much impact on the island?'

'The islanders helped the makin' o' the film. It was a fine break from normal work.'

'Anything else remaining from their time here?' I asked.

'They left the wooden huts the maist o' them lived in; the hoose at Mucklegrind was built wi them, haven't you been in Mucklegrind?'

'No,' I replied, 'but I've seen it from the outside.' It looked as if it was built with several huts, and Elizabeth had told me Alasdair Holbourn had built it. He lined the inside with panelling from the *Olympic*, a sister of the *Titanic*, buying the panelling when the ship was finally broken up at the yard of Thomas W. Ward at Inverkeithing in Fife during 1937.[24] To help preserve the huts, it looked as though wire mesh had been fixed to the outside before a cement harling was applied to the mesh. The huts were secured to the ground by wire ropes otherwise they would blow away during winter gales. Alasdair used to stay there during the summer but as his health deteriorated he hadn't been able to return for a few years, but all reports indicated that he was a likeable and active character who had been the island school teacher and missionary for a number of years.

After a brief chat Harry would leave and I'd carry on alone in the engine shed, but I looked forward to every visit. He was a mine of information, although

The toon of Ham from Hamnafield. The submerged reef on which the *Oceanic* lies is marked by the white water at the top right.

reluctant at times to part with some of it from concern that he might say something out of turn – which was never the case. He only once came close to giving too much information when I asked why a large fuse had been added to the circuit on an electric cable that disappeared through a hole in the side of the shed. He explained that in the event of the nurse's generator failing this cable would take electricity from Elizabeth's small generator to power a few lights and the fridge that contained medicinal drugs, and hinted this cable was the cause of the generator burning out. Elizabeth's generator was small and could only be used for lights and her twin-tub washing machine if nothing else was switched on; it did not have the power to boil an electric kettle. If Dal had switched on any additional appliances other than the fridge and lights, and the fuse did not blow, it would almost certainly have overloaded the generator. I replaced the fuse with a much smaller, manual, resettable switch that was more suited to the size of the generator. This was later named by Simon as the "Dalometer", and would trip if overloaded. My sympathy also lay with Dal, as after my last trip south I realised how easy it was when you had been used to mains electricity just to switch things on without giving them a second thought.

Several months after fitting the Dalometer we were sitting with Elizabeth in the evening when her phone rang. It was Dal asking if he could connect up to Elizabeth's generator as their generator had broken down. Elizabeth put the phone down and turned towards us. 'I reminded him it's just the lights and fridge, nothing else,' said Elizabeth.

Simon smiled in his sometimes annoyingly knowing way and walked across to the window to look at the nurse's house in the evening dim, then there was a slight flicker of the Ham lights. 'The nurses lights have just gone on,' said Simon, 'they're running on your generator now.'

After half an hour passed, Simon and I were preparing to go back to the Haa when the Ham lights dipped and quickly recovered. The three of us rushed to Elizabeth's window to see the nurse's house in darkness. Elizabeth shook her head in disbelief.

'The Dalometer's tripped,' said Simon, with a smile. 'I bet he's switched the kettle on.'

'At least your generator's not damaged,' I said to Elizabeth, just as the phone rang.

'It must be Dal,' said Simon, enjoying the situation.

Elizabeth answered the phone and spoke for a few minutes. She put the phone down. 'He says he's not going to use the electricity, the fridge has cooled sufficiently and he's coming over to borrow my Tilley lamp.'

Simon and I waited for a few minutes to see Dal. When he failed to appear we walked back to the Haa.

'I wouldn't go to bed, Alec, you're going to be called out.'

He was right.

I received a letter from Mary at the end of February. She was never far from my thoughts and seeing her over the Christmas period had kept us in touch. I knew she was ambitious, but I was besotted with Foula and could not see my work allowing me the time to see her in the foreseeable future. My father had always told me that I should not get married until I could support a wife. Perhaps this was outdated advice as most marriages of my generation had both partners working and in my line of work it was unlikely I would ever be able to guarantee anything.

Although Mary and I had been going out when our lives converged over the last three years, we were now 550 miles apart, over 200 of those by sea. I enjoyed her company, but as a young man it was difficult to tell what percentage was from the heart, what was natural instinct, or maybe just easy love from afar. Was I clinging onto a relationship that required no commitment? How could I ask a girl with a good job and secure future to come and live with me while carrying out financially-risky work on a remote island in a house with no electricity, water or plumbing? It seemed an impossible situation as I could be here for several years. I was not prepared for the alternative: to go and work in England. But like anything remote, not making a decision was an easy and faint-hearted option. I once overheard an aunt say to my parents, 'Who on earth is going to marry Alec?' It was another of those throw-away comments that swilled around my brain.

Simon was so laid back about girls, never outwardly appearing to get emotionally involved, and was popular, probably for that reason. He was quick to tease me if I said something deep or slightly philosophical about any of the girls we knew. Fortunately his teasing was always brief, and we rarely discussed each other's girlfriends knowing it might cause a rift.

'Relationships just don't work in this business,' he would say.

'It surely depends on the girl?'

'You've just got to look at Tony and Chris [divers we had worked with] to see it makes things difficult.'

'Their marriages work,' I replied.

'But that's why we're here making good money and they're not,' said Simon, as he spread out his arms, and I knew what he meant. They were restricted by having other people to consider; they were quite rightly limited in what they could do, but willingly.

There was no simple answer to Mary's letter when it arrived. It took several days of thought before I even started a reply, and then days to write it. There was no doubt our lives were going in very different directions. She was city orientated and my life was perhaps more sheltered by staying in Foula, or just very different. We were like two trees planted in different soils, and Foula was putting its mark on me. I knew I was changing irreversibly.

Eventually I sent a reply in the form of a poem. Perhaps it is the fictional aspect of poetry where reality can be damped down or gently manipulated making it easier to express feelings. Relieved at last to have written a reply, and yet still unsure whether I should give it to Harry to put in the post bag, I became unsettled and Elizabeth sensed it.

'Has thee a problem with thee work?' she asked.

'No, it's just the planning for the summer,' I lied, as she scrutinised my face wondering if I might be catching a cold.

'Mind, you'll tell me if there's anything I can do,' she replied, with genuine concern.

Next time I saw Harry I gave him the letter to put in the post. Harry, in his normal discreet way, put it in his pocket as if he would never dream of looking at the address to see who I was sending it to, which was probably true.

# Chapter 6
# Survival on Foula

As spring approached and the weather improved Simon regularly phoned Elizabeth with messages for me, asking me to call back if a decision had to be made. At times I felt I had the luxury of escaping to Foula, although at the Shetland end I also had to make arrangements for the coming season. The phone was essential to our work and even more important to the island. It must have been a different island before communications were available, particularly if anyone was seriously ill. The red phone box had been installed in 1955, but before that, in 1937, a wireless station was operational to help with communications.

Simon had been trying to arrange for someone to live in our spare room and cook us a few meals each week. In Fair Isle, Deirdre, a student working as one of the Bird Observatory temporary cooks, had often visited our hut and cooked meals that she would eat with us. When we first went to Foula she came across to see the birds and stayed briefly in our spare room in the Haa which worked well for all of us. This was before the common practice of mixed flats at universities and initially I thought some irate parent might contact us about their daughter, but in reality people trusted their offspring, appreciating that after 18 they were capable of looking out for themselves and could make their own judgements. Shetland was as practical as any society and it had always been nice to see how well Deirdre was treated by the islanders and fishermen. Generally, islanders are broadminded and, with Foula's lack of strong religious fervour, the arrangement had never been alluded to in anything but the best of terms in front of us.

Deirdre, still a student, was persuaded by Simon to come back for part of the summer; the arrangement was to cook one meal a day for five days a week and in return we would pay her a small sum for her work, along with free board and lodgings. We knew Deirdre well enough that there were unlikely to be any problems as she only had one fault – she continually beat us at board games.

The islanders advised us that April was the earliest time the weather might be settled for us to be able to work, but we were both raring to go and had no intention of missing any working days. By the beginning of March I was rushing to complete jobs on the house. I had rebuilt the fire, cleared all the drains, replaced missing slates and was beginning to reinstate the wood in the partly-collapsed roof of the baronial front porch – a place where we intended to store some of our equipment, but only if I could make it watertight.

On the 12th of March I took the inflatable to Walls and went by bus to Lerwick to meet Simon off the steamer. We shopped for food and in typical fashion I used a list while Simon went round exploring the shelves and adding treats to our trolleys. We stayed that night in the Fishermen's Mission. The following day we managed to get all our new equipment to Walls where we had a load of gear stored in our vehicle that we'd never managed to get onto the island. It was at times like this that we appreciated having both contacts and experience to be able to live and work on islands. Kenny, the owner of the small fishing boat *Lustre*, had laid it up in Walls as he was now working on the

*Bountiful*, a large Orkney fishing boat. He allowed us to use it to take all our gear to Foula. We worked into the night loading all the equipment along with some sheep feed Elizabeth had ordered, and then drove our vehicle onto the deck. After a few hours sleep in the Foula hut we set off at 7am, Simon putting his red, white and black striped bobble hat on as we left the pier – like a symbol that he was about to start his island life again, or that it was extremely cold. Arriving at 9.30am in Foula, Jim gave us a hand to unload by using the crane to get the vehicle off, and what we could not carry up to the house we left on the pier, knowing it was safe. Harry had said, 'You could leave a £5 note under a stone on the pier and it'd be there until it was blown away or rotted.' He was right.

With the quick turn round we were back in Walls by 1pm. After tying up the trawler we returned to Foula in the inflatable to find Harry and Elizabeth standing on the pier waiting for us, Elizabeth asking us up for a meal.

'When's yon cook lass comin?' Elizabeth asked. Word must have got round that Deirdre was coming to cook for us and this was Elizabeth's idea of being first with the news although she'd probably heard about it when I was on her phone to Simon.

'She'll be here in about two months,' replied Simon.

'It'll mak' a difference to you,' she answered. Simon looked at me with a knowing look. Elizabeth would surely phone Maggie to tell her as soon as the door was closed behind us.

Racing each other down to the Haa in an attempt to beat a heavy rain cloud coming over the hill, we both paused to catch our breath where the road splits, with one track going to the pier. We looked out to sea and watched the heavy swell breaking over the reef before making a final sprint, bursting through the back door with Simon slightly ahead of me. I relaxed in a chair to recover while Simon pumped up the pressure and lit the Tilley lamp. The wind was quickly freshening, the noise on the windows increasing until it was blotted out by the battering of a heavy shower.

'It looks like a wild night, Sy,' I said.

He picked up one of our new newspapers, flicking through the pages to get to the sports section. 'God, it's been a rush,' I heard from behind the newspaper. 'I don't think there'll be any chance of working tomorrow with the bad forecast.'

'No,' I replied, lying back in my chair, quite content to do nothing. 'I'm looking forward to an easy day.'

As our inherited stock of peat diminished we either had to ask for our own peat bank or import coal. We already supplemented the peat with bits of broken fish boxes and the odd wooden spar found on the rocks. Foula was not in a main shipping route, limiting the debris washed ashore and, with much of its coast dangerously inaccessible, recovering anything was a game of luck. But materials for building or repairing fences were always in short supply and any functional looking wood, like planks or posts, were not burnt but kept for use around the Haa.

The peat-cutting was controlled by a "peat marshal" designated by the landlord. As we were not considered residents or crofters we had no entitlement to take peat from the main peat-cutting area. We discussed it with Elizabeth, who suggested we cut peat from one of her crofts, Sloag, which was close to the Haa, but there was no road to it. We started to learn how to cut the peat, although it did not take long for the peat marshal, Rob, to come and investigate. He didn't want people cutting peat on the crofts, even with the tenant's permission, so instead he directed us to a disused peat bank close to those cut by the rest of the islanders. After he left us at our new bank we gave each other a knowing look, suspecting Elizabeth had known this would happen.

'What d'you think, Sy, was it part of Elizabeth's plan?'

'Good for her, if it was,' he replied, 'but I wonder if she's that scheming.'

'Mmm,' I answered, not sure that she was.

'Whatever,' he replied, 'it couldn't have worked out better.'

Rob had been right in not allowing us to cut peat next to a croft. In the past it had been cut as close to the crofts as possible for ease of transport, which would have been in kishies[5] (a woven basket) and later barrows when the roads were built.

Sometimes the forming soil beneath the peat was taken to add to the croft vegetable patches or as bedding for cattle. This had caused erosion which was noted by Captain Vetch in 1821: 'The Island of Foula, at Stanisfield, a portion of the Noop Hill, the covering of peat-moss being scanty, the natives have managed by perseverance to get down to the naked rock. This system of carrying off the soil, so prevalent in Orkney and Fair Isle, cannot be sufficiently deprecated, or soon put an end to, as hundreds of acres of good land are every year consigned to sterility, although abundant of peat-moss is never far distant.'[25]

Cutting peat can become competitive and Simon and I were no different to anyone else after we learned the art. The first step was the "flaying" of the peat banks that involved cutting sods of the growing heather and moss off the top, and placing them neatly in the "gref", which was the bottom of the bank where the peat had been removed the previous year. This gives the ground a layer of growing turf and allows plants to bind together preventing any erosion caused by the heavy rain. The removal of this top turf also leaves a solid peat face to cut into.

Harry was the best peat-cutter on the island; they said he could cut 1,000 peats an hour and throw a peat 40ft without breaking it. It was typical of Harry that he used this skill to help most of the older folk who were unable to cut their peats by cutting them himself, or arranging communal cutting. When it came to Elizabeth's peats, the "cutters" asked were Eric, Jim, Ken, Harry, John-

The author unloading their vehicle onto the Foula pier.

Andrew, Jock, Simon and I. We were pleased to join in as peat-cutting was still a novelty to us and it acknowledged our peat-cutting was at a sufficient standard to be useful. One of my great pleasures in life is learning something new and becoming skilled at it.

We all stopped cutting in the early afternoon for a break, and finished in the late afternoon after we had cut at least a year's supply, amounting to more than eight tractor-trailer-loads of dry peat that would be carted to Ham later in the summer after the peats had dried. Elizabeth then offered us a full meal with tea and beer at Ham, during which she gratefully fussed over everyone like a mother hen. It was one of her endearing, and sometimes embarrassing traits that she did not fuss over Simon and me as if we were just children, she fussed over us as if we were *her* children.

Weeks or months later, when the peats had partially dried, the women and children would "raise" them into small piles and, after further drying, they were taken home, or built into roogs (stacks) with the peats placed neatly on top to shed the rain so that they could remain on the bank until there was an opportunity to transport them to the croft. Some still used a barrow but most people asked Jim to use his tractor and trailer, and Simon and I would help by using Elizabeth's. After our first year of cutting peats and raising them ourselves we never had any concerns over peats for our fire, and looked forward to the work of cutting and raising because of the satisfaction it gave.

One fine evening the Haa door burst open and Ken appeared. He was Jim's older brother and just as tall, but he spent much of the time off the island. He was happy, but looking cold, having just crossed from Shetland alone in his small yoal.

'How's it going boys?' he said cheerily, as he closed in on our fire and passed Simon the latest *Shetland Times* newspaper.

'It's been good, we've had a productive run in the fine weather. You'd have had a good crossing?'

'Aye, an' I've thought of a good money-making scheme,' he said.

Simon, between glances at the paper, handed him a cup of coffee and offered a plate with some of our few remaining digestive biscuits. 'What's the scheme?'

'It's that simple I can't see how nobody's doin' it on Shetlan'. It's growing carrots, they're a hell o' a price and easy to grow.'

'Where'd you grow them?' I asked.

'On Niggards (his croft) to start, and then get others at Hametoon, use their land, rotating the crop round the crofts. The unsold carrots the sheep would eat.'

Ken always had schemes, often grasping at straws for some quick money. He was a bright, charismatic person but bored, with a tendency, when circumstances allowed, to stay on the mainland. In his late thirties, he was unable to settle to anything, and while his life was flashing by other people streaked ahead in a race where he had inherited the intelligence to be up at the front, but the pull of the island coupled with the lack of something interesting to absorb his large reserve of energy had dragged him back. If he had been born two generations before, he might have been climbing cliffs for birds' eggs, or sailing miles offshore to fish, and enjoying an exciting life, but the Foula men of those days were gone – the island was now more renowned for its unhurriedness than gusto. Past generations of his family on the island had acted like an anchor, holding him back from settling to a job or business on the mainland that would absorb his energy. Now, he was finding people of his age on the mainland buying and skippering fishing boats, making a good living and having a challenging life. It needed a yielding temperament at Ken's age to start again at the bottom, which was never his nature.

As he warmed up he continued his good form, excited by the project he hoped to start. I knew how he felt – I had that enthusiastic feeling every time I started a new project. His croft would be several acres, dug over for centuries and fertilised with the dung from cattle kept in the byre, and lay in the Hametoon area that was bounded by a wall and contained about 65 acres of arable land. It was only in the last few years that it had nearly all reverted to pasture.

The "toons" were good land and in 1874 it was reported that Foula 'was capable of producing finer crops than any other island in the group. Much of the soil being naturally good, and the climate affected more by the Gulf stream than that of any other part of Shetland. Crops of bere, oats, and potatoes grow luxuriantly; while the natural pasture of the steep but grassy hills is rich and varied in the nature of its component plants.'[26]

This is often qualified by further reports where the crops can be stunted or destroyed by mists of salt water sweeping over the island during storms. It was said that the soil being continually subjected to salt spray was the reason the first crofts to be abandoned were in the north of the island.

I expected the soil to be ideal for carrots with few stones to twist and distort the root. For a crop not using artificial fertilisers he might obtain a yield of nine tons per acre. I didn't know if pests like carrot root fly existed on the island but I expected they might be blown away by the wind. The carrot's great advantage over other vegetables is easy storage, which would allow them to survive the irregular mailboat service. Island life was about getting a number of projects going, each yielding a small amount of income. This, on a small scale, sounded feasible.

'Would it pay well?' I asked.

He ran off some figures which sounded good but his costs were based on using island labour and equipment, mostly his brother Jim's.

'You've maybe got a bit too many zeros on the end,' smiled Simon. This was a bone that Simon would definitely chew.

Simon, John-Andrew and Rob cutting peat.

Ken returned his smile. 'The figure's just rough, but you can see it works.'

'You'll be the Carrot King of Shetland,' Simon remarked.

Ken laughed, knowing Simon would make fun of it.

When Ken had warmed up in front of the fire and was completely drained of news by Simon, I ran him along the road in our vehicle. It was good to see him happy. Life had not treated him well; his wife had left the island and it would be nice to see him back on his feet, getting stuck into something that would use up all his energy.

Returning to the Haa, I found Simon still looking at the sports page of the *Shetland Times*.

'It'll never happen,' he said, 'as soon as he gets started he'll get bored. It's too long a wait to get his money back.'

'Maybe, Sy,' I replied, knowing he was almost certainly right, but hoping Ken would attempt the scheme and make it work.

'Let's go up to Lizzy's?' Simon suggested. It wasn't a question, and he started to put his jacket on.

'You're just wanting to swop some gossip.'

'She'll hear anyway,' he said, 'if she hasn't heard already. Ken will have talked about it in Scalloway.'

I put on my jacket, imagining Elizabeth's concentration and response. 'Naw,' she'd say, her head cocked to one side and leaning forward not wanting to miss anything. But it was not to be, much to Simon's disappointment Elizabeth had already heard.


When we arrived in Foula it was apparent that making a full-time living from crofting was a near impossible task. I was taught that a farmer can have 40 years' experience if something new is learned each year and the techniques are changed accordingly. But the same farmer can also have one year's experience 40 times if no changes take place – the old farming methods continuing with no improvements as if the person had never been there, other than to repeat each year. Foula crofters were more akin to the latter, the work spiralling into an ever-decreasing financial reward, the only benefit being the peace of mind that comes with little change. As people died or left, the amount of cultivated land was reducing, allowing the improved land to deteriorate, making it sad to see the overgrown remains of someone's dream. It was as if the islanders deceived themselves on a daily basis about the decline, with little if any positive measures being followed to reverse it. But the abandoned crofts showed that nature cannot be fooled.

As we were gradually assimilated into the ways of island life, every day learning something new, it became apparent that Foula had used the crofts and peat for their basic survival. The additional resources that had allowed the population to rise in the late 1700s and 1800s had been the fishing and the birds' eggs. But as the fishing declined so did the inhabitants.

In 1774 Reverend George Low pointed out how they were unable to grow enough corn, and with potatoes recently introduced, and growing well, they were able to save the meal obtained from the grain crops by eating fish with potatoes rather than bread.[27, 25]

During the 1800s the population had grown well above the ability of the island to feed itself and in 1883 Foula agriculture was described as an island

The east part of the Hametoon. From the right the Baxter chapel, Punds croft, Dykes, and Niggards. Much of the land would have been cultivated in the past. *Lesley Timings*

dug with the Shetland spade, the harrows drawn by women, who also carried almost all the peats home, often from a great distance. The low temperatures and violent gales from the sea made husbandry a precarious business, the yields of the crops like oats and bere (a form of barley) were only able to supply the island for four or five months of the year, but the milk and butter lasted longer.[9, 5] As the island was not self-sufficient in grain, it became a serious problem in the winter if the inhabitants did not have the money to buy enough to store, as the boat service was unable to make regular trips. Several times it had to rely on imported gifts of meal from a specially chartered boat.

This was accentuated by the truck laws that were peculiar to Orkney and Shetland. In simple terms, it was a form of barter where the landlord sets the price of the fish and also controls the shop prices which the tenant is obliged to use to buy his food and equipment. The landlords either charged a high rent to a merchant running the shop or conducted the business themselves. The relative absence of money in the truck system restricted the freedom of the islanders to use other markets.[28] From a report made during a visit in 1867, it was deduced that if the inhabitants were allowed to buy and sell in any market they chose they would live in comparative comfort.[29] Small islands were in the worst position as the trade of the island was a monopoly, and was conducted almost entirely on an account with one shop, which kept the trade by giving the islanders credit.[30]

In the 1880s the Established Church catechist Robert Gear, who was a local missionary, was publicly fighting the system. As a result he ended up being taken to court after receiving a summons to be removed from the island, issued by the truck merchants.[31] This was followed by a show of island unity when a court officer went to Foula for the purpose of "poinding and rouping" his effects. No violence was offered to the officer but the islanders refused to purchase a single article offered for sale, and the officer was forced to stop the proceedings.[32]

But the islanders were caught between a rock and a hard place as they needed a merchant to buy their produce and, as most were in debt to the existing firm, their hands were tied. The minister, Reverend Morrison, claimed to reply on behalf of the islanders in 1883, but appeared to justify the benefits of the existing system.[9, 33] It was not until the basic truck system was abolished in 1886 that anything changed. But many outlying areas remained with only one merchant, like Foula, and the people in those areas had little option but to use them.

The truck reform came along with three main pieces of crofting legislation in the crofters' favour over the next century. The first, in 1886, gave the crofter security of tenure and the right to a fair rent. Up until then the landlord had a considerable hold over the tenants with the threat of putting them out of their homes. Crofters all over Scotland had got into arrears with their rents, but the Crofters Commission had the power to wipe off a large amount of these debts, and did so in Foula, reducing the rental of the whole island from £140 to £90. At that time, with up to 266 islanders in 42 families,[34] half of them occupying the best land at Hametoon, the rent for each croft varied between £2 and £4 pounds a year.[13] The rent was mostly taken in barter by the crofter supplying a cow or a few sheep.

By 1976 crofters were given the right to purchase their individual crofts and later, in 2003, as part of the Land Reform (Scotland) Act 1993, crofting community bodies were provided with the right to purchase eligible croft land associated with the local crofting community. In Foula these acts were particularly significant as all the islanders were connected with crofts, while elsewhere in Shetland and rural Highland areas crofting activity was significantly less.

In Shetland the croft was treated as the family home, the land usually worked by the women as the men had traditionally gone fishing to generate the bulk of the income. But crofting was in most people's blood, they found pleasure in working the land, turning over the soil and caring for plants as they grow. It was a definite way of life, and in Shetland it had a bonus in that it gave women an economic independence with the men free to undertake other work and projects, knowing they had a home and a small amount of land to supplement or even fulfil their food supply. Traditionally, in Foula this had allowed the men to go to sea when the peat-cutting finished in May, and return in August or September to help with the harvest.

Over the years many items of everyday life were designed to suit the strength of men. The boats had to be pulled up and down the beach, although no longer rowed or sailed, maintaining their unreliable engines was an essential skill, and often male. Even the old tractors on the island required physical strength to steer, with a substantial force required to operate the clutch and brake. On the other side of the coin the Foula sheep were small, and when contained on the crofts they could be handled by anyone. Women derived other income from knitting, curing skins, salting fish and meat, allowing them to have a degree of financial independence. The job division appeared to be based on the need for strength on the one hand and child-bearing on the other, with the women having little choice in the past of the type of work they could do as there were few paid jobs. This gender bias on the island was not considered as inequality, just different roles and a culture developed over centuries, but it was quite rightly becoming outdated as equipment changed and islanders were forced to alter their way of life. The men no longer went off to sea for months, but the women continued to work the crofts, from digging the soil to bringing in the hay.

I was surprised how physically hard the women worked. On one of our walks we had watched the heavily pregnant wife of an islander sitting on a three-legged stool as she scythed the hay, moving the stool as she worked her way across the field, even when her husband came across to stand beside her and chat. I knew this was traditional female work and she seemed neither to be requiring help nor wanting it, and he did not appear to offer it. Many years later, when we had a salvage ship based on the north-west coast of Spain, I was walking up the hill behind the harbour with my family when I offered to help an elderly lady who was carrying a load of hay in a net on her back. She turned me down with thanks as she considered it her job. I thought how similar the rural cultures of a fishing community might be.

The major contribution women played in the croft work was acknowledged in an 1891 *Ladies Journal*: 'It is not a little astonishing to notice the active part taken by women in the Shetland economy; with the husband at sea, the whole care and work of the croft and household devolves upon the wife, and this is no child's play. Not only does she dig and plant out the whole ground herself with such help as she may get from her family, but she looks after all the livestock and otherwise attends to her own work proper about the house and croft.'[35]

The Isbisters still used Shetland spades. The three of them worked in a row, each turf having the three Shetland spades behind it as they pushed together turning the long clod over in unison. It looked so easy but I knew croft work was not always easy, with many tasks repetitive and endless, although from a visitor's perspective it was often seen to be romantic. Machinery would make life easier but it required capital and it was difficult to justify the expenditure without some form of co-operation to maximise its use.

The earnings from a croft, relative to other work, were being continually eroded, with additional part-time jobs growing in importance. Elizabeth was the school cleaner, Jim ran the mailboat, Rob the mailboat crew, Mary was the school cook, Harry the postmaster, Edith relied on knitting, and others on the pension, and there was work for a carer for the elderly. All were prepared to accept a low standard of living for their choice to stay on the island, but as an outsider I could see the crofts were gradually being accumulated in the hands of fewer people. It was probably inevitable, but it resulted in many of the old houses being abandoned as only the one croft house was required. Like the croft work it was the women who held the island together, they were the ones who were difficult to replace, and they were often the hardest working, rarely asking for help and having few complaints about their work. Although Elizabeth was a definite exception, welcoming any work on her croft by any person male or female, and complaints would be numerous, although bound up within her usual conversational mutterings.

A reason for many people to try and live off the land is the strong feeling of independence it gives, although I realised that any form of financial independence is now an illusion. With agricultural subsidies, the health service, and education, we have all become more dependent on others than we ever have been. The only real achievement can be the self-reliance on much of the food from a known source that in itself is satisfying.

It was obvious to outsiders that change was inevitable, something new had to be brought to the island if it were to encompass new people. Rob was trying to construct a fibreglass boat in the only available premises of an old byre. If it worked he intended to design, and build more, but he was finding it a struggle due to the lack of electrical power and the unsuitable and unheated shed which was barely warm enough to allow the fibreglass resin to set. His elder brother John, before he left the island, was digging the foundations for a hostel, a project that had the makings of a future business that could have included a shop and museum, but it was not being followed up.

New ideas are rarely helped by resistance to change and the obvious emotional adhesion to the land, embedded by generations of families who had lived on it. It may bear no economic or social logic, but the family connection was undoubtedly one of the major reasons for people staying on islands. This was not a new feeling. In 1797 it was stated: 'This island is inhabited by 26 families, who, although there is not sufficient land for supporting them with provisions, yet, they are so attached to the place, that they are unwilling to leave it; rather choosing to put up with its many inconveniences than to emigrate.'[36]

It is that resilience, the love of the island and family, their wish to die and be buried on the island, that keeps many of the elderly population who would undoubtedly live a more comfortable life on the mainland. That tie is difficult to break. It is as if their life's purpose was to pass their croft on to the next generation, which also seemed true of the landlord with the land. I realised that great courage must have been required by some of those who left when they sought a better future for themselves and their families. A new family or individual coming to the island lacks any ancestral tie, and this can only be countered by creating better living conditions, otherwise they may wish to leave on the first occasion when life becomes difficult.

I dreamed of rebuilding a croft and took the opportunity to have a good look at the derelict buildings during bad weather when I had time on my own. Simon preferred to relax in the house and listen to sport on the radio. Even if it was blowing a gale and pouring with rain, I'd often follow the rocky coast north passing the "spooty holes" where the water was funnelled into a small, partly-submerged cave at the end of a seaward facing gulley. The cavern had a small hole in its roof, causing the air, compressed by the incoming wave, to force the water out in a great spout. When at its peak, it created an irresistible appeal. I waited for each wave to rush in, causing a great thump within the cave before the water shot out. Standing as close as possible, I'd tell myself I would just wait for one more, one more, one more … eventually dragging myself away to wander further north to meet the Sloag burn where it entered the sea. At this point I turned inland, following the burn to the ruins of Sloag croft which lay on the extreme edge of land that would have been cultivated in the past as part of the "toon of Ham". Behind the ruined buildings lay the remains of peat banks that merged with the heather, leading onto poor quality grassland and the rocky coast.

After I read Powell's book about filming on the island, I realised he had the same feelings when he first saw Sloag in 1936: 'The scene of the most ambitious sequence in the film was Sloag, a thatched croft in a brae north of the Haa, only about two hundred yards away. A burn ran down into the sea from Rosie's Loch and the three hills of Foula were all visible from Sloag, one behind the other, Hamnafeld like a black wall, the Sneug over its shoulder and, beyond, the top of the Kame. All around the croft were smooth grassy mounds and fields of oats and barley. In front was the brae running down to the sea, at the back was a noble cabbage-patch. It was a place to dream about ...'[37]

In 1954 the school teacher, Chris Mylne, made a similar statement: 'There were ruined crofts to the north of Ham Voe: Veedal and Sloag ... I explored the derelict house at Sloag where the last inhabitant had been found lying dead on his potato patch, felled by a merciful heart attack as he worked. Only the weather had touched his house in the interim, but much of the roof was intact and many of his possessions, like a pair of boots and his bible were still in place where he had left them.'[38]

The ruins of Springs croft at the north end.

Unfortunately, the writer who had paid so many compliments to the island, and had been popular, only lasted 1½ years, defeated by the very nature of the isolation of the island he had spoken so well of, deciding Foula was too remote to cater for his health.

Now the oats and barley were long gone, the land reverting to rough pasture where Elizabeth's sheep roamed freely. The roof no longer existed, and the sheep had sought shelter within the walls, pushing stones over as they clambered in, and trampled their manure into the floor where grass had taken hold. Gradually the square lines of the building were reverting back to nature, the work of man was being re-absorbed beneath a stunning outlook, the senses enhanced on this day by the slight taste of salt in the air. Whether imagined or real, it reminded me of the power of creation as I looked around to take in the unforgiving ruggedness of Foula where nature will always remain both king and queen. With little concern for time or place, even the sheep became less wary of me as they grazed around the broken walls.

I could see no hindrance to my dream of rebuilding the croft; it was as if it had already happened, and I imagined it standing in front of me. I wondered how many strangers had dreamed this dream, and yet, in the back of their mind, they would know that it would be near impossible to fulfil. There would be financial reasons, let alone numerous others. I was told when I studied agriculture that the only way to become a farmer was patrimony, alimony, or matrimony. It had been much the same for the island crofts.

I had an aunt and uncle who were hill farmers on the west coast of Scotland. They had previously been tenant farmers on an island and thought life would be easier and have more opportunities for their children if they moved to the mainland. They grew a field of oats for winter feed and several fields for hay, the rest of the farm was made up of bog, bracken, rock, and very rough grazing with ancient oak, alder and birch woods covering any ground where their roots could latch on and their leaves could survive the ravages of the sheep. The farmhouse contained a small dairy at one end for handling milk and butter, and each morning my aunt would milk two cows, always watched by the farm cat expecting its daily share.

My mother arranged for us to stay at the farm most summers. My father preferred to be at home; any talk of distant holidays and he would say 'we couldn't afford it' or he was 'too busy'. One of my clear memories was setting off from the east coast of Scotland to travel the 110 miles to the west coast where my sister, brother and I could spend endless hours of exploration along the rocky coast. Our cousins showed us sea creatures beneath the stones, golden eagles that lived at the top of a cliff, and the cracks in the rocks where we could hide from the continual nearby presence of an adult. When the tide covered a sandy part of the beach we all swam in the water, unaware, at that age, how cold it was.

Every few years we would go back, noticing the farm change. An old Land Rover with a power take-off was the first piece of machinery for farm and personal use, a small grey Ferguson tractor with its trailer similar to Elizabeth's appeared, followed by equipment for turning the hay, and an elevator for building it into a stack. Like some of the past population in Foula, their children were not interested in taking on the hard work and the poor return they would have to accept if they ran the farm. But it was a way of life to my aunt and uncle who, similar to those in Foula, were bright, intelligent people who had chosen a living where physical skills were in more demand than intellectual ability.

Sloag brought back those childhood memories as I explored the ruins, enjoying the thoughts from the past and relaxing in the comfort of this majestic island as if it was embracing me in its arms. Whether Sloag was abandoned because of complicated ownership or the position of the croft I did not know, but it made me wonder if it was possible to be lonely in Foula. I had not experienced it, even in those dark, winter nights on my own, but Michael Powell described a few people as: 'sunk into melancholia and others with no relatives, no money and no prospects equally sunk in apathy.'[37]

But now, 40 years later, I did not think this was the case. I thought of Harry, Peter Gray, Edith Gray and Kitty Manson, who all lived on their own and seemed content, but maybe Tom was downhearted or bored, just living each day, content to be alive.

Within the ruin lay lengths of decaying timber from the roof, probably made from drift wood; they say it was the best of materials as the saturation of salt water helped preserve it and prevented it from becoming infected with woodworm. The rafters may have been cut on the island. The remains of a saw pit stood at the head of the voe, near the noosts that the boats were pulled into.

It had been used to cut the large baulks of timber washed ashore into planks, one man standing in the bottom of the pit while another stood above holding the top end of the long saw and pulling it up after each downward cutting stroke.

In a sea cave further south there was enough timber to build a roof. The large baulks of squared wood had initials carved into them to denote the person who had made the recovery and taken ownership. Most of the initials were of the long dead or those who had left the island. We asked about getting a piece of the timber to reinforce the winch bed on our salvage boat, intending to tow the timber round to the voe at high water, but it all became too complicated in identifying a single surviving relative as most people were related. Not wanting to offend anyone we purchased a new piece in Shetland, realising that the wood in the cave would probably lie there until it became unusable from being flung about during storms; already many of the edges were badly rounded and the ends abraded.

Fair Isle attracted more wrecks and timber than Foula because it is in the centre of a sea route and, over the years, they had become well organised in

Sloag croft. Behind it from the left are the tops of of Hamnafield, the Sneug and the Kame.

recovering and using salvaged material. During the winter before our arrival in Fair Isle, a ship had lost most of its deck cargo of timber when it was washed overboard in a gale. Some of it had come ashore on the island and Jerry, whose croft was near a small inlet, quickly recovered as much as he could and built a complete shed with it. When the Customs officers appeared on the island a week or two later to investigate if any wood had been recovered, Jerry showed them inside his new shed, explaining that if he had recovered any it would be kept in the shed. They went away, possibly none the wiser, but probably knowing the islanders had learned to be experts in salvage and smuggling over the centuries. The Customs had fulfilled their duty without making a pointless example of someone for salvaging a bundle of salt-impregnated timber that would have little value after the cost of removing it from the island.

As I stopped dreaming and walked back to the Haa, I thought how lucky we were in having it as our home. We could not have chosen a better house, mainly because of its location, but whenever I dreamed of a future on the island my imagination contained images of Sloag.

# Chapter 7
# Birders and Visitors

When Simon and I first arrived in Foula we concentrated almost entirely on our work and the tides and weather that affected it. This allowed the island to creep up on us, making me unaware of its growing influence. We were both happy to accept and enjoy any part of island life, unquestioned, but before we arrived we had been slightly concerned as some on the mainland could only see its negative side – a failing island of reclusive occupants, which was partly true – but with the time and space to be exposed to it we gained an understanding of the more sensitive side. The island community quickly became familiar, like a friend that we trusted and continued to like, overlooking any shortcomings that appeared. I hoped in turn they would overlook our deficiencies. There was little that surprised us, but this was not true of our experiences with some of the visitors.

Travellers, mostly ministers and doctors, had visited Foula throughout the centuries. They moved easily through the islands as they had the luxury of being accommodated, fed and looked after, usually at no cost to themselves but paid for by the lairds and the kindness of parishioners. In 1774, the Reverend George Low wrote on his visit to Foula: 'Our boatsmen and my servant were distributed among the different families of the isle, and I together with a gentleman who accompanied me had lodgings assigned in the Bailie's Booth, where in a short time we had everything for the table sent us in plenty, such as fish of several kinds, fowls, milk, butter, and eggs, without any expense. When I offered to pay for what we had they were much affronted, and told me no such thing ever happened in Foula as to pay for eatables.' [27]

The visitors usually observed, counted, and shot samples of its famous bird population before writing reports for books or papers. Later, in 1880, when travellers were looking for accommodation, they were advised to write to Mr James Garriock of Reawick, the factor for the Melby Estate, to obtain permission to occupy the rooms reserved at Mr Peterson's that consisted of a sitting room with one box bed in it, and a smaller closet with similar accommodation. Failing the factor's house, they might get accommodation at the Congregational Manse.[12] Visiting was still under the control of the owner and it was not until the islands became more accessible in 1886, when the crofters had security of tenure removing any fear of removal, that other keen travellers started to visit and ornithologists were able to indulge their interest on the island enjoying its unique bird life.

In more recent times, besides the wildlife, a purity and romantic side to the island developed because of its remoteness and lack of change; it offered a taste of the past, and a look at a way of life that was vanishing. The offshore fishing and cliff climbing for wild birds' eggs had long been given up, but the cliffs remained impressive and undisturbed, except for the power of the sea that had not diminished. They say the only constant in life is change, and Foula had changed, but at a much slower rate than the rest of the country, allowing a few visitors not only to see what was there but also what they imagined should be there. Where else in the country could they see people scything a crop of hay or fetching water from a well? Some onlookers occasionally made the mistake of thinking the people must be primitive, of a lesser intelligence or badly educated. This was not the case. Life on the island for most, if not all, was a positive choice, not a default position.

As the island became more popular, coping with the extra visitors without even the thought of generating any revenue from them may have made the strangers harder to accept. At times it became easy to see them as an unwanted intrusion, but this was rarely the case. Foula had a good relationship with the visitors, treating them courteously, realising how much effort and cost they had incurred to get to the island, which eliminated all but the most determined.

I asked Simon, 'Why d'you think people have this fascination with islands?'

'Everyone wants to see something unusual; we're not much different from them,' he replied.

'But it must be expensive for them to get here.'

'It's the birds most of them want to see, they're unique in Britain. The island comes as a bonus and it gives them the illusion of being liberated from the rest of the world.'

'If they're stuck on the island and they miss their ferry south,' I replied, 'it's definitely not an illusion.'

I thought how fortunate we had been on islands in having a purpose, rather than just coming here to look – which we never would have done. Although fascinated by the island and its way of life, it was our work that drove us, and it had the fortunate aspect of being of interest to the islanders and not competing with them, making it easier for us to become friends and be involved in their way of life. We were lucky.

During previous summers a Scalloway boat called the *Hirta* was available for charters to Foula. It allowed groups of people to prearrange trips, weather permitting, but Hance, the owner, retired and no-one had considered it profitable to continue. As a result the travellers had started approaching commercial fishing boats, which would pass Foula on their way to the fishing grounds, to ask them if they could drop them on the island.

With the weather improving we were occasionally distracted by the noise of a fishing boat coming into the pier. Curious, we ran down, occasionally seeing a passenger being dropped off or picked up. Sometimes, after a few days, a visitor to the island who looked wet, frozen and fed up would be standing on the pier looking for the opportunity to jump aboard the deck of a fishing boat that was returning to the mainland. Our first experience of being involved occurred when a camper appeared at our door, soaked through, and carrying a tattered tent half-jammed in the top of his rucksack.

'Is there a chance of getting dry in your house?' he asked.

'Come in,' Simon replied, ushering him into the back porch.

'I couldn't find anywhere to stay on the island, but an islander suggested you might help.'

'No problem,' said Simon, leading him in as water dripped off both him and his rucksack.

After drying himself in front of the peat fire he stayed the night in our spare room. It was obvious how Foula needed accommodation even though our camper left on the first fishing boat that came into the pier, relieved to be returning to the comfort of Scalloway. He became the first of a few, both male and female, who sought refuge in the Haa. Word soon spread that 'the divers might help if the weather gets too bad.' It was never a chore as we nearly always enjoyed the company, and we had the space to make anyone welcome as long as they could look after themselves, and we never charged. Females brought a pleasant change from the male-orientated conversation, and if we were lucky our dull cooking ingredients were turned into exciting meals that we all shared. Our visitors rarely stayed long, sometimes just an afternoon to warm up. Having experienced the inaccessibility of the island they usually took the first opportunity to leave in case they were stranded for weeks or months.

But sometimes an unusual visitor could be useful, and professional men occasionally appeared with bird groups or on yachts. The pier was unsuitable for yachts with their deep draught and soft sides because they would scrub against the rough concrete as the swell induced a continual motion. But the more adventurous crew would anchor off and row ashore. We spoke to a top Dutch surgeon who had briefly taken his yacht alongside at high water and after Simon told Elizabeth about him she rushed down to the pier. Slightly curious, we hung around and found out that she had just delivered a large lamb that had a badly dislocated shoulder which she had been unable to put back. She persuaded an initially reluctant surgeon to go up to Ham to have a look at it. First, he took down one of the salted and dried legs hanging in the rafters. He felt the movement of the shoulder, cutting it open to gain a closer look. He then went back to the lamb and slipped its shoulder back into position as if he had been doing it all his life. Simon and I laughed; it was typical of Elizabeth, she would never let an opportunity slip through her fingers.

On a sunny but windy day our breakfast was disturbed by a loud clatter; the sound of chain rattling down a ship's hawse pipe as an anchor was dropped. We hurried to the window to see what ship it was.

'That will have woken most of the island,' said Simon, as we watched a small cruise ship swinging on her anchor about half a mile from the shore, close enough to get shelter from the heavy westerly swell. Simon reached for the binoculars and scanned the ship trying to make out a name, port or flag that would indicate where she was from. 'It's called the *Stella Maris*. She looks like one of the west-coast MacBrayne ferries,' he mused, as he passed me the binoculars. 'How many passengers will she have?'

'She'll maybe have a hundred to come ashore,' I guessed, realising this was a lot of people for Foula.

The news would spread like wildfire, but I was surprised that no one on the island had known. Simon was certain to have heard from Elizabeth if she knew. We watched two boats being lowered from their davits, and a gangway placed over the ship's side before the passengers started to embark into one of the tenders.

'Let's go down to the pier,' I said.

'Okay. D'you think many of the passengers will be foreign?' Simon queried. 'They'll maybe need an island guide. I wonder who'll do it.'

As we walked down the slipway we saw Elizabeth half running to try and cut us off at the start of the pier. She was completely out of breath, we waited for her to recover as we watched the first boat making its way towards the pier with a uniformed man standing beside the tiller.

'Yon boat'll not get in,' she said, pointing towards the Scalloway trawler *Alis Wood* blocking off the end of the pier with a rope which stretched across the voe to keep the stern in the deeper water. The three of us hurried down intending to wake one of the crew, but before we could get there the skipper had emerged from the wheelhouse. He waved to acknowledge us, and went aft to slacken the rope.

The tender stopped opposite him. The uniformed man shouted across to him in an officious tone of voice. 'Did nobody tell you we were coming?'

The skipper, in the process of slackening the rope, stopped, and turned slowly towards the boat before replying 'No,' and then added, 'but I'm surprised nobody told you we'd be here.' He let the rope sink, allowing the boat to go over it. He looked tired, I knew they had been fishing all night and the last thing he wanted to do was wake his crew to shift the boat.

We waited for the tender to circle round the bow of the trawler and approach the steps where he threw us ropes to secure to the rings. Lingering in case they needed some help, I scanned the passengers to see if there were any of our age. Unfortunately they were all middle aged people dressed in "sensible" clothing with hiking boots.

'Hello,' Simon said cheerily. 'Welcome to Foula.'

'Good morning,' one of the ladies replied, with an obvious Edinburgh accent.

With no further help required, and no young passengers, Simon and I looked at each other, a mutual look that said, 'there's nothing of interest, let's get out of here'. We walked up towards the Haa only to see Jim and Ken arrive. Jim headed straight to the winch shed and started the engine to pull the mailboat all the way up the slipway to give the passengers more space for disembarking. It was typical of Jim, he was always considerate.

Ken spoke to the person in charge of the boat. 'Do you need any fresh lobsters?'

'You'll have to ask the cook,' the officer replied.

The passengers looked up at Ken, a tall charismatic figure. They were having their first look at a real Foula man. Jim came to join him and the two massive brothers surveyed the passengers before they went off to fetch a flattie and take Ken's lobster boat off its mooring. They would go to Ham Little, where they kept the live lobsters stored in boxes partly-submerged in sea water.

'Cup of tea, boys?' asked Elizabeth, who was still standing beside us. It was the time of day when she was normally busy and we looked at each other suspecting this could mean she had an urgent job that she was unable to do herself.

Simon asked, 'Are there any small jobs needing doing?'

'Naw, only if you had a moment, the teacher asked if you'd use my tractor to tak' the manse peats hame.'

Simon looked relieved. 'If you could ask when it's to be done, we'll fit it in.'

We knew from past experience that if we took the tractor and trailer up to the peat bank and left it there it would be filled with peats, and then we would drive it to the manse and help unload.

It would have been easy to sit all day with Elizabeth, and she would have loved it, chatting away about the cruise ship, enquiring whether we knew anything about it, or the people on it. Any morsel of information would please her, and Simon, not wanting to miss the opportunity, would fill in the gaps by telling her about Edinburgh while she studied the groups of passengers with her binoculars from the window, making comments on their clothes and the likely sort of people they would be. She was enthralled by the whole bustle of activity, the island suddenly became alive for her and she couldn't get enough of it. When the boat returned to the ship for another load of passengers we took the opportunity to slip back to the Haa, deftly avoiding groups of people. We were not island stock and felt that it would be sensible to lie low while we prepared to do our own work, starting on some domestic chores.

The influx of so many people ruled out the worst job – clothes washing – as they would see us at the burn and almost certainly ask questions and photograph us as we rinsed our clothes. Further down our list was washing dish towels in the sink. By late afternoon we had long before lost interest in our chores. Simon was sitting on the settee, bobble hat on his head, reading the sporting section of a two-week-old newspaper while I had started reading a book. We were both distracted by a shadow cast from the window and looked to see two faces pressed against the salty glass.

'Look, he's reading a newspaper,' said one of the ladies.

We didn't move, but looked at each other, Simon pushing his bobble hat further back on his head, no words sufficient to express his astonishment, but he could not contain himself. 'If we'd looked into their house in Edinburgh we'd be locked up,' he quietly hissed so that they would not hear.

'It's the state of the house,' I replied. 'They probably hope to see something really squalid to go back and tell their friends.' I looked around at the diving suits lying on the floor, old magazines and newspapers piled on the table next to dirty coffee cups, with the recently washed dishcloths hanging over the back of wooden chairs. Yes, I thought, they will have something to tell their friends.

'Let's go down and see what's going on,' said Simon, his blood warmed up by the incident.

'Right,' I replied, moving from the window and grabbing a coat from a chair.

Groups of people were making their way to the pier and a prolonged blast sounded on the ship's foghorn as two tenders shuttled passengers out to the cruise ship. Passing the mailboat I saw John-Andrew ahead of us, standing behind two returning women, one of them holding a dead shag and showing the identification ring on its leg to her friend. When John-Andrew mimicked the cry of the bird, it was instantly dropped to the ground, both women shocked by the sound. A smiling John-Andrew, looking very much an islander with his dark tousled hair, black beard and Shetland accent, laughed. They relaxed, one of them saying in a friendly tone, 'You devil,' as she picked it up and asked him a question.

At the pier a few of the islanders were speaking to some of the passengers. Maggie, the nurse, whispered to us that one of them was a bishop. He was a friendly, affable man who was keen to talk and ask questions of his fellow travellers. We listened to him as he held court, a new opinion offered for every question asked. A female islander, wearing her usual clothes, stood beside Maggie who was also dressed in working clothes, suitable for being down at the pier. The two women caught the bishop's roving eye.

'Do you make a living off the island?' he asked.

She nodded yes in a shy manner, as if concerned at being picked out of the crowd, although she had a university degree and the nurse beside her was at the top of her profession. The bishop must have assumed they were destitute and, digging deep into his pocket in an exaggerated manner, he gave them fifty-pence each from his loose change. I was shocked, expecting an outburst, but thankfully they accepted with grace and I breathed a sigh of relief until I looked across at Simon who could hardly contain himself. I knew he would be bursting to discuss it with Elizabeth who was at the back of the crowd. I could imagine her whole body shaking with laughter, saying, 'Boys, boys, an' he's given Maggie and Sheila fifty-pence each. What does the man think we're like?'

As the last tender left for the cruise ship, Jim and Ken came back, their boat filled with empty lobster-storage boxes. By the look on their faces at least they had made some good money out of the cruise ship, and there was a distinct lightening of Ken's step.

I rarely missed the mainland for evenings out or the different food we might have eaten, but I was aware that our company was especially masculine with conversations swinging round primarily-male subjects – vehicles, boats, engines and sport – not that it particularly bothered me as I knew I was part of the cause. The lack of a female touch and conversation was noticeable in the house and although it did ease when Deirdre arrived, she was just one woman among many men and I suspect she became bored with us at times, but was too polite to say. We knew Deirdre was due to leave later in the summer to get on with her own life, but after the luxury of having her with us, we thought it crucial to find someone to replace her.

Simon intended placing a notice in a shop window on the Shetland mainland, or if that was not successful, advertise in a paper, but in the turmoil of our immediate work this had been forgotten. Towards the end of the summer when we were in Scalloway luck was on our side as we met two girls wanting to stay for a short time in Foula. This seemed a perfect opportunity; there was no need for me to say anything to Simon, I could sense him working towards it. I wondered which, if either of them, might be interested in the job. But after hearing about their travels through Shetland, their time at university and Lesley's life in Birmingham, I doubted either of them would want the summer job. Roz appeared to be quieter than Lesley, maybe not so confident with strangers, but they both appeared too independent, too organised, too city-orientated, and exceptionally academic to be interested in cooking for us in Foula. Lesley had studied maths at Cambridge University – not that we thought it was a required qualification for our cook.

By the end of the evening they both wanted to come and stay in Foula the following summer. The arrangements for their return to Shetland and then the trip to Foula were easily agreed; the same arrangement had worked well with Deirdre. I then wondered who obtained the best deal. I think they did, but only an enjoyable summer for them would tell. Perhaps similar conversations had occurred over the centuries with young men from the Foula boat crews and the eligible young ladies from Scalloway or Walls. But, of course, I wasn't consciously looking for a partner like they might have been.

When we first arrived on the island Eric was a bachelor at 29, and his aunt Edith, the only unmarried young woman, was aged 54. I was 25 and Simon 27 – there was no chance for either of us to marry a Foula lass! After being caught out with some ribald remarks from our friends in Fife when making the simple statement that Foula's population had increased by 28 per cent after we had been there for six years, we became careful how we phrased the comment.

The islanders had a concern about the future population and were proud of their past where Foula was reckoned to be the last place in Scotland to speak Norn – an extinct North Germanic language that was derived from the Vikings and was originally spoken in Orkney, Shetland, Caithness and in the far north of the Scottish mainland. After Orkney and Shetland were pledged to Scotland by Norway in 1469, Norn was gradually replaced by Scots. In 1774, Reverend Low noted that William Henry of Guttorm in Foula had the most knowledge of Norn and could speak poetry and knew the words of songs.[27] But by the late 1800s the numerous appearances of smallpox, which in the 1700s had caused a rush of immigrants from the Shetland mainland to replace those that had perished in Foula, resulted in many of the traditional Foula memories being lost. The dialect spoken gradually changed from a species of old Scotch, with a considerable admixture of Norse, and by the late 1800s many Scotch words now obsolete in Scotland were still current in Foula.[9]

We found the Shetland accent pleasant and easy to understand and, like most folk, they moderate their accent when they believe we are unable to understand it. In the 1700s the common appellation in Foula to all acquaintances was "brother",[27] probably an influence of the church, but when we were there a greeting between islanders appeared to be "boy". 'How's thee, boy?' was often used between men, but the island accent and language was being subtly altered with the advent of English- and Scots-accented mothers. I liked it, as it took the parochial attitude sometimes remarked on by visitors to a more cosmopolitan view of the island.

Foula's greatest fear of something brought from outside remained that of disease. Their concern about their lack of immunity stemmed from smallpox that had a catastrophic effect on the islands before vaccinations became available. Shetland and Foula were often affected at the same time and Brand reports in the 1700s, "the mortal pock", as it was called, carried off whole families, and Foula had only a few persons left 'to perform the last office of humanity to their brethren.'[39]

The smallpox appeared again in 1720, and in Foula the mortality was so great that there were again scarcely enough people left to bury the dead. The disease would not go away, returning in 1740, and again in 1760. Inoculation was introduced in 1761, but 'being deemed a hazardous undertaking, it was confined entirely to the higher ranks.'[40]

Since 1770, inoculation had been performed by a number of Shetland doctors and, famously, by a person named John Williamson, called Johnny Notions among his neighbours. 'Unassisted by education, and unfettered by the rules of art, he stands unrivalled in this business. Several thousand have been inoculated by him, and he has not lost a single patient.'[36]

But in Foula there was a resistance to vaccination and it was reported by Reverend David Thomson in 1792: 'Being averse to inoculation, a very great number of aged persons have never had the small-pox. The young people avoid infection, in the natural way, as much as they can; and are not much inclined to inoculation, lest they communicate the contagion to their friends.'[36]

Dr Jenner gained the accolade as the pioneer of immunisation, publishing his results in 1798. At that time smallpox was said to kill around ten per cent of the British population, with the number as high as 20 per cent in some towns and cities.

As the disease was brought under control, Foula's population rose. In 1774, 130 people were recorded as living in Foula, by 1792 the population had increased to 143,[36] and by 1821 it was 165.[25] This rise in the 1800s was probably due to the profitability of the fishing industry as well as the overcoming of smallpox. In Shetland the population expansion was added to with the booming kelp industry, but when these industries collapsed at a similar time as the potato blight reached Shetland in the mid-1840s, it eventually resulted in emigration. The same happened in Norway where the emigration per head of population was greater than Scotland in the 19th century.[41]

The population in Foula reached a peak, in 1887, of 267. This increase in population was reflected in the whole of Shetland, but by 1901, when Holbourn had purchased the island, the numbers had already fallen to 230 inhabitants who lived in 43 households.[15] It gradually fell to 100 by 1936, to 71 in 1954, and now it stood at 28.

The Foula people always had an independence about them, and a sense of rivalry. John Sands, a freelance journalist and artist, expressed it in the late 1800s: 'A stranger might imagine that in an island only three miles in length the people would regard themselves as homogenous, and that there would be no room for pride of place; but human nature is much the same everywhere, and as Edinburgh speaks of Glasgow with disdain and Glasgow returns the compliment, so the Hametoun in Foula considers itself vastly superior to Ham and Harrier and the latter despises the former. Boys from the two ends meet as natural enemies at the school and engage in bickers (quarrels).'[29]

This is not to say the islanders did not have a good reputation as decent people. Captain Vetch, a surveyor, in 1821 during his stay in Foula states: '... And it is a curious fact, that during the last seven years there has been no marriage in the island, nor illegitimate children;– In every respect the inhabitants seem to be much at their ease, are decently clothed, and are of a cheerful, inquisitive nature. Indeed I met no peasantry in Shetland that equal them. Their frank, free disposition and simple primitive manners, render them a very amiable people.'[25]

This was echoed 58 years later when Robert Cowie, a physician, writes: '... than those of Foula a better set of people does not exist in the isles of Shetland. They are sober, industrious, hospitable, intelligent, and very attentive to the ordinances of religion.'[13]

One hundred years further on Simon and I received similar hospitality and kindness, and part of the reason may have been that the older generation had never been insular, with many of them better travelled than the people who visited the island.

The island continued to muddle on and it was always hoped that money would miraculously appear from government to help, but there appeared no active encouragement for new people to come to the island, although there was never talk of a mass exit, in fact the very reverse – they had no intention of leaving.

Foula was not known for smuggling or looting wrecks. Captain Veitch, in

1821, came to the conclusion that smuggling was the cause of the difference between the islands of Fair Isle and Foula. Fair Isle lay right in the middle of the major shipping route which ran between Orkney and Shetland, and had more than 80 listed wrecks, while Foula lay north of the route and only had seven that were positively known. There may be many unknown shipwrecks on both islands as the cliffs on the west side are unseen by any house and, from our diving experience, the boulders on the seabed would have quickly ground up a wooden or small steel ship resulting in its rapid disappearance, leaving little if anything to be seen on the seabed. The only noticeable aftermath could be the finding of wreckage, survivors or bodies.

Bobby had told us that in April 1834 the *Sarah*, a brig from Belfast bound for Leith, was driven by a storm onto the base of the Noup. The mate and a young man named Robert Black jumped from the vessel when she struck the rocks. The mate was crushed to death, but the young lad climbed to the top of a 200-foot cliff and wandered down the Daal past young cattle which were kept on the hill, making him realise the island was inhabited. John Henry, an islander, was out getting peats when, from the mist of spray off the sea an unkempt figure came

*Oceanic* **being launched at Harland and Wolff in Belfast.**

slowly towards him, all clothed in white as the shipwrecked man had nothing on but his shirt and trousers.

As he neared the stack of peats John shouted. 'Is du earthly or unearthly?'

'Earthly to be sure I am, and a poor man cast away on your isle.'

He was taken back and nursed to health by the islanders.[11, 8]

With the advent of steam engines and manufactured ice, fishing boats were able to travel further from their home ports and still be able to land fresh fish. This had the dual negative effects in Foula of their grounds being fished by boats from the south, and the risk of these fishing boats being lost in island waters. In 1899, the *Teal Duck* from North Shields, with eight of a crew, was fishing with baited long lines. Later some wreckage was washed up on the island and the wheelhouse and a small dinghy belonging to her were found on Shetland beaches, but no bodies were ever recovered or even seen. She was believed to have been wrecked on the South Ness of the island.[42]

With the high cliffs and enormous waves there was very little the islanders could do even if they knew of a shipwreck. Foula must have been reminiscent of hell when aboard a ship that was being driven towards the island in a gale. If it

Underwater on the *Oceanic* in the clear Shetland waters.

was at night, the dark waves would thunder against the rocks at the base of the cliffs, the crew knowing as the ship approached that they would meet the horror of a violent death.

But Foula's most famous wreck met her demise peacefully. She was the White Star Liner *Oceanic*, built in 1899 as the largest ship in the world, and wrecked in 1914 near the Hoevdi rock on the submerged reef known as the Shaalds of Foula.[13] This is the wreck Simon and I were working – our reason for being in Foula. The loss is described by Professor Holbourn: 'Occasionally wreckage is seen on the Hoevdi that no one knows anything about. Here side by side with many a humbler vessel lies the twisted remnants of the 17,000 ton armed auxiliary cruiser Oceanic, once the pride of the White Star fleet. On 5th September 1914, the giant liner was seen approaching the isle. The islanders watched with some anxiety for she was making straight for the sunken rocks. Anxiety gave place to admiration when it was seen that the vessel was taking a narrow passage between two rocks, and the islanders applauded such daring seamanship and intimate knowledge of the chart. Suddenly, however, the Oceanic discovered her danger and, instead of backing out in the same direction, turned broadside to a nine-knot tide and was swept to her doom with a crash that was heard all over the island. The launch of the *Lion*, a salvage boat which hurried to the scene, was capable of a speed of ten knots, yet she was unable to make any headway against the tide although she tried with full steam for fifteen minutes. Even then it was not the top of the tide, the officer in charge reckoned that the full tide would be twelve knots. Before long every able-bodied islander was commandeered to assist in the work of salvage. Troops and guns were safely removed and an attempt was made to take off some of the more valuable furniture and books. The salvage boats and the trawlers made 'a bonny sight' with their searchlights that lit up the hills. But before long a gale blew and the great ship slipped below the waves. We often think longingly of the many tons of coal, blankets, linen, pianos, and all the furniture of the luxury liner lying just beyond our reach, so near and yet so far. Although the Oceanic has altered her position and now lies in deeper water she can still be seen beneath the waves.'[4]

The *Oceanic* had not altered her position but broke up during a single gale and disappeared from sight.

# Chapter 8
# Gales, Gossip, and Cliffs

Our diving project on the *Oceanic* had expanded well beyond our original estimate because we continually found additional amounts of copper and brass when we had thought we had cleared an area. We were becoming experts in dismantling the vast steam engines weighing hundreds of tons that had propelled the ship and, with our recently acquired salvage vessel *Trygg*, we were hoping to extend our work as far into each autumn as possible. The islanders shook their heads when it was mentioned, even old Tom would tell us 'the heather had flowered well that summer and so we were in for a hard winter'.

We experienced Foula's maritime dilemma for ourselves. Throughout the summer we had run for safety to Scalloway every time the weather deteriorated;

although time consuming we enjoyed these trips, often taking islanders with us, and Simon would have the opportunity to pick up any local news.

Gossip was common in Foula, like everywhere, and as far back as 1899 it was commented that their monotonous life had made them very curious and inquisitive, and fond of gossip, but never anything malicious.[1] Today it was little different and, after returning to the island, we usually went up to Elizabeth's to deliver the items we had purchased for her and hear her news. She was always pleased to see us, her smile spreading across her face as soon as she opened the door. Simon would sometimes quote amusing statements he had heard or read and this would enliven Elizabeth like a warm up before the main show. Then he would deliberately let slip that he had heard some interesting happenings on the mainland. Her face quickly changed to an inquisitive look, with her head slightly tilted to one side as if she was desperately listening for an unknown sound. The rituals of giving her the shopping and sitting down for scones and tea were gone through and, as I chatted, I could see Simon waiting his opportunity, egged on by glances from Elizabeth, but she rarely wanted to show herself as being overtly inquisitive.

I continued to ask questions, enjoying Simon's frustration, but eventually he interrupted me. 'I have some "A1" gossip for you,' he'd say.

'Let's be hearin' it,' she'd reply.

'What have you in exchange?' asks Simon, in his usual, but pleasantly artful manner.

Elizabeth, anxious to hear new gossip, ran through a series of local happenings, much to Simon's amusement. 'I'll need better than that, Elizabeth, this really is good gossip.'

She racked her brain and divulged as much as she could think of.

Simon sat back in his seat with a satisfied grin on his face, feeling the full intensity of her anticipation. He began slowly, 'The fire brigade were called out to a fishing boat in Lerwick when smoke was seen coming out the engine room.'

'Naw,' says Elizabeth, with a slight frown, wondering how this would be relevant to Foula.

Simon took his time, enjoying supping his tea although I sensed that he was itching to know if Elizabeth had heard the story and wasn't prepared to tell him. It had happened before.

When Simon continued, Elizabeth leant forward on the edge of her seat, getting as close as possible, not wishing to miss the slightest detail. 'When they checked the accommodation hatch our island character appeared on deck, pulling up his trousers,' said Simon.

'Naw,' Elizabeth straightened up on her chair, anticipating something really tasty.

'You would not believe what happened next,' said Simon, drawing out the punch line, as if to make Elizabeth beg for it.

'Go on, Sy, go on,' cried Elizabeth, hardly able to contain herself.

'His girlfriend followed him out the hatch – with nothing on but a pair of wellington boots!'

'Naw,' repeated Elizabeth. 'Naw, I canna believe it, you're makin' it up.' Her short, stout body shook with mirth as she moved her head from side to side. The gossip seemed too good to be true – and perhaps it was, these stories tended to grow legs.

Gossip always goes both ways and a few weeks later I was up at Elizabeth's when she said, 'I hear you've stopped wearin' clothes for yir work.'

I looked at her, puzzled by her remark, before becoming aware of what she was referring to. I smiled but my mind went to *The Shetland Times*, envisaging the headlines: 'Naked divers seen working in Foula.'

I replied as if in mitigation, 'But he'd got his bobble hat on.'

Elizabeth smiled, 'Away with you, he was naked,' she answered.

It was true, and it all started with the child's rule for defining the number of turns of rope required for tying objects: one turn for a cow, two for a dinghy, and three for a battleship. On most occasions when Simon tied knots and they slipped, we had easily recovered the inflatable, but once during a fierce gale the inflatable had blown away from the inside of the pier and ended up badly damaged 30 miles away on a beach in Shetland. Since then, much to Simon's feigned annoyance, John-Andrew and I would often check the ropes as a precaution. This day our salvage vessel was lying on our mooring at the entrance to the voe within shouting distance of the Haa, allowing us to nip in for coffee and meals, giving us a break ashore rather than using the galley on the boat. Coming up from the engine room I heard the outboard and saw Simon motoring towards the pier in the inflatable.

'What's up, John-Andrew?' I asked.

'Sy's gone in for some more blades for the metal saw,' he replied. We both looked towards the pier and watched him tie the boat up.

'Let's get the hold finished before he comes back,' I answered, while glancing back to see Simon walk up to the Haa. We climbed down the ladder into the hold, helping each other to sort and stow the salvaged cargo. Simon appeared ten minutes later and shouted down to us.

'I've put the kettle on if you want to come ashore.'

'Great,' replied John-Andrew.

As we climbed out of the hold we were shocked to see the inflatable drifting away from the stern of the boat. 'Sy!' I shouted, as I pointed and ran to the stern in the hope of jumping the distance into the inflatable, but I was too late. Turning round I picked up a grapple, but before I could throw it Simon had stripped off his clothes and was running full tilt to the stern, leaping into the water with nothing on but his bobble hat. The inflatable was drifting towards the rocks in front of the Haa as he swam towards it, but it was touch and go whether he would make it in time. I held my breath.

Reaching it, he caught it by the grab rope, hauled himself aboard and tried to start the outboard. The boat was so close that it was doubtful whether the propeller would clear the rocks. The outboard failed to start first pull – this was usual – but on the second it burst into life. He quickly put the boat astern to keep her clear of the breaking water and neatly turned it to motor back towards us as he pulled his sodden bobble hat firmly on his head. We had been watching with concern for his safety, but no longer. Now John-Andrew and I looked at each other, both coming out with a smile and the word 'camera'. I nipped into the wheelhouse to fetch it. John-Andrew and I smiled at each other as the camera clicked.

Elizabeth laughed when she heard, thinking it was a good story, but even so she said with a smile, 'It might not be big enough for a headline in the local paper.' Not that she would ever feed any gossip to the press?

As the weather deteriorated we knew we had to leave *Trygg* tied up in a safe place for the winter, but in a location we could carry out repairs on her. If Foula had a secure harbour we might have left her there, ready to work if there was a break in the weather. But this was not the case; the harbour was the weak point of the island and by the end of September, due to the deteriorating weather, we had to sail *Trygg* to the safety of Tayport harbour in Fife. We had chosen Tayport because it was nearest to my home as a boy and I knew it well, and Simon wanted to stay in St Andrews, which was only a few miles away, for the winter. After leaving the boat, John-Andrew, Simon and I returned to continue our work in Foula, but soon found our operating days with the inflatable became severely limited by the weather. But it gave us time to enjoy the island and have another attempt at finishing some of the repairs on the house.

After Deidre left we had become quite lax in keeping the house tidy, although there were always regular domestic chores – bringing in peat, emptying ash, pumping paraffin out of a barrel into smaller cans for the Tilley lamp – but our most disliked task was washing clothes. It required bad weather for a few days to make me feel sufficiently guilty and shame me into making a start. I was never encouraged by Simon's attitude as he was even more laid back than me. Our clothes were washed for cleanliness rather than vanity as no one on the island cared what you wore; no judgements or offence was taken or given by appearance. I had been through my dirty washing so many times in an attempt

*Trygg* lifting over the bow a 14.5 tonne bronze central propeller boss and taking it into the sheltered waters of the voe.

to pick out the cleanest that I definitely had nothing remotely clean left to wear, and my clothes were always the worst as I was the engineer. We did have plenty of boxes of washing powder, but it was easier to buy than to use, and the large, industrial packets looked down at me from the kitchen shelf, stimulating my guilt. Distraction from the washing was easy. I might be starting to get the clothes and buckets ready when Simon would say, 'Alec, let's go and visit the south end.' I readily agreed, abandoning all intent to continue. This was the one time I missed electricity, running water – and a washing machine.

I would start on the laborious task by heaping the fire with peat to heat several kettles full of boiling water to fill two buckets, then stir the detergent-soaked clothes with a driftwood stick before leaving them to soak for at least half an hour. At this point I might take any excuse to go off to do something else and abandon them in the bucket under the illusion that the longer they soaked the cleaner they became. Eventually the two buckets of soaked clothes were carried on a five-minute walk down to the burn where on route I would nearly always be caught by Tom. But on these occasions I was glad to stop for five minutes to rest my arms and pass the time of day. When I moved on, Tom would follow me up the slight incline towards Ham, leaving me where the road turned into the croft and down the hill to the burn. If there was a big tide or swell causing the salt water to mingle with the fresh I would move further upstream, tipping the clothes out next to the vertebrae of a whale that had been washed up the previous year.

First, I pummelled the clothes against a rock to get the dirt out, before pinning them down with a stone at one end, allowing the water to flow through them, rinsing out the dirt and washing powder that could then be seen drifting down the burn in clouds. Leaving them for at least half an hour, I lay on the bank behind the Ham kale yard, enjoying the shelter from the wind and feeling the heat from the sun if it shone that day. If it was windy and wet, a brief visit to Elizabeth's croft was preferred.

Returning, I'd wring the clothes out and carry them back to the Haa where a mangle was used to squeeze out the final dregs of water. If it was dry and windy they were hung on our washing line, or thrown over a wall with a heavy stone on top to hold them down. It did not always go well – the occasional sock would disappear down the burn, and the wind was often so strong that items like shirts were blown off the line and into the sea. In wet weather, the sitting room would have clothes hanging everywhere, giving off a pungent yet clean smell of detergent. But the greatest satisfaction of the washing, apart from cleaner clothes, was the relief at completing the work; I no longer had to think about doing the hated task.

I wondered how the islanders without electricity or running water coped with their washing. Did they hate it like us? I suspect it was traditionally done by the women with an old washboard – I can remember my mother having one – but I'm sure no-one's clothes were ever as dirty as mine.

When south for a few months in the winter we made up for our island seclusion, probably like islanders in the past who had gone fishing, whaling, or on cargo ships around the world. The contrast between their working environment and the island life must have been great and if they had found a potential partner elsewhere it must have led to difficult decisions. Fortunately I was busy enough, with my mind concentrating on preparing for our return, not to be unduly distracted by personal emotions but I was still unsure in which direction I wanted to take my life. I often thought of Sloag.

After completing the modifications to *Trygg* at Tayport, we began loading her with our stores and various items arriving for the islanders, including a "dozer blade" for a tractor, wire rope, cylinder head gaskets, special tobacco for Dal, and gunpowder for Jock's home-made shotgun cartridges. We also loaded a large quantity of food from the cash and carry for ourselves and islanders as the shop had finally closed.

The Aberdeen papers during February had reported that a deep water trawler called the *Coastal Empress* had been damaged 16 miles south of Foula by an 80-foot high wave. The wave smashed through the wheelhouse into the skipper's cabin, down the companionway into the engine room. It also tore away the lifeboat, safety rails and fittings. It was stated that if there had been a second wave they would definitely have gone over.[43]

This report made us hesitant to return until the weather became more settled. We knew we were a bit quick off the blocks when we set off in the middle of March and encountered weather too bad to approach Foula, having to divert to Scalloway. After waiting for ten days we risked a trip, taking with us additional cargo that had been sent to us at Scalloway, including a pram which we thought was a good omen, along with bags of layers mash for the hens, bread, cigarettes and boxes containing food.

It was a rough crossing with a gale forecast, but the pier was on the sheltered side of the island and with the help of the islanders the boat was quickly unloaded. Simon then jumped ashore to stay on the island and I returned to Scalloway with Ken, who needed to go to the mainland. Arriving back at Scalloway, Ken and I then visited the Lounge bar in Lerwick to relax after a rough trip. There was always someone playing the fiddle upstairs, making it a real treat and reminding me of some evenings in Foula.

Leaving Ken, in the early evening I went to the Fisherman's Mission to get a warm shower and a clean bed for the night. I was still in my dirty clothes and the washing facilities aboard *Trygg* were worse than those in the Haa. It was almost worth being exposed to the dirt and grime to enjoy that refreshing feeling of washing away all the worries along with the smell of the engine room before changing into clean clothes which made me feel and act like a different person. Mr Simmons, the person in charge of the Mission, was getting used to our visits from the previous summer; sometimes it was just a quick shower, other times we might have a meal and stay the night, all of which he allowed us to pay for as he considered us in a similar category to fishermen. If the Mission was full I am sure he quite rightly would have given them preference, although Simon reckoned that with our work we were definitely "deep sea fishermen". 'Maybe,' the kindly Mr Simmons would reply with a smile.

The following day, after securing *Trygg* on moorings in East Voe at Scalloway, I was offered a berth aboard the fishing boat *Spray* as they were intending to sail to Foula early the next morning to fish off the island. The sea was too rough to drop me at the pier, but after signalling Simon with the boat's fog horn, he and John-Andrew picked me up in the inflatable.

In the Haa, as I warmed up, Simon and I discussed how John-Andrew had made a wetsuit over the winter to practice diving with a snorkel in the Voe. As proof, he had recovered bits of brass that had slipped over the side of *Trygg* when we were working in the voe. We had always been worried about teaching him to dive but after that effort he joined the team as a diver as well as working on deck, and we planned his first diving job – the laying of a massive mooring for *Trygg* in the entrance to the voe. We could hardly stop talking about the coming summer as I wandered round the sitting room with pleasure, touching familiar objects and feeling at home, delighted to be back on the island.

We both took an interest in and enjoyed the island birds and, with a new camera, Simon was intending to go to the cliffs to see if he could take some unusual photographs. John-Andrew was keen to take us on the first day we weren't working – and it wasn't raining; an essential requirement we thought, when near the cliffs, as many had slippery, close-cropped grass near the edge. Foula had been famous in the past for the islanders who scaled the cliffs for birds and their eggs, when human fatalities had been frequent, but now John-Andrew was the last of the islanders that took a serious interest in climbing.

In 1700, the Reverend John Brand wrote of the Foula people: 'they are judged to be the best climbers of rocks in all this country, for some of them will fasten a flake or knife, as some say, in the ground on the top of the rock, to which they tie a small rope or cord, and so they will come down the face of the rock with this in their hand sixty, seventy, or eighty fathoms (480 feet), and do return bringing up eggs and fowls with them; but indeed very many of them lose their lives this way; yea it is observed that few old men are to be seen there, they being so cut off before they arrive at old age…'[39]

The climbing was carried on throughout the century and reports continued to mention the lives that were lost as they were also 'catching wild fowls for their feathers.'[36]

Feathers were mostly bought by the government. After fumigation they were immune to lice and bed-bugs and could be used by the military, but in the mid 1800s the market collapsed because of the use of different materials.[44]

By 1822 they had coined a phrase: 'It was formerly said of the Foula man, – his gutcher (grandfather) guid before, his father guid before, and he must expect to go over the Sneug too.'[45] The Sneug was the highest point on the island – 1,372 feet and nearest to the Kame, which was the second-highest vertical cliff in Britain.

The primitive rope they used sounded unsafe and is described in 1832: 'Their frail tenure of existence depended solely upon the support of a rope of hair or bristles and hemp mixed together, which latter is by the rockmen considered much less liable to be cut by the sharp projecting stones than when the 'tow' is composed exclusively of either.'[11]

Bobby Isbister stressed how the islanders all co-operated in the past, whether it was on the croft, recovering eggs or when fishing, but there was always rivalry to be the best. A Foula man in those days, with the danger of climbing and going many miles out to sea to fish, must have been an exceptional person, very different from the type of person required to survive on the island or anywhere in Britain today.

But life was not always straightforward even then, and an unusual incident occurred 150 years before was told to us by Bobby: 'A Foula man and his wife were upon the same rope, and the gude wife was farthest down, when the thread of life showed evident signs of holding out no longer. Without delay he sacrificed his rib away, she flew whirling and screaming like a wounded sea gull, and her husband returned home to mourn for his departed spouse. Great indeed was his affliction and as usual the neighbours had assembled to offer all the consolation in their power, when the door burst open and in rushed the gude wife herself, dripping from the salt sea, and giving convincing proof by means of her fists and tongue that she was no disembodied spirit, but true flesh and blood. How matters were made up with her now perhaps still more disconsolate husband, history does not inform us, but she escaped from supposed certain destruction by the wind having caught her petticoats in the descent, and thus held her supported by a parachute, till she sank gracefully into the ocean's bosom, where by good chance a passing boat picked her up.'[8]

This infers that women, and in petticoats, were lowered down the cliffs. It does seem incongruous to their normal lives, although the women may be considerably lighter than the men for supporting on a rope.

Few people survived a fall and on 23rd May, 1885, an accident is reported: 'As three fishermen were rowing their boat off the Noop in the afternoon they saw a dark object floating in a *geo* at the foot of the rocks. From its appearance the men imagined it to be the remains of some drowned seaman cast up on their shore, and they at once proceeded to make arrangements for bringing the corpse to land, so as to give it a decent burial. When taking it in tow some suspicions came into one of the men's mind that the clothes were not unknown to him. On examination the suspicion proved to be only too well founded, there being no difficulty in recognising the body as one of their nearest neighbours – James Paterson, crofter, Shodels. From the place where it was found, as well as the crushed condition of the body, there was no doubt that death had been caused by a fall from the cliffs, where deceased was often in the habit of climbing in search for wild fowls and eggs …'[46]

One of John-Andrew's past relations, James Andrew Ratter of Braidfit croft, was said to have talked about fowling around 1920 when he was at the age of 18.[38] But the purpose by then was merely to keep up tradition and to test their skills, rather than a mainstay for survival.

For our trip to explore the cliffs, we met John-Andrew at his croft. There was no defined track from Hametoon leading to the west but he knew the easiest route through the bath-shaped glen called the Daal. On the south side was the Noup, that terminated in a cliff, and to the north lay Hamnafield. We picked our way round peat bogs and hidden wet areas that snaked down the hillside as if in wait for an unwary walker who could end up knee deep in a sodden mossy mush. The extraction usually required help to pull the legs out, often resulting in the walker falling over in the bog and even losing the boot off his foot, and then having to fish it out on his hands and knees. Fortunately we had been through this phase when we first came to the island, but this time John-Andrew, who was extremely agile and well used to the rough ground, knew exactly where to go.

Reaching the west side of the Daal we looked out at the heavy swell, the sea stretching uninterrupted by any land all the way to the south tip of Greenland. In the northwest of the island we could see steep, sloping ground called the Ufshins, the angle being close to the limit of standing, but at a later time I saw John-Andrew's father running along sheep tracks as he chased sheep, even when the slope was around 65 degrees. It was covered with close-cropped grass which was slippery, and ended abruptly in a cliff. The Reverend George Low in 1774 wrote: '… the ascent is so steep that one is forced to take fast hold of the heath to prevent tumbling down, as there is no such thing as stopping till he is dashed to pieces, as happened to a poor woman in gathering dye stuff a short time before I went there.'

This was probably the dye known in Foula as "coreolet", as there was a history of using and selling natural plants and mosses, particularly this fine reddish moss which was the main saleable dye from the island at that time.[27]

We moved away from the Ufshins and made our way towards the edge of the Noup, where we found John-Andrew managed the steep land with confidence, rarely putting a hand down to support himself, whereas Simon and I held onto heather or clumps of grass on the steepest parts as we looked for sheep tracks that gave a better foothold. Angling down towards the top of the cliffs we'd leave one sheep track, cross the steep, sloping grass and heather, before picking up another lower down as they always ran along the contour of the slope, parallel to the cliff face. Tumbling down was a phrase not far from my mind as I thought it was getting quite tricky, although John-Andrew remained unfazed by it. We stopped near the edge where we could hear the sea crashing against the base of the cliffs far below – which made me even more cautious.

Poking your head even obliquely over a cliff edge while lying on a grassy slope is not something I would recommend; not only do you feel you might slip over the edge but I was also concerned that my weight might cause the edge to collapse, taking me with it. We crouched down to take pictures of the mass of birds that flew within a few feet of us. John-Andrew, who knew which areas were safe, beckoned us to move to a better position where we could get close to the cliff edge on relatively flat, rocky ground and be able to see the ledges beneath, packed with birds.

'How about a close up of a bird?' John-Andrew asked, and before either of us could reply he was over the edge and out of sight. I slithered closer to the face, carefully leaning over to where I could see him standing on a ledge about two feet wide, five feet below us. Beneath him were a series of ledges like narrow shelves and then a drop straight into the sea. The birds either side of him looked on curiously, not unduly concerned; some had taken off but many remained. It was a fantastic sight. There were literally clouds of birds and, like a small incident in a busy street, few took any interest in us as they continued to wheel round and glide in the updraught. The guillemots and razorbills lacked the flying skills of those that soared and would return to their ledges in straight flight lines that came to an abrupt halt as they landed. John-Andrew had captured a live razorbill in either hand and started to climb up the ledges using his elbows, before finally wiggling his way over the top where he stood up with the birds. He gently passed one over. I was surprised how calm it was and thought back to when the island had relied on them for food; perhaps the birds were now less frightened as generations had passed since then.

We made our way back, passing the areas where Arctic skuas (commonly called allens) and great skuas (commonly called bonxies) nested on the ground. These are aggressive birds that give you a nasty thump on the head by dive-bombing you when approaching their nests. They have been written about throughout the centuries by most visitors to the island whose main purpose of coming had been to see them. In 1774 it was written: 'The hill tops … are covered with thousands of the Arctic skuas, which build among the heather, and lay two eggs of an olive colour … and also we find that remarkable bird the great skua; I no sooner approach his quarters but he attacked me and my company with so great fury that every one of us were forced to do him obeyance for every stroke. He beat my water Spaniel quite out of the pit, insomuch that he fled to our feet for shelter, and could not be forced out again, tho' a bold dog and well used to encounter Otters, … … In Foula this is a privileged bird, no man will dare shoot it, under penalty of 16s. 8d. Sterling (from the landlord), nor destroy its eggs; when they meet it at sea, whatever fish they have in the boat the great skua always gets a share, and all this out of gratitude for beating off the eagle, who dares not venture to prey on the island during the whole breeding season.'[27]

We normally carried a stick over a shoulder as a static protection to prevent our heads being hit by the birds. When we took some visitors along the road to the north of the island in our pickup, one of them asked if he could walk as he was not very happy with the smoke coming up through the rusted floor in our old vehicle. Within minutes he was signalling wildly for us to come back and pick him up as the skuas attacked him unforgivingly for entering their territory.

In 1821 there were 150 pairs of Arctic skuas and only 30 pairs of great skuas, and the kittiwake and the puffin numbers probably exceed all the birds in Foula.[25]

By 1832 Dr Edward Charlton, a naturalist, had reported: 'Soon after a man came down from the hills with six eggs of the skua gull [great skua], however I told him, I did not wish any more of them, being anxious to preserve that noble bird from destruction.'[11, 8]

This was becoming a serious issue as by 1880 there were only two places left in Britain – one of them Foula – where the great skua still bred because of people taking their eggs.[10] Their population in Foula had remained fairly steady at 30 pairs during the 1800s but by 1976 it had increased to 3,000 pairs.[47] The Arctic skua breeding pairs had also increased from 60 in 1890[48] to 253 in 1975.[49] These were encouraging figures.

We noticed the great skuas were starting to breed around the crofts and in these areas some islanders removed the eggs for eating. The skuas were believed to be decimating the kittiwakes, which they harassed during their flight back to the island to make them bring up the fish they had swallowed, the great skua catching the vomited fish in the air and eating them. But recently they had started to feed on the kittiwake chicks and drove the lambs off the land near their nests as well as feeding on any weak lambs. By removing the eggs the islanders intended the birds to move back onto the scattald outside their crofts where they would lay for a second time.

During 1954, legislation had been passed in the form of the Wild Bird Protection Act that covered many birds and their eggs found in Foula, but unprotected fulmar eggs could lawfully be taken from their nests which were

Looking from Hametoon west towards the Daal and the Ufshins where the steep grass bank meets the cliffs.

often accessible on rock ledges or steep grassy slopes. The angry fulmars would defend themselves by vomiting a noxious liquid that is known to take the waterproofing from other birds' feathers, but even so, it was relatively easy to gather a basketful of their eggs just by leaning over the edges of the lower cliffs and grassy slopes on the east side.

There has always been a market for wild birds eggs in Foula, almost entirely for eating, and in 1955 Chris Mylne, the teacher/missionary, found that the collecting of eggs for sale on the mainland was still part of the island way of life. I personally suspect they all ended up as a gift to members of Foula families who lived on the Shetland mainland. He states that: 'One Friday they were preparing baskets packed with grass and announced these were the first collection that weekend of the skuas' eggs, which were traditionally gathered at three week intervals, to allow the birds to re-lay a new batch for their larders. Great skua eggs especially, are much larger than hen's eggs and just as tasty. Moreover I was assured this couldn't do much harm as the birds always laid again so all they were doing was delaying the breeding season by about a month.'[38]

The Noop at the south west of Foula. *Lesley Timings*

Often given wild birds to eat, I was pleased to see the islanders' love and care of wildlife was not diminished by their need to use them as part of their diet. Simon and I watched John-Andrew shield an eider duck from a great skua that was aggressively attacking her young brood of cheeping ducklings. She had emerged from her inland nest and they were waddling in her wake towards Ham Voe. Using his arms to deflect the angry skua he saw the ducklings safely onto the water, and watched the mother until she had carefully ushered her newly launched family to the safety of an overhanging bank.

The Brathay Exploration Group arrived at specific times throughout the summer, undertaking studies, mostly on the bird population, but at one time they had also helped the islanders on their crofts. They all stayed in Ristie, which was rented by the group. It looked out on the famous Gaada Stack, originally a giant, three-legged arch at the north end, and as the area had no permanent residents they had the place to themselves. We rarely saw them as they formed their own group of friends amongst themselves and spent most of the time counting and ringing birds, but after Hance stopped running the *Hirta* it became difficult for these parties to reach the island and, even worse,

Looking over a steep grassy edge. *Lesley Timings*

once they were on the island it became impossible to guarantee getting them off within the time window required to catch a ferry or plane south. At these times we were occasionally called in to transport them with *Trygg*, combining it with a run to Scalloway or Walls to collect fuel or stores. Although it might cost us a day's work in good weather, it felt part of an enjoyable duty when staying on the island not to leave visitors stranded.

Many of the ornithologists were keen photographers – a hobby also becoming popular with the islanders – giving them the opportunity to capture not only the scenery but prove the sighting of rare or unusual birds. A German birdwatcher called Gunther was a regular visitor in Foula and stayed in Elizabeth's Loch cottage from where he walked around the island with multiple cameras and lenses slung around his neck. It was towards the end of May when an islander was fortunate to catch sight of a snowy owl. Although two nesting females and one male had bred on the island of Fetlar in the northeast of Shetland in 1974, this bird was normally found north of the Arctic circle. As soon as word got out there was a rush as people attempted to reach the island. It was not like the mainland where flocks of birdwatchers were able to arrive within hours, or even

**Guillemots on a ledge.**                                              *Lesley Timings*

131

Fair Isle where I had seen the numbers increase dramatically with rare sightings, but for Foula the most people learned from the sighting was how difficult it was to get to the island. They could have flown to the west coast of America in a quicker time, and at a lower cost.

The bird was eventually photographed at Loch cottage by an islander when, the rumour had it, Gunther was still looking for it two miles away at the south after a false sighting.

# Chapter 9
# Hard Work and Housework

When in Fife for part of the winter, Roz, one of the prospective cooks we met in Scalloway, came up for a quick visit in February and stayed with my parents. She arranged to arrive in Foula ahead of Lesley at the beginning of summer, travelling to Walls where she hoped to catch the mailboat. The short visit to Fife was all very casual, but Simon and I thought we were getting the "once over" to check we were safe people to stay with during the coming summer. She was right to check, and we respected her for it.

When Roz turned up at Walls the boat was a day late from its printed schedule, which was not unusual, but it suffered from another delay at Walls, so it was 6.40pm before Jim phoned to say they had left. In Foula the visibility had only been about half a mile all day as fog shrouded the island, but it was quite common for the island to sit in its own cloud attracted by the land mass, and a mile off it could be a bright, sunny day.

Half an hour before the boat was due, people started collecting at the pier and wandering up to the Haa. We placed a Tilley lamp in a window hoping the light might help guide the boat. After a long wait, Harry went to find out if there had been any word from Walls, only to return with nothing to tell us. The boat was now more than two hours overdue, and we were all concerned.

The most likely explanation was a breakdown as the mailboat engine had been temperamental for a long time. The boat had no radio, and was unable to communicate with anyone, and no radar to guide her. Her sole instrument for navigation was a magnetic compass. Our boat *Trygg* was on a mooring in East Voe at Scalloway at the time, and if we or an islander had set out in our inflatable or a small boat we would almost certainly have become enveloped in the mists and become lost as well.

'You'd think they would get a radio and radar fitted,' said Simon.

'Jim said they get paid very little for the contract, so I don't suppose they can afford it.'

'I'd have thought a radio was essential when carrying passengers,' answered Simon as he put on his oilskins.

We had a VHF radio on *Trygg*; it had limited range, about 24 miles at worst, but we found it useful for forecasts and finding out the actual sea conditions from other boats in the area.

Taking two good torches we walked up the coast in case they had come ashore on the island, while Harry called out the Aith Lifeboat in the west of Shetland, the most northerly lifeboat in the UK. I thought of Roz. We hardly knew her but we felt responsible that she was at sea, even though I had every confidence in Jim and knew that he would take no risks. He was a good mechanic; it might take him a while, but he would fix the engine if it could be fixed. After returning from our coastal search having seen nothing but fog, we didn't go to bed, instead we waited in the sitting room in case we were needed.

It was three in the morning when we saw a torch coming towards the Haa.

'They've had to return to Scalloway,' Harry said, when he looked in to tell us the news.

'What happened?' asked Simon.

'They thought they'd missed the island and turned back.'

I knew it was the sensible decision to make, and felt the feeling of relief flow over me that they were unharmed.

The following morning Elizabeth hurried down to tell us that her friend had phoned to say that one of the newspaper headlines was 'Foula Mailboat Missing – With Divers' Cook on Board.'

Roz arrived on the mailboat two days later, none the worse for her adventure. In fact, she was more buoyed up than concerned, the excitement still apparent when we had a small party for her birthday later that week.

The next time the mailboat left for its run it only managed half a mile before it broke down. We watched it for ten minutes with binoculars before setting out in the inflatable to see if we could help. Jim emerged disappointed and oily from the cramped engine room after deciding it required lengthy repairs. We towed it with the inflatable, making slow but surprisingly easy progress back to the pier. This was the day Lesley was due to arrive, and the flat calm sea looked beautiful, with perfect visibility. I set off in the inflatable to pick her up at Walls, the trip taking less than an hour. The mailbags had been made ready for the mailboat so it seemed prudent to take them – common sense still triumphed over regulations – although we did joke with the postmaster that we were so much faster than the mailboat we should only be carrying first-class mail. Lesley and I stuffed the canvas bags into plastic sacks to keep them dry and set off for a quick return trip. Back in Foula, we were met at the pier by Harry, Elizabeth, Jim, John-Andrew, Roz and Simon. As expected, Lesley and Roz received a ribbing for being Jonahs.

With the weather improving each day, life was busy for everyone and gave us massive appetites as a result of the physical work. There were normally five of us – John-Andrew, Simon and myself, plus the two girls – but seven or more when John-Andrew's relations, Andrew and Magnie, came to the island for a break and helped us. We required endless supplies and nothing went to waste. It was late spring and the time for eggs; omelettes, fried eggs, cakes and natural custard were now a regular feature in our diet. In the morning, instead of porridge we might have an omelette stuffed with grated cheddar cheese cut from one of our large wholesale blocks. Some eggs had a slight fishy taste, so if we wanted them boiled we used ones taken from the fulmars, known as "mallies", whose eggs were white and tasted similar to those from a hen.

On occasional evenings Jim or Harry might bring their fiddles along, and at other times we were joined by crews from the fishing boats. I wasn't sure we were the attraction, but the girls certainly added to the company, making events feel more like a party. It made me wonder if Foula had been like this when its population was greater; if so, it was a good life for the young.

Sometimes intense and frank discussions would liven up the atmosphere during the evenings, the islanders having a different slant to a topic, challenging the complexity of a situation to render it down to simple logic. Everyone was tolerant, as if the bright pulsing light from the Tilley lamp, with its perpetual hiss, instilled a calmness that seeped into all our hearts. The outside world was so far away that the larger life events were never taken too seriously. It was as if only Foula existed, our little island completely detached from the worries and daily decisions that had to be made in the larger world. I found my eyes opening as I saw the world through the girls' perspective; it was so very different to the one I had been brought up with and stood in stark contrast to the very masculine traditions of the island, and my own family. Fortunately, times were changing both on the island and elsewhere.

Lesley and Roz usually baked cakes or scones on the mailboat days because we expected more visitors as they waited for the boat to arrive. Lesley was a perfect cook, unflustered by anything, particularly Simon's teasing, and Roz was gaining experience fast. On one occasion they baked an enormous Victoria sponge using our ample supply of eggs and used the last of our sugar knowing it would be replaced when the mailboat returned. Pleased with their creation, considering the inadequacies of our kitchen, all was well except for Roz's slight reservation about the eggs. This was provoked by one of Simon's jokes on the previous day when he had said, 'we'd all be led away in handcuffs for eating the eggs'. We reassured her they were better used than wasted.

When Lesley brought the cake in from the kitchen, I was sitting with a steaming coffee and Simon, complete with bobble hat, sat on the settee sipping a cup of tea. Roz stood with four plates in her hand and a very sharp knife. Simon and I had finished work for the day and were considering whether we should start the cake or wait until others appeared. Suddenly, Simon was distracted by someone passing the window. He got up and rushed out to catch them before they went down to the pier. I knew he was up to something when I heard them come in through the passage. Roz looked at me like a startled rabbit. I returned the look with one of concern, putting my coffee down as I rose from the chair. An eminent ornithologist and his equally qualified wife came into the room. Simon smiled craftily. I looked at Roz. She was trying hard to compose herself, her eyes glancing between the ornithologists and the illegal cake. Roz was an honest girl who visibly showed her feelings, and I knew this must be a nightmare for her. I watched her body sway as she transferred the weight from one leg to the other. I began to worry. Would she say something? I looked at Lesley. She was unfazed by their arrival, the perfect poker player.

'We're just about to have a piece of cake,' said Simon. 'Would you like some?'

'Yes, please,' was the eager reply from the ornithologists, who were two nice people and easy company.

Roz started to cut the cake, but I could see her hand shaking. Simon, unable to let the moment go, had another dig, remarking how well the girls coped with a shortage of ingredients.

It was too much. I could see Roz had stopped cutting, I took the knife from her as a red blush started to envelop her face. Pointing to the kitchen, I asked if she would mind getting some more plates. Lesley cut the cake, Simon grinned, and I handed the existing plates round before rushing off to the kitchen to join Roz.

When we returned I could hear the ornithologists chatting about the birds and remarking on Lesley and Roz's ability to have the time and the ingredients for cake-making in Foula. 'Staying at Brathay, we're running low on everything, particularly sugar,' The man remarked.

Roz, now completely composed and back on form, quietly replied, 'Simon organises all our ingredients.'

Simon, sitting down with a large piece of cake in his hand poised for a bite, used his other hand to pull his bobble hat slightly further down his forehead – a guilty habit.

In the middle of May gales set in. Lesley and Roz started painting the house and we all made an effort to reduce the endless list of jobs designed to make our life in the Haa easier and more comfortable. Anything from painting inside to cement repairs on the outside walls, the work was always taken in a light-hearted manner, stopping at times for chats and cups of tea, along with enjoyable delays when a visitor appeared.

At times we might urgently be asked if we would clear nets from the propellers of Shetland fishing boats. It was easy for us and we never charged but were always given fish – the *Brighter Morn* giving us haddocks and the *Provider* an enormous cod, and other boats regularly gave us a mixed fry. We felt like past generations of islanders who must have enjoyed a bountiful spring feasting on the eggs and carcases of migrating birds, and catching fresh fish when they could get out in their boats after struggling through a long winter of salted food, meal, potatoes and limited vegetables.

I often asked myself the question, 'What if I lived on the island permanently?' Simon thought me foolish to even think of it – but I did, and it became a recurring, unanswered thought. I knew it would be different from our present life as we had been lucky with our house, its position next to the pier gave us the opportunity to see all the comings and goings on the island; it was the first port of call for lost visitors, a refuge to those battered by the weather and a place where people were always welcome to wait for a boat. Our work, too, was an attraction. In a place that was often bereft of any island news, people were curious to find out how we were progressing. If we had been in another house, like Sloag, and working on a routine job, I would miss our visitors; my life would become less inspired and undoubtedly less enjoyable, unless there were more people on the island.

I was aware of the limited opportunities for myself or the islanders. Eric had never been off the island, except when he was born, and it looked as though it would be sheer chance if he found himself a partner and, if so, would he be happier? I felt the recent island marriage failures stood like a dark cloud lurking in the background. Although never talked about I could sense the wounds had cast a shadow over the families involved. It was a cautionary tale, and I wondered if it would affect Eric. At present he appeared wholly satisfied staying in a tidy but un-serviced house with his parents and sharing the croft as a stable base to eke out a living. He was also learning all the old stories from his elderly parents that would make him an undoubted authority when they passed. There would be many that might envy his way of life; the alternatives if he left the island might not be so attractive. For entertainment and worldly news he had purchased a 12-volt television that ran off a car battery which could be charged by the Limpet. I was curious whether it would affect the whole family, changing their musical talents and evenings spent together. We had no television in the Haa and had no intention of getting one – we liked life the way it was.

Many people came to Foula to find pleasure from the birds and the magnificent landscape provided them with a unique and unsophisticated experience, but I was surprised how few came from the countryside. This may have limited potential partners for islanders as country folk would likely make the most suitable partners. It was easy for Simon and me to live here, just two bachelors with no dependants, but bringing up a family must be difficult in domestic terms, otherwise it was a wonderful place for the children to grow up, if you didn't mind the lack of sport and social interaction.

None of the visitors I had met so far had ever mentioned the possibility of having any wish to stay on the island. Very few would enjoy the natural restrictions that put limits on their way of life. They all seemed such free people, like the migrating birds, who having explored Foula were ready to fly away to investigate new and exciting lands. In my heart I was just a boy and knew the wanderlust remained within me, as it did with the girls who walked all over the island taking an interest in the tens of thousands of birds as well as visiting the islanders. When in the Haa the girls read, and Roz was also curing a sheepskin under differing instructions from the Isbisters and Elizabeth. We never worried that they might not like the island or enjoy sharing the house with us as they always appeared happy entertaining themselves.

We became familiar with the few stalwart visitors who came for a few weeks each summer. One in particular, an elderly lady called Vera, always tried to travel by boat to islands as she claimed it gave a true feeling of their isolation compared with a quick flight by an aeroplane. She became a familiar sight with her dog as she enjoyed endless miles of walking, the scruffy-coated dog being referred to by Simon as her "scabbie" dog, as it had the misfortune of having its tail removed when it caught in the propeller-shaft coupling on a small Shetland yoal. But Vera and her dog were like a beam of sunshine, always happy and helpful wherever she went.

Occasionally the girls, instead of going for their usual walk, would stay in the Haa and watch for our return. It was one of the pleasures of their company, when the three of us returned from the wreck absolutely exhausted and the adrenalin rush from our diving had faded during the cold trip back in the inflatable. Our hearts would lift as we saw the girls running down the pier to take the ropes, Roz with arms and legs everywhere, Lesley more contained. We would all be smiling broadly. It was nice to be welcomed back and have them helping to unload the inflatable. Harry would be examining what we had recovered and Tom watched from a distance with a smile on his face. Once the inflatable was secured, Simon, with his diving hood pulled back, woollen bobble hat on his head, would always make some remark about 'how well they looked' before we all walked up to the Haa. Pulling each other out of our diving suits we dressed before joining the girls in the sitting room, where we stood thawing out in front of the roaring peat fire. Food would be produced and we would celebrate together as we all chatted about each other's day. It was on these occasions I knew my life was moving on. The days of sudden decisions and at times irresponsibility were passing as I became more stable, more realistic, although at times it was difficult to get out of ingrained habits from the past.

Simon was daft about anything at all that represented sport – he loved it, and followed the Sunderland football team. As a cub reporter for the *Sunderland Echo* he had regularly watched Sunderland play in order to write about them. He also followed the main players of other teams and was a George Best fan. When he was not listening to sport on the radio he was happy to kick a ball about, playing "keepie uppies", or on dry, windy days when the sun shone he was keen to drag me off to play. We'd use a cricket bat made from driftwood, or shot putt using old aluminium trawl floats, and we'd toss cabers made from washed-up spars. Elizabeth's sheep looked on with cautious interest as pieces of driftwood were assembled with an old piece of trawl net that had been washed up on the rocks in front of the Haa to make a junior-sized goal. Simon's game of goalies rarely stopped until he had won decisively. He relied on accuracy and skill, whereas my only asset was brute force behind a hard kick.

'George Best coming in to score,' was his commentary as he dribbled the ball towards me.

'Gordon Banks prepares to save,' I replied, joining in his fantasy while I moved nervously from side to side with all the pretence of a real goalkeeper, not sure where he would kick the ball, but putting a bit of acting and distraction into it.

'Goal!' he shouted, as the ball whizzed past my ear into a corner of the net, then he followed up with a little dance as if it was a real game. However hard I tried, I knew in the end he would always win; he had excellent ball skills and yet had poor balance when on the boat. I had limited football skill but excellent balance, I could have been a tight rope walker. I never worked that difference out, or was it just confidence?

Surprised to find the four children at the Foula school were not taught football, and had rarely kicked a ball, Simon was encouraged to pass on his "footy" skills. He included the older children in the occasional "goalie" sessions in the Haa yard where anybody that happened to be about – visitors, schoolchildren or islanders – were commandeered if possible.

After the football we might fly a kite. It was also something new for the island and worked well for a while, providing us all with entertainment. It took a lot of skill as the wind was never steady, often falling and quickly rising in gusts, eventually destroying the kites beyond repair and ending another saga. But Simon was not to be defeated, taking up another interest that appealed to him – fishing. He took heart from seeing people catching sillocks from the rocks or pier; these were young coalfish that can grow up to three feet long. During the summer we were visited by Peter Gray, a regular rod fisherman who had advised me on rebuilding the fire. He lived at Burns, a 1½-storied house which had been built by his father and lay about 15 minutes' walk from the pier. The croft was beautifully kept and always had flowers in the garden. Peter, in his 80s, was happy to quietly live out the rest of his life having little contact with others except his late wife's brother, Harry. When we saw him fish at the pier he looked relaxed and enjoyed himself as he held a long pole with a fixed length of line, often catching six- to eight-inch long sillocks every time he cast. He quickly took them off the hook and threw the line back to catch more. After filling a bucket, he put the rod over his shoulder and slowly walked back to his croft. He knew the tide, weather and time of year sufficiently well to practically always appear when the fish were there. It seemed too good to be true and I wondered if Harry told him whenever he had seen shoals of fish at the end of the pier.

Simon had watched Peter catch fish with a certain fascination and decided this was for him. His mother, in her later years, had enjoyed the times she had been able to fish with a rod. Although Simon had not fished with her, he became fully bitten by the bug when he heard of a trout that was reputed to live between the entrance to the voe and the Ham burn. Duncan, the skipper of the trawler *Avrella*, would tie up at the end of the pier during good weather to rest the crew before the night's fishing and spend hours standing on the bow, casting his line for this trout.

Using an old rod found in the Haa porch, Simon went up the burn with a hook and a worm to try his luck. After several hours I watched him return from the comfort of the Haa window. I could see he was not carrying any fish, and heard him return the rod to the porch before coming into the sitting room. 'Well?' I asked, while making tea for him.

He sat down thoughtfully on the settee, waited for me to bring the cup along with a piece of freshly-made bread covered in a thick layer of jam, before answering in a slow deliberate fashion, as if he was upset. 'When I was at school, we were studying the works of the Orkney poet George Mackay Brown.' He paused to take a sip from his tea. 'Mackay Brown had written a story about going fishing on a burn with his "wand" and the teacher asked us to write an essay on our interpretation of what he meant.'

'What did you write?' I asked, not sure how relevant this was.

'Every person in the class wrote about the rod representing some magic tool for extracting fish. The teacher agreed, expressing how clever and subtle was his use of the word "wand".'

'It sounds quite sensible,' I said.

'So I thought,' replied Simon, 'until John-Andrew came along to see what I was doing.' He asked, 'Has thee caught onything wi thy wand an wurry?' (Wurry is a worm.)

'What did he mean?' I queried.

'Apparently,' replied Simon, 'in Shetland and Orkney the fishing rod has been called a wand for generations.' Simon shook his head, 'It's enough to make you lose faith in your teachers.'

Although Simon had ended up as head boy at school, he must have been a tricky student. He previously told me that he had written to T.S. Eliot to ask the meaning of a passage of poetry because he disagreed with his teacher's interpretation. He had been disappointed when he received a reply stating that the meaning should be "whatever the reader thinks it is." I could see why he went into journalism.

After several days of gales with the heavy rain battering against the windows, we became slow to rise in the mornings as the days showed all the symptoms of a lazy time. It was on these occasions I sensed boredom setting in. When I had been on my own I loved these days with the sound of the wind-driven rain, and if I had to go out for anything I found pleasure in struggling back to the house, looking forward to shaking out the waterproof clothes before enjoying a big fire with no guilt whatsoever for having an easy day. I would listen to the radio or read a book, my day usually broken by one or more islanders dropping in, pleased to share the heat and shelter before leaving to check their yoal in its noost or collect something from the pier. I imagined them relaxing in their crofts after they had attended their stock, the usual pointed remarks would be made to each other about the weather before settling down in front of their stove, the men might play the fiddle, read a book or just sit in silence, some with a pipe held loosely between their teeth. The women, who always had work to do, would bake or tidy round the house before taking their turn at the fire.

For us with the two girls, it was different if the bad weather kept everyone inside. We all knew there had to be a semblance of order and co-operation to make life work. Breakfast on a bad weather day was rarely later than nine, but often taking an hour to finish before the first hint came that no one wanted to go out and face the driving rain. I usually took the opportunity to fill in my diary if I had not made any entries for the previous day. There was nothing confidential in my diary, I recorded what had happened each day along with the working tide times, and made sketches of our work, accompanied by a detailed description of the progress. At the bottom of each page was a list of all the consumables used and occasionally an estimate of our remaining stores. There were also details of highlights of island life such as cutting peats, mail-boat departures, and minor jottings on repairing fences, games of bridge at Maggie's, silly stories and gathering sheep. There was nothing of a personal nature, it was more like a ship's log, although Simon always referred to it as 'dear diary': 'What's dear diary saying about the tides today?' he would ask.

Simon's preference was to listen to sport, sometimes giving the appearance of napping on the settee, his bobble hat pulled down over his eyes and his legs curled up to his chest, and the radio pressed against his ear if no one else wanted to hear it. Roz and Lesley sat at the table, books open in front of them. All of us warm and snug as we watched the kettle hiss for its umpteenth time from its position on top of the banked up fire, with no one making a move to take it off.

When by ourselves, Simon and I had occasionally resorted to competitions, once competing to extend a twelve-foot retractable steel measuring tape vertically, finding the greatest height that could be sustained for 30 seconds before it bent over and fell down. Simon, being very competitive, after he lost Champion of the World would want to compete for Champion of the Universe, but that was one game where he couldn't beat me. It reflected how low we'd sink. If we had been south we would have watched the television, gone to the pub to meet friends or strangers, maybe a cinema in the evening or just drive round – the choices were numerous. I thought boredom in the south was more

From the left Alec, Simon and John-Andrew on the pier.

work related, from jobs that gave little satisfaction, rather than during spare time when people had leisure opportunities in abundance.

Today Simon asked the girls if they minded if he turned the radio up. When they said it was fine, he levered himself up from the settee, an old newspaper and magazine slipping off his legs onto the floor. He fiddled with the radio to see if he could find any football matches or other sport by checking the limited channels available, switching it off after finding nothing that interested him. Placing the radio back on the table he then paused before re-tuning it to Radio 4 to catch the news. None of us were reading now, we were all watching as if we were expecting something to happen.

Simon returned to the settee and resumed his curled up position. 'What day is it?' he asked.

'Thursday,' came back in chorus. It was easy to forget the days as we had nothing to define our weekends. If the weather was suitable we worked, a habit most of the island had fallen into.

A silence fell over us as we listened to gale warnings on the radio: 'Fair Isle; north-westerly 7 to severe gale 9, decreasing 4 or 5, then backing south-westerly 5 to 7 later. Very rough becoming moderate or rough. Rain. Good, occasionally poor later.'

'Well it looks like no work for another two days,' said Simon.

'And the rest,' I answered pessimistically, knowing how unsettled the weather seemed to be at the moment.

The girls looked at each other. I wondered if they were thinking 'how are we going to get rid of these two bored boys over the next few days?' They normally had the house to themselves when we were working.

Simon waited for the sports results to finish before he clicked the radio off. Taking the kettle off the fire, I returned to my chair feeling tinges of guilt for not soaking dirty clothes or washing saltwater off my diving suit to make it ready for the repairs it required. It was the perfect day to do all those jobs; there would be plenty of water today, the rain was filling our tanks to overflowing, but I lacked energy and the will to do it. There was always tomorrow.

I looked across at Roz and Lesley. They were always cheerful and smiling, appearing like a sparkle of gold in among all the minor problems encountered with being on an island. I often wondered what the islanders thought of the divers' cooks. While the young enjoyed their company and the Haa was always a happy place, everyone knew the girls were only here for a few months; perhaps they treated them differently to other island women?

But the miserable weather had just gone on for so long that even Roz and Lesley were reluctant to go out. I wasn't complaining, it was refreshing having them in the house, lifting my spirits, making life less serious and, at times, marginally intellectual. If anyone took things too earnestly, like me, it was often made fun of. They both had a good sense of humour – an essential trait for living on an island – and it was nice that they had each other for company. It worked well, but at times I would have been pleased to see more of Roz on her own. There was that unexplainable attraction, although I kept telling myself we were very different. I knew she would never live on a small island, and was not the most practical of people, more the intellectual, but … god only knows, attraction happens.

Simon came back to life. Restless and bored he half-heartedly asked the girls if they had heard any local gossip. With no new gossip, the old news was dissected. An abstract artist who had won an international art prize was discussed. I had an ear to the conversation although I was pretending to read my book. I knew Simon too well, anticipating parts of his conversation and instinctively knowing in which directions it was likely to lead. I had heard Simon's art theories a few times. They were less theories than ruses to get the conversation going.

He lifted his feet off the settee and said, 'I wonder if the artist can paint a duck?'

I glanced at him, giving a slight shake of my head. I then buried myself in my book just in case this discussion went on for a while. I had been dragged in before and did not wish to be dragged in again. The girls looked at each other; they were also getting to know Simon and resisted the temptation to continue, perhaps thinking it would be too energetic for such a miserable day.

He pushed his bobble hat to the back of his head and put his glasses back on. Dropping the subject, he started flipping through old magazines and papers searching for sporting articles. After finding he had seen every article he threw the papers down on the floor and looked around for a book. We all stopped reading and watched. I wondered if young islanders behaved like this in bad weather. I am sure they had the same quirks and useless ploys as us.

'I'm going to read a book,' announced Simon with a flourish as he picked one up and flicked through the pages, indecisive about its contents. After a few minutes he lifted his head from the book and said, 'I don't think I'll read it.' He pulled his bobble hat level on his head and removed his glasses. 'I'll maybe walk up to Elizabeth's and catch up with any gossip. Anyone coming with me?'

Lesley tidied her books on the table. 'I'll come,' she replied.

I looked at Roz. She caught my eye and smiled.

The room appeared smaller and more intimate when Roz and I were left alone. She took her book and moved to the settee opposite me, nearer to the fire. We sat in silence for a few minutes listening to the wind and rain.

'Could you throw me my note book, Roz?' Reluctant to throw it, she leant over to pick it off the table beside her and handed it to me. 'Aren't you going to fill in your diary?'

Roz kept a proper diary, the contents unseen by anyone but herself. This had led to a bit of teasing as we suggested entries she should make, causing her slight embarrassment if one of the remarks came near the truth.

Watching *Trygg* on her mooring in bad weather.

'I'll do it later,' Roz replied, a bit too hurriedly.

I smiled and asked, 'Have you ever missed an entry?'

'Never,' she replied.

'Why not miss today out? As the only missing day, you will always remember it.'

We started chatting. It was nice to be alone together, and then I heard the outside door open and a blast of air came into the room causing the fire to flare.

'Anyone in?' came a call.

'We're in the sitting room,' I shouted back. Rob came in, removing his oilskin top and holding it under his arm where it dripped water on the floor. He pulled his waterproof trousers down to his knees and sat on Simon's vacated space on the settee, putting his oilskin jacket between him and Roz.

'Oh heck!' I thought, surprising myself as I was always pleased when Rob came into the Haa. I got up to make some coffee.

# Chapter 10
# Crofting and Fishing

Late spring and early summer were a beautiful time in Foula – when it was not raining. The colours of the land started to change, everything brightening as the dormant vegetation was invigorated with new life by the increasing temperature. The lighter winds allowed us more working time and the mailboat had gone out for the first time in three weeks, everything seemed good. But then we heard what sounded like another blow for Foula – Leraback croft was being sold.

Our first indication was seeing a visitor looking over it, followed by a rumour that suggested the asking price was £2,500. All immediate thoughts were of the loss of Andrew Umphray to the island – one of the older inhabitants – and Nita, his live-in carer. But on the brighter side a young family might settle, bringing new people and new ideas. It was one of the better houses, and housing is a key to population growth on an island. Few people today are prepared to accept the conditions of past generations, and the cost of building a house had far exceeded the reach of the income that a person settling in Foula was likely to generate.

The croft lay at the top of a steep bank at the south side of the Ham burn. It overlooked the post office and school to the north, and to the east on a fine day it was possible to see the Shetland mainland. The house was well maintained, substantially built of stone with a bituminous felt roof that was regularly tarred. Andrew had installed a small generator and there was running water with a proper bathroom and toilet. It did not have older buildings attached to the back of it like many of the other crofts; in the case of Leraback the steep bank down to the burn may have prevented any more building. This gave it the advantage that it could have windows on both the north and south sides.

Andrew was in his 70s, slightly built, and usually seen outdoors in a long, old-fashioned waterproof coat when he wheeled his barrow around the island to collect peats or parcels from the mailboat. The barrow was typical of those in Foula – made of wood with a large-diameter spoked wheel that had an iron hoop shrunk onto it to act as its tread. After Foula had its first road built, islanders perfected the making of various barrows for different uses, the main adaption being the position and size of the wheel, which affected the load the user would bear and the volume of the box on the barrow. The wheel diameter was determined by the conditions in which it was used with the larger, wider wheel for the boggy ground when it would be used for collecting peats. Andrew required no encouragement in explaining the merits of them to anyone prepared to listen, and we soon learned that he, the barrow, and his long waterproof coat, appeared inseparable.

He had never married, but during our time on the island Nita had looked after him, having replied to his advertisement for a home-help. Also in her 70s – probably older than him – and from England, she had spent most of her life abroad. She'd had a tragic life, losing both her son and husband, that left her with no close relatives. She smoked continuously in a very distinctive manner, taking the cigarette from her mouth in a quick, sweeping motion like a 1930's film star. They were an unusual combination, but the arrangement worked well and we suspected Nita ruled with a rod of iron. She always appeared content and sociable, often playing bridge with the nurse and her husband, Simon being called in as the fourth player. Andrew would regularly collect a box for Nita from the mailboat which "swinkled" and "chinked" as it was passed up to be placed gently in his barrow. We all knew she enjoyed the occasional drink – it was impossible to keep secrets on an island.

Leraback croft had been advertised in the national papers and after it was sold Nita and Andrew planned to move into special housing they had pre-arranged at Bixter, only six miles from Walls. When they left, Nita's loss to the island had its repercussions on me – I was reluctantly taught to play bridge to complete a foursome for the occasional games at the nurse's house and the Haa. This caused me humiliation in the south as Simon had not told me that the rules played in Foula were unique to Dal – who I had stupidly believed when he claimed he had been a party to the World Bridge Federation. He was convincing, or I was just plain stupid.

Discussing Leraback at Ham, we all had different expectations, but I was sure there was potential for anyone with the right dream, particularly if they were interested in birds. We speculated on the character of the purchaser, but I hoped it would be an active, practical couple with young children, perhaps from a farming family, experienced with working land, and having a smattering of know-how in all the trades such as building, plumbing and wiring.

But Elizabeth had her own views which were pessimistic. 'They'll have their work cut out to survive in Foula,' she said.

'But the island can do with some more people,' replied Simon.

'I hope they're young,' I said, as I rubbed Dusty's ears. Elizabeth's sheep dog was getting old and deaf and I wondered how long he would last. Perhaps longer than the new incomers.

'Nay point tryin' crofting, it's been done afore, for the last few hundred years, and all that's happened is they've left,' said Elizabeth affirmatively.

We all agreed there was no way that Leraback on its own would provide a liveable income, and the new occupants would have to create something else to survive. I thought of my time on the Isle of Barra where croft houses had been sold. Initially a few houses were bought or rented by artists and used as places to escape with the intention of working. This new world of art was sweeping over some of the other islands with potters, painters and writers arriving. They had no need to physically work the land or sea as they could sell their works reflecting the beauty of the place, either as accurate depictions or creating a different perception of their physical surroundings. They may not have gained the same admiration or interest as traditional islanders who worked at sea or struggled to make a living on a croft, but their work had encouraged tourists to follow in their wake. Some incomers using the phrase like students do, of "travelling in the hope of finding themselves", a phrase the girls were sceptical of, quoting various sources where "self was a consequence of life's experience", and therefore you never find it because it changes all the time as new influences have their effect. This certainly rang true with my experience in Foula where additional knowledge was continually altering my awareness of a much broader and mindful life that I had previously been oblivious to.

We knew of "exotic flowers" on islands and in remote areas who rarely survived for long unless they had sufficient independence of wealth to maintain their status. Individuals like Gavin Maxwell and Compton Mackenzie who wrote *Whisky Galore* being the most famous. Mackenzie experienced many islands before finally settling in Barra, but even then he spent much of his time on the mainland. I suspect he required the accolade that numerous friends, wealth and fame attract, only retreating to the sanity of an island when he had indulged too much. Barra was big enough to cope with unpractical people as there were tradesmen available, but in Foula any person who could not look after themselves might become a burden to the rest of the community.

The gap between the dream and the reality can often be too far to bridge, and Foula had the perfect ingredients for a wonderful dream. Perhaps Professor Holbourn had kept his dream alive by not becoming a full-time resident on the island, just enjoying it during short stays and refreshing his fascination and interest at a distance during his lecture tours. I felt my dream was still being fulfilled and would only reach its conclusion when our work ended and I had to make a decision.

'They're not using it as a holiday home?' I queried Elizabeth.

'Naa, naa,' said Elizabeth, dismissing the suggestion with a wave of her hand, 'there's nane that wants a second home in Foula.'

'How d'you think they're going to make a living?' asked Simon.

'They could start a bed and breakfast,' I said, knowing how people had stayed with us in the Haa after their tents were damaged.

'Island stability lies in diversity,' Father MacLennan had said in Barra when he was promoting various different enterprises, two of which – a fish processing factory and a hotel – became major successes. Further north in North Uist the digs we stayed in were run by the wife of the local fish factory manager. They had come up from the south and were making a good living on the island, as well as enjoying the lifestyle. Accommodation was always required in Foula in the summer, and even if the croft had been bought and let by another islander it could bring income to the island from visitors over the summer months, and always be there for island families or relations if they wished to return. Elizabeth let Loch cottage regularly each year to birdwatching Germans, but it was a poor specimen of a place and only gave them slightly better shelter than a tent.

'You could sell Loch cottage,' joked Simon.

'It's a peerie hoose,' Elizabeth pointed out, 'but at Leraback they'll maybe take couples in.'

I could sense she was feeling slightly uncomfortable with this change in direction and wanted to shift the subject. Then, out of the blue, as if she'd just remembered, she said, 'The new owners will take over Leraback at the end of November,' and looked at Simon with a grin.

Simon remarked with a laugh, 'If they've been expecting "the good life", this could be considered the poverty package.'

The only person who felt it essential to obtain help on a regular basis was Elizabeth. Her hiring requirements from the mainland were based on an attempt to seek out the perfect female agricultural student at very little cost. It included free board and lodging and, we thought, an experience of a lifetime, never to be repeated! She didn't advertise but spread word around her friends in Shetland, and this usually resulted in a young, totally inexperienced traveller coming for a few weeks. By the time they had learned enough to become of any use, they left. Some had never learned to sweep with a broom let alone be able to operate her petrol-paraffin tractor. Simon referred to them as "Lizzie's slaves", and considered Ham like a remote beach that threw up interesting bits of driftwood – except in this case it was people.

I don't know where Isabelle appeared from and why she stayed so long, although she was one of the best helpers to appear at Ham. She was from France, in her early 30s, and spoke English with an attractive French accent. Unfortunately, Elizabeth was quick in finding fault with any of her helpers; it wasn't that she scolded them to their face, it was more the telling of their faults to others as she expected them to have some sort of telepathy in knowing exactly how she wanted the work carried out. Isabelle at times became very excited about her work, especially handling animals, when Elizabeth would shout totally unintelligible instructions from the other side of a fence. One day Isabelle found Simon and me walking up to Ham. We could see she was agitated and excited at the same time, shouting and pointing toward Ham, 'Harry has zee knife, Harry has zee knife.'

'He's only going to kill a sheep,' replied Simon.

'I know, I know, but all the bloody parts, we will have to clean.' Isabelle held her hands up to her head, 'It's terrible, terrible.'

Neither of us was sure whether it was killing the sheep or the work afterwards that concerned her.

Harry always used a humane killer before the knife came out. I had previously helped him when Elizabeth caught a particularly wild sheep by using her guile and a bucket of feed. We found the unlucky creature hobbled and tied to a post to prevent it escaping. Harry killed it immediately with the humane killer before cutting its throat and bleeding it. In this case the blood was not collected. I helped him carry the carcase back to a shed at Ham where the animals were usually butchered. He carefully skinned the sheep, working his hands beneath the skin to take the fleece off in one piece before the guts were removed and every organ was carried to the house to be thoroughly washed. I could imagine Isabelle being at the scene of carnage, with Elizabeth flustering about and shouting confusing orders at her which she had little chance of understanding.

As a boy I was never keen on tripe, but Elizabeth saved all the organs with eager hands as she thought of the times in winter when food was scarce. The best of the meat was salted and dried while the remainder would be used to give her and Joann a brief time of plenty over the following weeks. Any parts considered inedible were kept for Dusty, her sheep dog. Nothing was wasted. With the electricity limited to the evening use of her small generator, she was unable to have a deep freeze, otherwise it would have certainly changed her eating habits.

There was always sadness if one of her caddie (pet) lambs was either sent to market or killed, but once the meat was on the plate it was all forgotten. One year she named a caddie lamb after Simon, calling it "Peerie Sy" (Little Simon). Simon was upset at the thought of it being killed, but partially relieved when it died of natural causes long before it was ready for eating. The slaughter of animals was part of island life that no one liked, particularly the outsiders, but it was necessary in maintaining quality food at a low cost.

We were never sure about taking alcohol into the island. Rob had told us the owners disapproved of it and, as we were in their house, we were cautious. There was only one islander that had a partiality for alcohol and this was limited to the mainland. None was available in Foula as the quantity of any brought in was so small that it was hastily consumed. Otherwise it was just the nurse, Dal and Nita who would order the occasional bottle, enjoying the odd glass without any visible signs of excessive drinking.

Neither of us was bothered about alcohol or the lack of it, and it was over a year before we brought in some bottles of South African wine, bought at a cash and carry in Dundee with the intention of using them for cooking. This small decision seemed to break our resistance and after that we often brought in cases of beer on our boat, but never spirits as neither of us enjoyed them. Our main use of beer was to mark an occasion or to hand round a can after a busy day and we never bought a sufficient quantity to last any length of time. We hoped this moderate use might allay any concern by the island owners in case word got back that their house was not in safe hands.

There was only one occasion when we consumed our load of beer in one go. It was on a beautiful summer's day when we left Scalloway to return to Foula. As we cleared the islands off Scalloway *Trygg* slid into a rhythmic, lazy roll in the light swell. We had a few passengers lounging on the deck, leaning against boxes of food and cases of beer that we had dumped randomly on top of the hatch, knowing it would be an easy crossing. After an hour's steaming I was relaxed in the wheelhouse, my knee against the wheel to keep her on course, and a cup in one hand as I watched Foula gradually rising out from the great expanse of sea ahead, when we passed a fishing boat on her way back to Scalloway and *Trygg* suddenly took a steep roll as we were hit by the wash from it. I glanced at the hatch to see our passengers rushing aft as the wave slapped against our bow, sending a shower of spray over the deck. She soon recovered her steady rhythm, the passengers dried off the places they were sitting and a silence gradually unfurled over the deck as everything returned to normal.

An hour and a half later a passenger noticed beer spraying from the top of a can. I went out to look, thinking we must have damaged it when we were loading. I looked at the others and spotted some with small bubbles on their surface – the salt water had literally eaten the unpainted aluminium tops on the cans, creating small holes in them. The holed cans were handed out to avoid waste and when we reached Foula the remaining cases were taken to the Haa where immediate action was taken to consume any others that had a hint of damage, to mitigate the possibility of further loss.

Alcohol was consumed during a few events – the infrequent "hamefarin" when an islander returned, and occasionally when Maggie and Dal held parties at the nurse's house. Dal, with his life shrouded in mystery, was an excellent host and when they held a party he had such a reputation that most of the island young would turn up, but only a few of the elderly. The numbers were often added to by the fishermen from the *Juna* who would come across from the mainland with their wives, some staying in the Haa if they were short of bunks on the boat.

Dal was always smartly dressed, walking round like a ship's steward with a tray of drinks and a white dish towel over his arm while he persuaded people to drink different concoctions, rarely taking no for an answer. Strength contests and other party games would follow, but the highlight was persuading Dal to do the haka as one of his many claims was that of ancient New Zealand heritage, although you could not find a person who looked less like a Maori rugby player. After much feigned resistance he could always be persuaded to perform. His gymnastic contortions and shouted commands bore little resemblance to the haka I had seen at rugby matches, but it was a brilliant performance that must have terrified any sheep that roamed within hearing distance of the house. We cheered him on as it always warranted a second performance, and another rowdy toast, assuring the party lasted well into the next day and even Harry would stay to near the end.

I don't know if it was boredom or sheer devilment but Dal had an unusual habit of claiming to visitors that he was Desmond Bagley, a well-known author at the time, but of more concern to us was his outrageous claim that other people on the island were connected with famous personalities. When passing his house I was invited in to be introduced to Karl, a tourist who was a policeman back in his home country, an occupation reflected in his dress with brown, knee-high leather boots, smart military-like clothes, and carrying enormous binoculars for studying the birds. Dal assured Karl that I was the brother of famous violinist Yehudi Menuhin. His English was not sufficient to grasp that it was untrue, however much I denied it, and considering I was scruffily dressed with dirty overalls I thought it was obvious that I was no relation. I knew the British sense of humour was difficult to understand, but Dal's, at times, was beyond even my comprehension. He sat there with a grin on his face as he egged Karl on, enjoying my embarrassment as I reluctantly stopped denying it and tried to turn the conversation.

No-one on the island took offence at these antics, and Simon laughed about it, relating it to Elizabeth with great glee as she shook her head in the pretence of disbelief while uttering, 'Na, na, I canna believe it.'

Simon assured us that Dal's antics benefitted the island by giving us something light and harmless to talk about.


There was a massive resource of fish off Foula which in the past had fed the inhabitants and also sustained the vast bird population. These stocks had once been the mainstay of island life, providing the money or credit from a merchant to keep the islanders in supplies during the hard, winter months. In 1774 it is recorded that the inhabitants caught vast numbers of fine middle-sized cod, and at one time they had as many as 12,000 fish on the rocky shore laid out to dry after being cleaned by the women and children, and those unable to go to sea. They belonged to the landlord who bought every marketable fish that was caught by every boat belonging to the island.[27, 45]

During the summer of 1792, Ham Voe was occupied by 16 fishing boats, 11 of which belonged to Walls. If the weather became so bad that the boats could no longer lie in the voe there were plenty hands available to pull them up the beach clear of the water and, in severe weather, they would be pulled into a "noost" – a pit dug into the bank in the shape of a boat where they could be secured and weighed down with stones to stop them blowing away.

By 1799 the average clear profit reported for each of the six-man crew during the season (May to August) was £12 - 10s and 4/6 Scots[36] – equivalent to 83 days wages for a skilled craftsman at that time.

The summer accommodation in 1832 for the fishermen is described: '… we walked out to the fishermen's huts on the opposite side of the little islet of Ham. Of the numerous fishing lodges that I had entered in different parts of Shetland, none equalled these for comfort and convenience. The huts which would barely hold six people, were partly sunk in the ground, I suppose to prevent their being overturned by the violence of the wind. In the centre, of course, was the fire, and around were arranged couches of green turf, soft and pleasant, whereon the tired fishermen reposed at night, and sat during the day when not employed at sea.'[11]

The deep-sea fishing grounds that lay beyond the coastal waters were referred to as "haafs". The Burra haaf lies between Foula and the Shetland mainland and is one of the most prosperous fishing grounds around the Shetland Isles. North of the island lies the Foula haaf, another good area that the island boats used to work.

In 1899 the vessels were of a Norwegian type, described as 18 to 22 feet at the keel, with a single, large square sail which is hoisted nearly amidships, and is supplemented by six oars manned by six men. They are called sixerns. One remained for us to see on the Ham beach. It had originally been used as the Foula mailboat and was now weighed down with stones to prevent it blowing away. In the early 1800s, as there were no trees in Shetland, these boats were imported from Norway in kits and assembled when they reached Shetland, but later they were built in the islands. By 1883 only six of these boats worked from Ham, and two from the north of the island that was described as a 'nice wild exposed fishing-station.'[12] The boats go out until 'they sink the land below the horizon, about 45 miles, and when the weather is favourable they remain at sea sometimes for two days. The fishing lines are laid in a depth of 80 to 120 fathoms, and are sunk to the bottom by stones, and left for two or three hours.

To take in the lines two men ply the oars, a third pulls up the line, while a fourth pulls in the fish as they come to the surface using a "huggie-staff", a stout piece of wood with a hook fixed on the end, and then they remove the head and the intestines. This takes three or four hours, after which the lines are again laid, or the boat returns to the shore.'[1]

Many Shetlanders lost their lives in these boats when unexpected gales blew up, and one mainland boat was blown as far as Norway where the crew stayed for the winter until they could safely return in the spring.

Peter Peterson, a crofter in Foula, set up a fish-curing business in 1898, but the landlord at that time, Gilmour, obtained a court order for him to give up the occupation of his premises and the coastal area he used for drying fish. It was difficult to think this was not done to prevent him from competing with the owner's preferred buyers as they wished to keep a monopoly on sales and purchases,[3] although by then the truck laws had been abolished. The Foula men had never found it easy to obtain a reasonable share from their fishing, and as their relatively simple methods declined with the advent of steam, and later diesel-engined fishing boats, it was inevitable the island population would decline.

The large trawlers not only reduced the stock but also made it difficult for islanders to operate with long lines, as they presented such an extensive area for trawlers to snag. An inshore limit was enacted in 1889 that banned trawling within three nautical miles of the British coast, but later it had to be strengthened by the Illegal Trawling (Scotland) Act, in 1934, that brought in serious penalties if this rule was broken, including prison time. The fishing grounds were patrolled by fishery protection ships up to the time we were working there and a large patrol vessel often gave us a fright when it would suddenly appear at full speed from behind the cliffs.

Many trawlers had been reported to the authorities for illegal fishing and, in 1894, there was a report of the gunboat *Cockchafer* firing across the bow of the *Stephenson* of North Shields when only 500 yards away.[50] The gunboat then asked the trawler why he had not stopped the first time; the skipper replied, 'Not while my lum [funnel] remained up. If you had hit it I would have given up.' He was charged with fishing within the prohibited limit and not stopping when demanded by a British warship.[51] But the fishing was so good the trawlers were happy to take the risk, even with the possibility of being hit by a shell or a jail sentence.

By 1936 the fish were said to be not so plentiful. When the film director Michael Powell asked Alasdair Holbourn why they were not eating fish on the island, he replied that, 'Nobody on the island ate fresh fish any more … not since the trawlers cleaned out our banks.' But some of the Foula men continued to make money out of fishing, but on mainland boats.[37]

We often watched Shetland trawlers and seine netters working off the island at night, with the smaller vessels lying at anchor or using the pier during the day while the crews slept. The space at the pier could accommodate two boats. If it was near high water and exceptionally good weather I had seen a maximum of four. Like us, they knew the pier was inadequate to keep a vessel alongside for any length of time. Our solution of placing a heavy mooring at the entrance to the voe resulted in us occasionally waking in the Haa to look out the window and see up to four fishing boats tied alongside us. Not that it was ever any problem – the main anchor had held the *Oceanic*.

The three-mile limit never applied to lobsters or crab fishing which used

The lobster boat *Juna* approaches Ham Voe

static gear such as creels, it was free for anyone to fish when they used a registered fishing boat. But in the late 1970s the sandeel fishery had come into full swing and we would see numerous small boats trawling off the east side of Foula. They loaded up until they were almost sinking before sailing to the "gut factory" on the isle of Bressay, on the east side of Shetland, where the sandeels were rendered down for animal, pet and fish farm foods. On the island, the fish caught had their stomachs filled with sandeels, and the puffins and other birds carried the small eel-like fish crisscrossed in their beaks to feed their young. The islanders realised a large reduction in the sandeel numbers was likely to have a knock-on effect on the bird population, which caused genuine concern.

**The north end with Mucklegrind on the right and Riste on the left.**                    *Lesley Timings*

# Chapter 11
# Classroom and Kirk

Elizabeth's final summer helper came during a spell of good weather when we were incredibly busy. We missed seeing Jim bring her to Foula in his yoal *Happy Voyager*, which he was now using as the mailboat because *Westering Homewards* still required spare parts for the engine. Simon heard from Elizabeth that this was one of the few occasions when the weather allowed Jim to turn up on the correct day and at the right time at the Foula pier in Walls. This was fortunate for the passenger who had never realised the unreliability of the mailboat times, and had appeared on time, not realising how lucky she had been. I noted in my diary: 'Jim brings in young lass on mailboat.'

On our first break from work Simon suggested we went up to Elizabeth's 'to see her new slave'. We pushed past the caddie lambs that barred our way to the door, while Elizabeth fussed over us. Moya, the new girl, was sitting on the resting chair next to old Joann, watching and learning how to spin wool. Behind her lay two cards – flat pieces of wood with steel pins like needles on one face, and a small handle at the end – which they used to tease the wool and align the fibres before spinning it into yarn. Her hair was tied up with a piece of leather, a pin through it, keeping it clear of a thick, woollen polo-neck jersey, and her jeans were slightly grubby at the knees from the croft work. She looked young compared with Elizabeth's previous helper.

Simon discussed the latest island news as I discreetly glanced at Moya. At times our eyes met. I knew from past experience that caution was required when drawing one of Elizabeth's helpers into the discussion as she might be sent off on a small job or errand. Elizabeth liked to be the centre of attention – she was the queen bee, Moya was a worker.

I found my thoughts were far from Simon's conversation as I gleaned small details of her journey and her reasons for going to Foula. She lived on the west side of the isle of Lewis, and had been on a trip to the island of St Kilda when she had read the book *Life and Death on St Kilda* by Tom Steel. From this she learned of Foula as a similarly remote island, but populated. Determined to see it, she crossed from Lewis to the mainland at Ullapool, made the long trip to Aberdeen and finally boarded the ferry to Lerwick. With fast-reducing funds after visiting the north of Shetland, she managed to get a temporary job waitressing in the Queen's Hotel in Lerwick while attempting to arrange a trip to the island. At that time the Queen's had a "reputation", caused by the influx of a few badly-behaved oil workers, but she was treated well and, surviving the work for a few weeks, she met a school teacher who had been born and brought up in Foula. He suggested phoning Elizabeth, knowing she was always looking for help on her croft. Following up on this suggestion, and accepting the predicted offer of work, she crossed Shetland by bus from Lerwick to Walls to arrive at the Foula pier as if she was to meet any other mode of transport.

'You were lucky,' I said.

'When I saw the size of Jim's open boat I wasn't too sure,' she replied smiling, before Elizabeth sent her out on an errand.

Walking back to the Haa we passed her carrying a sack of hen feed and looking as though she enjoyed the work. I asked Simon what he thought of her. 'She's just a schoolgirl,' he replied, and looked at me with curious interest. Simon was often initially dismissive of people arriving in Foula. He liked to have some time and opportunity to find character flaws he could use to make some fun. I had to be careful, any hint of weakness or affection and Simon might pick on it, but I could not believe she was that young considering her determination to get to the islands. For the first time in my life my head and my heart were working in unison. I really liked her, but how could she like me as one of the first things she said was how boorish and loud she found the oil industry divers that used the Queen's Hotel.

'D'you think she'll last long, Sy?'

'No, she'll be like the rest, it can't be easy working with Elizabeth and she pays them practically nothing.'

My heart fell. 'Being from an island will give her a better chance,' I replied. I knew working with Elizabeth would be an interesting but trying experience, but she looked as though she'd cope well and, in my heart, I was hoping she'd stay for a while.

When Moya first came down to the Haa I was out. She went in to chat with Lesley and Roz, sitting in what was usually my chair. We had become creatures of habit – Simon, John-Andrew and I always sat in the same places. Most of the island knew this and found other chairs, but Moya never moved when I came in and Simon and John-Andrew made comments, aimed more at embarrassing me than her.

'Alec's back hurts if he doesn't sit in that chair,' or 'Alec really likes to sit there,' Simon would say, but it had no effect.

I would reply, 'No, no, no, I'm fine where I am,' and I respected her for not moving – although I might have respected her more if she had moved.

She didn't stay for longer than 15 minutes, knowing Elizabeth would look for her if she was away too long. Unfortunately for me, the pattern was repeated with Elizabeth keeping her busy during the days and evenings because she was so useful, making personal meetings difficult. Simon and I snatched odd moments of conversation with her as she repaired a fence or came down to the pier to fetch something for Elizabeth from the boat. When we had *Trygg* alongside the pier discharging cargo I would lean out the wheelhouse window and, sensing her watching me, I hoped she would come to speak to us. She was hard-working and bright, undoubtedly had a good future before her, and I knew she intended to go to university as Harry had mentioned she left school at 16 with sufficient qualifications to study medicine. With such good prospects ahead of her it was unlikely she would have any interest in me, but it did make me think about my appearance. Now I wished I had cleaner and smarter clothes, although I balanced this with the good things about the island, where no one indulged themselves excessively. There were no fancy cars or clothes; we were stripped bare, everyone knowing our characters. You saw and knew what you got, there was no pretence.

On the few occasions Moya visited the Haa, she brought fresh interests from her knowledge of the island she lived on. Turning over the conversations and images in my mind, I noticed how different she was from others who came. I considered myself a logical person, an engineer who examined all the evidence before making a decision. I hoped I was determined, not impulsive, and yet suddenly my life was changing. I was intrigued with this girl. There was no logic in this dream, other than the empathy I felt. I had no indication that she felt anything for me, or even liked me. Perhaps I was wasting my time.

After six weeks she had to leave and I realised how difficult it must be for islanders to choose a partner, with all the opportunities for a relationship passing by, with no possibility of meeting in a pub later or going out to the cinema. Elizabeth was paying her so little that she scarcely had enough money to get home and I took the opportunity to discuss it with her. But she refused assistance, leaving my offer on the table as a last resort. Helping would have been the excuse I required to keep in touch, but Tom unexpectedly settled the financial issue by kindly insisting on paying her for chores she had done for him, saying, 'You'll be needin' this as yon ald wife'll no be payin' thee much.'

I missed her when she went. The Haa changed for us all as Roz and Lesley had also left to return south, Roz attending another course and Lesley starting work. This left a great hole in our lives, making me seriously question the direction I was going.

Although Foula had no tradition of a purely religious settlement it was easy to understand why religious groups established themselves in small islands. I could feel my own emotional instincts being touched in many islands where they provided a natural theatre with a sense of spirituality. There was a remoteness from other temptations, allowing freedom from criticism and the enactment of personal expressions of holiness in complete seclusion. In many cases this was contrary to the religions they espoused – which required temptation to prove faith. But Foula did not escape completely from the ancient hand of religious zeal; there were ruins of a very old chapel and burial ground near the north end, and as time had passed the island entertained its share of radicals.

In 1774, when the population was 130, the Reverend George Low made a tour of the island and described the church: 'In the middle of the easternmost enclosure stands a little neat Church, where divine service is performed once or twice a year, either by the parson of Waes (Walls), to whose charge they belong, or by an itinerant, sent by the Society for Propagating Christian Knowledge. Thro' the rest of the year the parish clerk reads the Scriptures. In the Church-yard I observed a large round stone which I could just easily lift, formerly of great use to the inhabitants. This was the Putting Stone of the island, and here the whole community met on Sunday afternoon, the younger sort to try their strength at putting. They have a fixed stone, which is the standing goal, and I observed several marks, by driving stones into the earth, which they told me was the distance where such and such an old man, now gone, threw the Putting Stone, at the same time lamenting that now none in the isle could come up with them.'[27, 45, 13]

The old never believe the young can be better, but they would definitely be beaten today. I remember Simon saying to the enormous Gear brothers that 'if they could lift one of the 700-pound bronze bearing shells we recovered they could have it.' A worried Simon quickly adding, as they rushed towards it – 'using one hand.'

But this sport was later frowned upon as the church attempted to get a grip on the island. By the 1790s it was said that the inhabitants had 'degenerated in their morals, and Christian knowledge.'[3] Records from the early 1800s show how vigorously Sabbath observation was enforced when some Foula men had noticed part of a wrecked ship drifting past the isle on a Sunday, and launched their boat to recover it. They were hauled before the Kirk Session but let off with a reprimand on condition that the money obtained from the sale of timber should be handed over to the church to be used in connection with the work of the parish.[23] It seemed even on the remote island of Foula they were unable to hold out against the officialdom and authority of the church.

Many of the early reports on the island have been written by preachers and therefore slanted towards their point of view, but the island's religious teachers appeared to be winning over souls in 1879: '... The island is provided with a Society School, a Parish Church, and a Congregational Chapel ... No feature in the religious life of the people of Foula is more remarkable than their scrupulous observance of the Sabbath.' This continued and, by 1909, the 230 population was again described as: '... a sober, industrious, hospitable, intelligent people, remarkable for their scrupulous observance of the Sabbath. Few of them leave the island: in no place is love of country stronger.'[15]

The Baxter Chapel[12] (the church I was married in), originally the Independent Congregationalist Church, became the main building of worship and was eventually taken over by the Church of Scotland. It had previously used the building at Hametoon that remained complete in 1936 and lay in such a stunning situation that Michael Powell was able to use it when making his film. His description extolls its beauty: 'There were two windows behind

Moya on Elizabeth's peat bank

the pulpit, where the round bulk of the Noup and the stony waste towards Stoel and the Daal showed through the small panes. In the north wall were two long windows, with hinged panes. The congregation, seated in pews, could see the whole sweep of the island watershed and the valley of Hametoon, with the crofts rising out of the sea of barley and the long, white grass. All the windows were recessed the full two feet thickness of the wall. Through the open door to the east the burn could be seen wandering down the valley until the waves of yellow iris met the Atlantic at Grisigarth ... There was a three sided plaster ceiling, forming a hexagon with the floor and walls.'[37]

Its roof was still intact in 1954[38] but by the time we arrived in Foula the roof had gone, and only the walls remained, surrounded on three sides by the graveyard that remained in use.

In Fair Isle, the Church of Scotland and Methodist Chapel played a major part in the life of the community with few people doing anything but essential jobs on a Sunday. But in no way was the religion extreme; it was gentle and in tune with the liberal views of the islanders. But when we worked on Sunday we were "mentioned in dispatches" as Simon put it. They had no issue with us working, but the preacher in the Methodist Chapel, Stewart Wilson, stated the islanders preferred to be with their families, which was true, as in good weather we would see them walking round teaching the children the names of the plants, cliffs and birds. In other islands where we had worked – like Barra, a strongly Catholic island – religion was more conservative, the churches also well attended and appeared to be run mostly by the womenfolk. Although the Catholic Church was part of a massive international religious institution, it was refreshing to see one of the priests, Father Callum MacLennan, become very active in promoting the island to create more businesses that were badly needed.

On one of our first Sundays in Foula I walked with Elizabeth to the Kirk, thinking it would be like Barra or Fair Isle, almost a social occasion where the islanders had an opportunity of getting together. I was disappointed to see only a handful of people at the dull service which had the awkwardness created by so few people singing. It was not communal enough to be enjoyed, but I was relieved to find out that it was a tolerant version of the Church of Scotland.

A few more attended when the Walls minister came in during September to christen Jim and Sheila's daughter, Penny. It made me appreciate why people enjoy the "theatre" of a full church with good singing, where, religious or not, you can indulge in the spiritual feeling that's created. This lack of any strong religious leanings in Foula had made it easier for us to plunge into island life without the thought of causing any offence about the times or days we worked.

Since 1945 the resident teacher in Foula had also served as a missionary, which involved taking the Sunday service in the tiny island kirk. It was not until 1990 that the two roles were divided and the pastoral needs would be met by someone living on the Shetland mainland.[52] If the teacher was married and male, his wife rarely had problems with her role, often joining in with the community. I had only met one school teacher's husband. He had previously been on the small island of Papa Stour before moving to Fair Isle where he took the role as Church of Scotland missionary and they proved to be a happy and successful team.

When we first arrived in Foula we rarely saw the teacher, Mr Vernal, who was on his own as his wife had already returned to Glasgow in anticipation of his leaving. With little reason to meet him, it was only when using Elizabeth's tractor to deliver his peats to the manse that we met in conversation and were asked into the manse. A relatively modern house for Foula, built in 1938, it had a peat-fuelled Raeburn stove for heat and cooking, although this must have proved inadequate as he also used an Aladdin paraffin heater. In his living room, on an easel, he had a carefully executed and unusual painting. Painted in oil with intricately detailed people it must have taken many hours to complete, keeping him fully occupied on wet and windy nights.

The island's organised education goes back to 1740 when the Society for Promoting Christian Knowledge granted to the Presbytery of Shetland the salaries for three schools in the islands, the teachers being transferred from one parish to another at the end of two years so as to give every parish an equal chance. The salary was £20 per annum which continued to be paid until 1877 under the condition that the schools, including the Foula school, were to be examined annually.[53, 36]

By 1872, an Act of Parliament had put an end to the parochial system of education throughout most of Scotland and ordered that schools in future should be managed by school boards elected by those who paid rates, and be supported by grants from the Government.[44] The new school is mentioned in

1883[12] and in the 1970s the same building was in use but with a classroom extension.

Mr Vernal was replaced by a new teacher-missionary who came from another Shetland island. He was a well-built, strong, dark-haired man with a bushy, black beard and came with his young wife. He appeared to shun many modern aids, being happy to use an oil lamp rather than the generator provided, and regularly took his peats home in a barrow. In his spare time he was building a high wall around the manse to shelter it from the wind and everyone was impressed by the skilled standard of his workmanship. It was a dry-stone wall to be admired, but it gave the visible appearance of solitude, an island within an island.

Considered a good teacher, we saw him rarely, but on attending the island church with Roz and Lesley he asked us all back for a meal. Simon was absent as he had gone to watch a football match with John-Andrew on one of the now popular battery-powered televisions. Perhaps Simon had suffered from too much preaching as his father had been a Church of Scotland minister.

When we later dropped off supplies at the manse the teacher's wife was outlining a painting under the light of an oil lamp. I was surprised how dull the wick lamp was compared with our Tilley, but it was silent, and I understood the attraction of living with just the sound of the sea and the birds, not having a noisy generator thumping away or the continual hiss of the Tilley. It appeared to suit their kind and grateful manner but, as with the previous teacher, we felt slightly uneasy, as if intruding on their lives, making me speculate that both the teachers I had met may have come here to enjoy the solitude.

I didn't know what was taught in the school, but generally the parents' generation – that was my generation – could be considered artistic as their home life usually included music and drawing. Part of their skill may have developed from the lack of television during their youth when all entertainment had to be homemade. We discovered this for ourselves, never reading or writing as much until we came to the island. I even attempted to learn the fiddle.

In 1892 an article stated that the 'arts are not altogether neglected in Foula. Many of them sing pleasingly, and a few play the violin with considerable spirit. Dancing, at one time a favourite pastime, was sternly tabooed by a well meaning but narrow minded pietism.'[10]

Much of it is true today, except for the dancing which they enjoy, but with only four school children and no specific music teacher the music taught at school would be limited to singing, anything else would have to be taught at home.

At the end of the summer term the school put on a concert. The teacher had spent a considerable time writing songs and themes and one of the schoolchildren, Bobby, came to the Haa to give us a copy of the light-hearted words he had sung that were written in the Shetland dialect. It was about the divers, and called in Shetland dialect *Da Divers*.

It started with the following verses (voars means spring):

> Der's mony a ene at needs a hand wi' work about da voars
> An mony a wife at needs a man to help her wi' her chores,
> An mony a derelick hovel boys needs patching up da floors,
> An it's all a day's work for da divers.
>
> *Chorus*
> If it wisna for da divers, whit should we do,
> We wouldna know da price of scrap in Glasgow and Peru,
> Da Bonxies wid be happy on da deid sheep rotted through,
> If it wisna for the work of the divers.

Several other songs had been written, with the teacher making sure the children received the best education possible with the limited resources of the island. It was obvious that he had a good sense of humour and was able to treat life in a light manner when required but, at times, it seemed quite the reverse. It may have been the effect of the island, but his taciturnity occasionally hid the "real person" that we liked to see. Having held the job for less than a year, he and his wife decided to leave and arranged with us to take them and their furniture across to Walls as soon as possible.

Three days after the end of term, on a sunny day with practically no wind but a heavy swell coming from the southwest, we decided to make the trip as it was the best weather we were likely to get. Everyone helped load the furniture – a difficult job as our hold was partly full. After the hold was secured, we helped his wife aboard. Not wishing to go below in the accommodation where she could sit down or lie on a bunk, we offered her a seat inside the front of the wheelhouse, but she preferred to sit out on deck on the edge of the hatch, just forward of the wheelhouse. The ropes were cast off, the islanders giving friendly waves as we backed away from the pier. There was no noticeable sadness from our passengers. In fact, the reverse: they both seemed happy to be leaving and he moved to stand beside his wife to make sure she was comfortable.

The journey started in relatively calm water, the swell getting progressively worse as we moved away from the shelter of the island. Although the boat rolled, the swell from our starboard side was on our stern quarter and I was not expecting water on the deck. But within minutes, she was violently sick.

'I'll turn round and take you back,' I said from the open wheelhouse window.

'No, no,' she said, insisting we continue to Shetland.

Anxious to return her to the quiet waters off Foula, I was rebuffed each time. As the trip progressed her condition worsened, but she was insistent. Finally, we reached the point where it was quicker to continue than turn back. It was agony

Never go off the track! Rob and Simon are pushing. In the background is the Baxter Chapel. *Lesley Timings*

watching her being so violently sick, knowing there was nothing I could do. Seasickness was common on *Trygg* when working round the waters off Foula, to the extent that it was often joked that we 'had a head count before we sailed and then a bottom count during the trip', but I had never seen someone so ill in such relatively calm weather and one's heart can do nothing but reach out to them.

At last Walls came into sight and the motion gradually reduced as we picked up shelter in the Sound of Vaila, but still her sickness continued. When we finally tied up alongside the pier – 'Thank God,' I said to Simon, who had been expressing the same concern throughout the trip – we helped her off the boat. She looked relieved but I knew it would be a while before she would recover.

In the store at Walls a pile of goods were waiting to be loaded. It was a quick turn round, setting off for a rolling and wet trip back as we pushed through the swell, but my thoughts kept returning to our seasick passenger. I hoped she had recovered; my heart still went out to her.

The teacher-missionary post was duly advertised, and a *third* teacher was sought since we had been on the island. Everyone knew it would be a problem recruiting a replacement as it was rumoured that there were few, if any, applicants. It must have been a thorn in the side of Shetland Islands Council, and yet it was a great job for a teacher who loved birds or remote islands. There just can't have been many of them who would commit themselves. I wondered if the missionary part might put them off. Eventually someone was found and the new teacher's furniture, including a piano, arrived aboard a fishing boat, the *Bairn's Pride*. One of the crew was heard to mutter, 'Next time they get a teacher who's musical, they need to make sure she plays the flute, not the bloody piano!'

Ten days later, after the teacher had flown in, we heard she was an elderly lady living on her own and appeared quite lame. Harry and I were asked to go to the manse to fix the generator as the previous teacher had rarely used it and she was having difficulty in getting it to start. I already sensed a feeling in the island, through small snippets of conversation, that the winter conditions, the loneliness, and the half-mile walk to the school would be too much for her. She had ticked all the boxes to get the job, but it appeared there was no box for common sense. Or perhaps she was the only applicant.

'I don't think she'll last long, Harry,' I said, as we walked back to the post office from the manse.

Harry sucked air through his teeth and shook his head, his normal habit when he was considering how gently he could state an opinion in his non-controversial fashion. 'Boy, boy, it seems wrong to send someone in her condition,' he replied.

I knew what he meant. It didn't matter if she was male or female, walking to the school in strong winds and heavy rain was bad enough for a young, fit person. I thought it was remiss that she didn't have any form of transport, but perhaps she was unable to drive. All the hobbies and necessities enjoyed by other teachers would be hard for her – peat-cutting, vegetable growing, and even being in the manse on her own where she might fall over or, as now, be unable to start her generator. Harry and I had already carried a load of peats into the house for her; thankfully the previous teacher had left her a year's supply but this would be a daily job if she was to keep warm and cook using the stove. She also had to keep the generator topped up using diesel stored in barrels outside the shed. I looked round to see that Harry was deep in thought, probably on the same lines as me.

'Is she to act as missionary?' I asked, thinking it would have been unheard of in the past when the Church was in full swing as women were barred from high office in most religions.

'So they say,' he cautiously replied.

'You'll have a female missionary for the first time,' I smiled, knowing Harry was not a church-goer and it would have no effect on him.

'It'll mak no difference to them that goes to the kirk,' replied Harry.

A pleasant silence fell over us as we walked, both deep in thought. I wondered who might have the time to look after her as everybody was busy with their own families. It seemed unfair on the island, as well as on her; she was a third of a mile from any inhabited house but at least she had a phone.

'The nurse will maybe look in,' I said.

'Boy, that one's a fine nurse, she probably will,' he replied, at the same time shaking his head to give me the impression he was not happy with the situation.

Later, we were unfortunately proved right when the teacher was unable to stay on the island. I don't think it was her physical limitations but the loneliness caused by them. If she had been fit she would have been made welcome in any of the crofts, but the elderly islanders rarely called on people and the men were unlikely to visit a single woman.

The children had to leave the school at age 12, when they became boarders at the Anderson High School in Lerwick. As the mailboat service was so infrequent the children would go for a whole term, with little opportunity of a break at home, making their school term longer than for those from other remote areas and islands. There was always a controversy in Foula. Most islanders would have preferred their children to complete their schooling on the island in the hope it might encourage them to remain. In Fair Isle, the general feeling was that they wanted their children to leave and learn a trade or profession, then hopefully bring it back to enhance the island after they had experienced life elsewhere.

There was no simple answer as the children were all so different. I could imagine some wanting to stay, and others just itching to leave, gain a trade or university degree and taste the outside world. But the most significant influence on their lives, whoever they might be, was likely to be the partner they hopefully found. And I was slowly realising it applied to myself as well.

# Chapter 12
# Changes and Tradition

In August *Westering Homewards*, the official mailboat, was still out of service and Jim continued to use his small yoal *Happy Voyager*, but even that was not trouble-free. On one occasion the small Stuart Turner petrol engine failed to start and Jock used his even smaller yoal. Neither of the boats were able to take more than the mail and a few parcels, and only in good weather as the boats were not decked in. But bad weather had been frequent and, as we were discovering, our weighty mooring in the entrance to the voe often lacked sufficient shelter for *Trygg*. Although the anchors were unlikely to move, the chain to the boat might break or tear itself out of the bow. Rather than risk an accident we were forced to find refuge in Scalloway or Walls at the peaks of the storms. It confirmed the island knowledge that no reasonably-sized fishing boat could operate consistently if based at Foula, even if it was held on a substantial mooring.

Now on our own, it became noticeable how empty the Haa had started to feel and, with our work giving us little time off, we were back to eating from tins and instant foods. But our lives very quickly took another turn when we met Karen and Jenni at the pier. They came from Leeds, had recently arrived and were camping on the island. Simon used his best manners to persuade them to visit us at the Haa, but we knew nothing about them and guessed they knew equally little about us. I had this innate respect for people who managed to get to Foula, always expecting them to be dynamic and full of energy, although there were exceptions.

Two days after our first meeting, they generously cooked us a meal and then added to the social life by having Karen's birthday party in the Haa. It felt like a switch had been thrown. It was not that the Haa was ever unhappy, but the girls brought back the elusive fourth dimension that had been missing, certainly for me. Part of it was the carefree tone that added perspective to our very male-orientated working life, and the cheerfulness they brought with them was contagious, spreading through the team which often included John-Andrew's cousins, Andrew and Magnie, who were on a few weeks holiday from Scalloway.

Because of this sudden dip and then uplift in our social lives it confirmed I had been naive in my thoughts on permanently living on the island, realising, like most of the visitors, that there was a difference between falling in love with an island and wishing to stay on it permanently. The two were completely different concepts, like loving going on holiday when the enjoyment of the event is as much to do with the circumstance as the place. This was Karen and Jenni's attitude, and it stared me in the face. It was the challenge of our work and the variety of people that I also required for happiness, a combination of circumstances rather than a single factor, although I still loved the island and its inhabitants and remained pulled to it like a magnet. But my mind was like a soup, perhaps the same confusion that swills around the brain of any young, unmarried lad as new experiences mix with all the other flotsam that enters the head.

On the first occasion we had spare time, we took Karen and Jenni round the island in the inflatable. It was a calm evening and we enjoyed a close-up look at the reefs, stacks and natural arches at the north end before turning down the west side. The sight of the second-highest vertical sea cliff in the UK was always stunning, making me feel quite dizzy as I looked up to see the clouds passing slowly over it. The conditions were so good that everyone landed on a small beach below one of the cliffs. We had been warned that we might fall over backwards when looking straight up at the overhanging rock, which proved true.

The year before we arrived on the island a naval team from Rosyth attempted to scale the near vertical 1,220-foot Kame. Described by a leading climber as 'sinister … one of the most unwelcoming pieces of rock in the country; the Kame is completely exposed to prevailing winds. The most difficult part of the ascent being a nightmare crawl up a 500-foot tower of fissured rock with forbidding overhangs and an inch-by-inch attempt on 120 feet of smooth sandstone.'[54]

The climbers were under the leadership of one of the most experienced climbers in the service but the weather deteriorated before they could reach the top and, leaving in a hurry, they left their climbing ropes behind. Apparently, on the first good weather day, one of the islanders climbed across the face and removed the ropes, descending completely free of any safety lines.

With the weather deteriorating as the summer faded we knew we would soon have to take the boat south for the winter. But first we had to sail to Scalloway to fill *Trygg* up with fuel, collect barrels and various stores for the island, and take a deck-load of sheep from the island. It was a quick trip and, after returning and discharging all our cargo at Foula, we topped up the hold with some of our recoveries before sailing south, dropping the girls and other passengers, along with another deck-load of sheep, at Fair Isle. When we eventually picked up the east coast of Scotland I sat on the hatch enjoying the warmth of the day, wondering if it would be best to stay in Fife and not return to Foula before the winter set in. I had been asked to go to California in November on a shipwreck project. It would be Christmas before I returned, and I'd also planned to visit Lesley and Roz when I went south to London to carry out some research.

All these trips were second to my wish to return to Foula as this was a time we could really appreciate the island. The work was less exciting without the salvage boat, but it was absolved of any worry, the weather could throw anything at us and it would not matter. Like Professor Holbourn, I was realising the island's limited facilities, that made us take the boat south, were a prominent factor in giving it part of its magic. We decided to return and try to work from the inflatable and enjoy Foula for the next six weeks.

The island population was ageing and deaths were not unexpected, but it was just five weeks after the arrival of the new teacher-missionary that one of the older women, Mary, died. She had been taken off the island when ill and later died in the Gilbert Bain Hospital in Lerwick. The body was returned to be buried – a desire of all islanders. The custom had been for the family to say goodbye to the coffin at the croft and the men would carry it to the church on a cradle of oars. If the death was in the north it could be more than a two-mile walk to the church, where a small meal was prepared in the vestry by the women and served to the men before the service. The men then continued with the coffin more than half a mile to the graveyard at Hametoon. When the first tractor and trailer arrived on the island it replaced the men carrying the coffin and now there were so few young it had almost become a necessity. The missionary was not sufficiently qualified to take the service and the funeral service was taken by a minister flown in from Shetland.

During the service I thought of the late Mary. I had been told that Harry had been courting her in his youth but was unable to marry because he had to look after his parents. By the time they died, he and Mary felt they were too old to marry. It was sad for Harry, losing that youthful opportunity of happiness. I wondered if his neutrality on the island was part of an inability to commit to anything, including marriage. In the quiet of the church I reflected on my life and that made me ponder if Harry now regretted the choice of not marrying when he was younger.

At the end of the service Dal leaned over and whispered to me that he had offered the use of the nurse's van to carry the coffin the final half mile from the church to the graveyard. He had also tuned the engine to run slowly; this, he claimed, would allow us all to walk peacefully behind. My heart missed a beat.

The coffin was carried out of the church and slid into the small van. The space in the back was limited, leaving part of the coffin unsupported where it stuck out of the back. Dal revved up the engine in preparation and, as there was a slight slope away from the church, the van slowly rolled forward until it turned up an incline on the road, where it stalled. From the strong smell of petrol it was obvious the engine had flooded. The starter motor ground away a few times before we all realised it was not going to start. The funeral party decided to push and as the van moved forward Dal let out the clutch, bump starting the engine. Off it went at a cracking pace with a few of us running behind, our hands on the coffin to prevent it sliding out the back. After 20 yards he slowed down, but only for the van to come to another juddering halt. The engine had stalled again. The young waited for the elderly to catch up and regain their breath. The broken journey continued until the road fell away, allowing Dal to coast down the gentle slope through Hametoon towards the graveyard at the old kirk. It was at times like this I really respected the people of Foula. There was no recrimination or humiliation as there might be south, life just continued, and the problem was understood and absorbed within their stride, giving it little meaning and therefore no effect.

He parked on the track leading to South Biggins where the coffin was lifted out and carried across the grass, a shadow being cast over us as we passed close to the ruined kirk. I wondered if its roof had fallen in unassisted, or had the materials been used for some other purpose as there was no sign of slates inside. Harry swung the iron-gate open, allowing the coffin to be carried through to where it was laid close to the newly dug grave. Eighteen of us shuffled past to stand either side of the open hole, everyone being careful not to trip over the small, rough-cut headstones that lay hidden in the unkempt grass. The grave was shallow, barely four feet deep. The remains of the previous occupant, a relation, had been placed discreetly to one side to await re-interment after the coffin was laid down. There was a pause as Jock picked a long stem from the uncut grass and set it across the coffin as a measuring rod, to ensure the hole was wide enough.

As the minister began to speak I could feel a sense of the vastness of the rocky cliff of the Noup. It appeared to dominate our small, male group, making us appear insignificant. The cliff was alive with seabirds circling and gliding in the updraught, their wings hardly moving as they passed the rock ledges that had been populated by guillemots and razorbills at the height of the summer. To the south was endless sea, white with foam where the heavy swell crashed against the solid rock of the island. The derelict crofts around us were reminders of the hundreds of people that had been here before, working the soil as they struggled to survive, the cycle continuing with each generation until they either left or ended up beneath our feet. For those that died abroad, I wondered if they had been happy to leave the island or whether there was always that nagging doubt making them long to return to their homeland and, on their deathbed, wishing they could be buried on the island. I hoped they had died happily in their new-found home.

It had always been a fight for survival on this unforgiving island; a constant struggle against the vagaries of the weather, disease, and death through climbing the cliffs or fishing. At present the population had never been safer, but now only a few islanders remained, with no sign of improvement. It was at its lowest ebb for centuries, perhaps since the island was first inhabited. Among the mourners were only four islanders of my generation. There was no pretence, no need for eulogies. It was simple: those that had known her paid their respects in the knowledge that they would follow. It was peace for her now and what better place to spend eternity than in the embrace of the island she had loved.

Everyone was silent, but the air was riven by the sound of the birds. It felt reassuring, their lively cries heard above the roar and pounding of breaking waves. This was the sound of life in Foula.

The earth was shovelled onto the coffin, the noise being like walking away on a gravel beach. It sounded final, becoming softer as the earth built up. The last verse of Bobbie Isbister's song, *Farewell, Fugley Island* (pronounced Foogly), was in my thoughts:

> When life's journey is over and my spirit is free,
> I'll re-cross the great Ocean, dear Island to thee.
> I'll revisit the scenes of my happier days,
> When fleetfoot and carefree I ran o'er thy braes.

After leaving Foula when the winter finally set in, Simon and I spent our spare time being social. I was 27 and, at a similar age, most of my Fife friends had married or become seriously involved with a partner. Simon, two years older than me, proved the exception. He was keen on going out but showed no attachment or talked of any favourite. My island life had become both my career and way of life – neither was conducive to a settled existence. But I was lucky. I now had a reasonable income and could make choices. My future was firmly in my hands.

When I travelled south to carry out research for our business, I visited Roz and Lesley. Roz and I had become strange allies when the island threw us all together for months. I had no idea whether our friendship would last in the "real" world, not even sure what the real world was. But the person I really wished to see was Moya, who I had not heard from after writing a letter to her from Fife. It had taken days to write, unsure of what to say, or what commitments to make that might result in a reply. But my mind relaxed after I posted the letter, as if I was admitting to the impossibility of a relationship as I knew she was intending to go to university, and I was committed to at least two more years in Foula.

Since meeting her we'd hardly had a private conversation, let alone gone out together. I thought of a time when I went up to Ham to collect a shopping order from Elizabeth who was out. Joann and Moya were in and Moya took

The Kame, the highest cliff on the west side of Foula.                    *Lesley Timings*

me through to the "ben end" to find the shopping list when she realised I had noticed Elizabeth's private hoard of Tunnock's Snowballs that were partly hidden from sight. She gave me a quick, knowing look before asking me not to tell Simon in case he teased her about them. There is nothing like sharing a secret, however small, to bring people together, especially as we were concealing it from Simon.

Receiving no immediate reply from Moya, I gave myself the benefit of the doubt and assumed the address was wrong, leaving me only one option – a trip to Lewis to see her. I had been there once, several years before, but this would be a good excuse to see the island again. At least the trip was easy from Fife; from Foula it would have been a major expedition to go to the island as the sea transport had no direct route. I thought of Simon saying 'You're never wrong when you do the right thing' but, as Simon knew, the result is only determined after the event. With no free time to go until after the New Year, I made no decision. It was not until I was staying in California that I received a reply from her that had been forwarded by my parents. Witty and chatty, it gave me hope and I decided to visit her on the Isle of Lewis in early January.

*Trygg* returns from Scalloway with a tractor, trailer, digger and oil drums for the island.

She would be easy to find; the village of Valtos where she lived had a similar population to Foula.

Moya had the choice of a career that could lead in any direction, as she "carried no baggage". I was already on a track leading in a specific direction, with Simon, and John-Andrew depending on us all working together to make our livings. I could not change direction easily, but most of all I did not wish to change direction and planned to return to Foula by the end of March. If I were to see her it had to be as early in January as possible.

The visit to the Isle of Lewis on my motorbike was planned to allow me four days on the island. It started with a storm force 10 on the ferry from the Scottish mainland which caused the ship to have a brief mechanical breakdown, making me appreciate the trauma of feeling sick. Landing at Stornoway I made my way to Valtos, a small village on the west side of the island that lay in a beautiful area with cliffs and sandy beaches, close to the Atlantic. It was not as basic as Foula in that it had electricity and water but, like the Haa, the wind whistled through the window frames and hot-water bottles were required to keep the bed warm. Unsure of my standing with her parents, I was relieved there was no hint of disapproval and I gained confidence when I realised they were entrepreneurs like myself.

During our time together we explored the beaches and cliffs on my motorbike and, in a brief spell of sunshine, enjoyed sitting behind boulders to shelter from the wind and watch the birds soaring as the heavy Atlantic swell broke over the rocks beneath them. Before I left Lewis, Moya said that she intended going to Edinburgh the following month and would look in at Fife on her return. This gave me a breathing space to think, which I needed.

My curious mother made Moya welcome, as she did with all visitors. She had become used to islanders staying when we came south with *Trygg* and required little explanation of Moya's presence other than she was paying a visit. The issue became confused when Harry phoned and I was out. He informed my mother that the mailboat had not been for nearly two months because of the bad weather and we would be unwise to come before the beginning of April. She then asked me directly if Moya was going to Foula with us. A question I couldn't answer.

While Moya was in Fife we had an easy, happy time taking life as it came, getting bits for *Trygg*, eating in cafes and pubs. I wanted it to go on for ever, but I knew the time would come when she had to leave and I would have to make a decision. There was no way I was going to ask her to come and cook – that was never an option – but I wished we were already in Foula. The unhurried nature of the island would have made my questions easier – or so I thought. I knew I was being weak about asking when the answers were important. It was the commitment that frightened me; being sure I was making the right decision from the head as much as the heart. This would be the most important decision I was ever to make in my life.

It was wet on her final day in Fife and we had a long, lazy lunch in a pub with Simon before taking a walk along the ancient stone pier at St Andrews. Returning to Tayport in the early evening, I parked the pickup among stacks of timber that had been discharged from a cargo ship and we stood on the pier looking down at *Trygg* lying 14 feet below us – it was low water. We climbed down the ladder, turned the heater off and shut the boat up for the night. I watched Moya leap several feet from the boat to the rusty, steel rungs set in the stone wall and clamber up the ladder as if she did it every day. The rain had stopped and it was becoming a fine, clear evening when we made our way round the stacks of timber to sit in the pickup. I saw this trip as decisive, and yet I could not believe she felt the same for me as I did for her. The quote from my aunt was ringing clear in my head: 'Who on earth is going to marry Alec?'

I looked out the pickup window at the stacks of timber surrounding us. The engine was running to keep us warm. I switched it off and leant towards her. 'Moya,' I asked, 'will you marry me?'

'Of course I will,' she replied.

My mother was good with Moya and genuinely pleased we were to be married. But I had given little consideration about the traditions involved, allowing my tactful mother to point me in the right direction, as she saw it. Asking if I had bought an engagement ring, and knowing me well enough not to wait for a reply, she produced a box with old, family rings and asked if I thought Moya would like one. I looked at the various rings with complete confusion. I was not even sure what an engagement ring should look like.

'There are only two that I think would be suitable,' she said, as she saved my embarrassment by picking out the two rings. 'But she might prefer one of the others,' she added, as if to keep all options open.

When Moya looked at the rings my mother explained that most came from my father's relations and there was no record of the original owners. It was a clever statement as there would be no personal prejudice in the choice. While they both looked I stood behind them, curious as to which ring Moya would choose. I had no intention of venturing an opinion, it was entirely Moya's choice and she, like my mother, had placed the same two rings to one side. One of the rings had two large diamonds – I think this would have been my mother's choice – it was impressive, almost ostentatious. The other looked more delicate with three small diamonds; the larger, centre diamond had a flaw in it. I had never seen a flawed diamond. In fact, I had never before looked closely at any diamond. Moya held it up to the light and I could only just see a thin dark line running through it. I was fascinated. It reminded me of people, where a flawed person is often more interesting than those unblemished. Moya chose that ring.

At Macgregor's auction house in St Andrews, Moya bought carpets for the Haa – large, old-fashioned rugs that would cover much of the sitting room and only cost a few pounds. We hoped they would help insulate the floor and stop the draughts blowing up between the floorboards. She quickly proved herself to be indispensable to the project and we were both fortunate that Simon was so easy going, accepting her as part of the business as well as my partner, but it was not without a bit of "ribbing" when he got the chance.

I had never considered Moya coming north on *Trygg*. As John-Andrew, Simon and I would be aboard there would be no privacy, but most of all there was also a risk. Perhaps it was not my choice to take these protective measures. Anyway, they were soon ignored by Moya. A few days before we intended to set off with *Trygg*, Moya left for Aberdeen to take the ferry to Shetland, planning to either catch the mailboat or a fishing boat to Foula, where she hoped to dry out the house and get it organised prior to our arrival. There was plenty to do in the Haa: there would be mould growing on the kitchen table, shelves, and cooker; outside rainwater drains might be blocked and a few slates would have blown off the roof. But I imagined her enjoying the peace, although I hoped she didn't mind the shadows from the Tilley lamp, the creaking floors, or the various noises that could become unsettling in strong winds.

Once *Trygg's* hold was filled we loaded either side of the hatch with our Morris 1000 pickup and a three-wheeler car John-Andrew had bought. Finally, just before we sailed, half a ton of explosives was secured in the forward end of the hold. We ploughed through a dark night of rain and snow to arrive at the Foula pier absolutely exhausted at 10am in the morning. Harry, Jim, Jock and Rob were there to meet us along with a smiling Moya. It was a tonic to see her looking so fit and full of enthusiasm. We quickly unloaded the boat, including the cars from the deck, before I was forced to take *Trygg* clear of the pier due to the weather. Simon, John-Andrew and Moya stayed in Foula, although Moya was keen to help me to take *Trygg* to Scalloway, but Ken and his son Davie, who had recently left secondary school at Lerwick, came with me as they both wanted a run to the mainland.

After we put the boat on a mooring I went to the fish merchant's office where Simon had left a phone message that the nurse was returning to Foula by plane that afternoon. I made the 40-minute bus trip to Sumburgh Airport to hitch a ride with her, also meeting two other passengers, John and Pat Smith who had taken over Leraback croft. The pilot, in usual Shetland fashion, flew around the island to give us a good look at the magnificent cliffs on the west as the large, rolling Atlantic waves crashed at their feet, sending clouds of white water up into the air. I was sitting next to the pilot when he told me that on his first flight to Foula he flew west around the cliffs towards the Atlantic after taking off, and someone on the island phoned Sumburgh airport to say he was going the wrong way! I suspected it was Elizabeth wanting to make some contacts at the airport, resulting in her having supplies sent in on the plane if there was space. With a smooth landing on the gravel strip, I was helping unload when Moya arrived with our pickup. I hurried across the gravel towards her. This was to be the start of our life together.

Back at the Haa I could smell wild birds John-Andrew had shot simmering in the oven. In the living room Moya and Simon had started improving the house; the carpets were laid and an old, treadle sewing machine from Fife was placed near a window to get the most of the natural light. Secondhand curtains, also bought at the auction, lay draped over a chair ready to be altered and in a brown paper parcel next to the sewing machine was a roll of cream silk she had purchased in Edinburgh – to make her wedding dress.

'Where's Simon?'

'He's off to flay the peat bank,' she replied. I looked around, pleased to see the place was deserted. It had seemed such a rush with the uncomfortable boat trip, then securing *Trygg* on a mooring at Scalloway, before rushing down to Sumburgh to catch the flight to Foula, and finally arrive at the Haa.

'We're on our own at last,' I said, as we settled down in front of the fire; the first time we'd been alone in the house together. The house had captivated me from the first day I arrived. I hoped it would work its magic on Moya.

After a few days our life on the island returned to normal, as if we'd never left. The weather continued to be unsettled, making it unsafe to work for the next 20 days – just what Harry had told us. The preparation of the peat bank was completed, cutting started and, on dry days when the wind temporarily dropped, Simon and I replaced the slates that had been blown off the roof while Moya puttied around the windows where the old hard putty had been shaken out by the winter gales. Inside, she was working hard to put the curtains up using lengths of brass tubes as curtain rods, these in turn were held up by bent plates of brass, also from the wreck. In the evenings letters were written, books read and there were the usual social times when we visited others and islanders dropped in to see us. We relaxed into a bad-weather routine, and enjoyed it.

There were plenty jobs to do and we helped where we could. I filled in more forms for Elizabeth's sheep subsidy. Simon suggested I would be put in jail for colluding with her on her sheep numbers. But no one knew how many sheep there were in Foula, or the numbers owned by each individual, least of all Elizabeth. It was unlikely they would ever know as it seemed impossible to round them all up and when I used similar figures to previous years I was unconcerned if they were a little high. If anyone deserved some extra cash to keep their small crofts going it was the islanders.

Moya and I walked along the rocky shoreline, wading bare foot in pools to see what creatures lay under the rocks, sometimes lying on the close-cropped grass near the clifftops watching the birds soar and the relentless waves breaking against the rocks – a continually changing but restful scene with the background music of the birds and the sea. Where the cliffs gave way to gravel and boulder beaches we picked our way down through the rocks to see if anything interesting had been washed ashore. A plank of wood or a fishbox would be considered a prize worth recovering. Hauling it above the high water mark it would be left until our return journey when we would drag it along behind us. Sometimes the sun would shine into some sheltered spot where we would sit and chat, or rest in silence, lying back and enjoying the total seclusion, as if the rest of the world no longer existed.

Our walks along the east coast from the Haa would gradually lengthen as we had time to see more of the island and explore each inlet. The north end with its boulder beaches and stacks always felt exposed. The remains of abandoned and now-ruined crofts lay on the lower ground where it was said the salt spray blown in from the sea made it difficult to grow good crops. In front of one of the crofts was the boulder beach where the crew of a Foula boat nearly lost their lives in 1881 when saving men from the German barque *Henrietta*, which lay four miles off, water-logged and rudderless during a storm. A flag of distress was seen and, although the Foula men knew they would never get back to Ham Voe, they did not hesitate to set out from there and row out to the vessel. On their return they had no choice but to land at the north of the island where there was no safe place while the sea was running mountains high. All the able-bodied men on the island came with ropes to assist and, as the boat rushed onto the rocks on the top of a wave, the men ashore got hold of her and everyone was saved.[55]

From the north banks it was possible to see the cliffs towards the west where it was said they were divided amongst the crofters in former times so that each had a frontage for collecting birds' eggs or fowls.[12] Walking close to the cliff edge near Soberley and looking towards the Kame – the highest cliff – we could see stretching in the distance a massive population of birds either sitting on the ledges or enjoying gliding in the updraught. It felt safer here when close to the cliff edge as the ground in some places sloped inwards, away from the cliff face, but we were always conscious of the risk of the earth collapsing beneath our feet.[56]

After the initial exploration of the island our walks became more random as there was no longer any specific place we wished to see. But our lives were to change after I had two accidents: a large steel beam falling on me in the hold of our boat, and later a diver's bend. Maggie was able to stabilise the situations before taking me to the ambulance plane on a stretcher in the back of her van.

After completing a time in hospital I was impatient to return to Foula where I was initially limited to the Haa before I improved sufficiently to roam the island with Moya. Our initial walks were short, not wishing to travel too far in case I struggled to make it back, the place or view shrinking in importance as we took pleasure in the enhanced feeling of being alive and the happiness of being together. We were never bored and were in no hurry to return to an interesting place as we thought we could always go there another day, but sometimes failed to do so. It became reflected in our later lives where we'd try not to procrastinate, always endeavouring to accomplish our exploits as we found it so easy to say 'we'll do it at a later date' – until the time runs out.

The Lum of Liorafeld, which lay on the hill of Hamnafield, has been documented over the centuries. A Church of Scotland minister in 1700 said that: 'In this isle, on the top of a hill, there is a hole, the mouth whereof may be [and some say now is] covered with a flat stone, going downwards to the bottom of the rock, which is said to be of a great depth; particularly a Dutch ship master is reported to have made a trial thereof, for the gratifying his curiosity, by taking up a barrel of lines with him, which he let all down, and yet could not find the bottom: some say he let down two barrels, which is very wonderful, considering a barrel of lines is reckoned to be several, some say nine, miles in length.' [39, 27]

Most Foula stories reflected the truth. The island was so stunning and the people through the centuries had taken such risks to survive that it did not require false stories. We thought there might be a moderately deep hole – the geology was such with contorted and upended seams of rock that there could have been a deep crack that had filled in – but on our walk we failed to find anything that looked like a blocked-off well. We may have been in the wrong place as the tradition was still strong, although no one claimed to have actually seen down the hole.

Another feature was the Sneck of the Smaalie: a stunning geological fault near the cliffs on the southwest of the island. It was worth regular visits to explore, but it required a full day free before we ventured so far. On the way we passed the church before turning west to go through the Daal, where Simon and I had gone to the cliffs with John-Andrew. At the west end we came to drier land, with well-eaten grasses which made for easy walking as we approached cliffs where the puffins lived in grassy burrows. On this ground lay the entrance to a deep fissure in the rock – the Sneck of the Smaalie. The fault had been formed by the parting of old red-sandstone cliffs, thereby earning the name of Sneck – a term for a sheer-sided crack – and Smaalie, which is said to be a Troll-like creature which has its home in the crack that measures 200 feet deep by seven feet wide and 300 feet long. It was an easy story to believe as the eeriness was enhanced by the dulled thunder of the waves against the cliffs on the seaward side.

Large rocks were jammed in the cleft near the top to form a narrow bridge that was concave, making it a risky crossing, but I could imagine that over the centuries young Foula men had crossed over it as a dare, including John-Andrew. The access led down a grassy slope before an awkward, wet and slippery climb over collapsed stones that were smeared with a green slime which had crept up the damp, stone walls either side. Drips of water and running streams from above gave life to ferns and other moisture-seeking lush vegetation which had managed to get a foothold on the vertical sides. It was like the tropical houses in botanical gardens – but colder.

Once submerged beneath the direct sunlight, we ventured through its dark

Waiting for Loganair to land. The manse is the house in the centre.          *Lesley Timings*

and eerie depth, at times being frightened by the sudden movements of a seabird disturbed by our presence, my heart missing a beat as the sound reverberated within the cleft when it flew off. Wet and spongy underfoot, we stepped warily over piles of bones and rotting carcases of dead sheep and birds that had fallen or become trapped within the crevice. It was easy to imagine the Smaalie lived there, catching and feeding on anything that came within its grasp. When the light increased I felt relief as we approached the west end where a rocky slope descended into the sea. To our right was a cliff face leading to Wester Hoevdi, which rose 507 feet from the water. Our only safe way back was to return through the Sneck.

Along the top of the cliffs beside the Sneck we were able to approach within eight feet of the puffins by lying down above the burrows and remaining still. We watched them land awkwardly on the ledges as if they were mere beginners at flying, before shaking themselves back into order and strutting into their burrows.

On these long walks it was easy to discuss our marriage. We had decided

Moya making curtains in the Haa using a tredle sewing machine.                    *Alison McLeay*

on something small and informal, and it was to be held on the island. This was unusual as many of the islanders had married on the Shetland mainland and only been blessed in the island kirk. Perhaps their wives came from the mainland, or they may have simply preferred it, but it was similar to the isle of Barra where I remember a girl telling me she wished to be married in Glasgow. I could never understand why, as their own island church was so beautiful. But the same could be said about my parents' local parish kirk in Fife that would be considered more attractive than the Foula kirk, but to us it was the attraction and simplicity of the island.

Most of the wedding organisation involved the preparation of food, which would fall to Moya, and we had no intention of making it more than an uncomplicated island wedding. Both sets of parents were happy with this. My mother, who I thought might be disappointed, told us she was married during the war when my father was on leave from the army and the only guests were one of her sisters with her Canadian husband, who was also on leave.

Back at the Haa, Simon added Moya as an extra player to compete in his

**Looking north on the west side where the cliffs were divided among the crofts for the rights to collect eggs.**
*Lesley Timings*

competitive sports. When bored he would drag us both out for a game of goalies, shot putting or tossing the caber. The cabers were different sizes, the selection made by Simon from timber that had been washed ashore. As the strongest, I had the longest one, Simon had the middle size and Moya the shortest. It was like daddy bear, mummy bear and baby bear. When the games finished we would race up to Elizabeth's. Simon was faster than me but not Moya and at times he cheated by tugging at Moya's jersey to put her off her stride, which made her cross. Badly out of breath and exhausted we would all arrive at Elizabeth's. From the doorstep she would cast her eyes over the three of us as we stood there, breathing heavily, with our hair dishevelled and, with a beaming smile, she'd say, 'Bairns, bairns, what have you been up to? Come away in.'

We enjoyed these bad-weather days and when we were exceptionally busy I often looked forward to hearing the wind blowing and the slates rattling on the roof – the precursor to an easy day with Moya. Life was calm, unpressured, and I could feel my life was different. It had changed for the better.

The Sneck of the Smaalie.

# Chapter 13
# A Delightful Wedding

The island gossip was buzzing when John and Pat Smith finally arrived at Leraback to stay permanently. They were joined by their daughter Annette and son-in-law Sam. The two men had been in the army. John, in his 40s, was rumoured to have a small pension. Sam and Annette Davis were in their 20s and after leaving the army Sam had worked as a painter and decorator. The opinion was soon held that the family had the potential to be real assets to the island, lifting everyone's hopes for the future. I understood the Smiths' enthusiasm and was pleased that Foula was a positive move for them as we never heard them complain about the place they came from. They were looking for a different way of life, not to escape from a bad one, and the crofting system was ideal in the way it allowed them to have a home with some land, giving them the opportunity to be creative in a multiple of ways.

Apart from teachers and preachers, as far as we knew this was the first time a family of complete strangers had come to settle in the island for 70 years. During previous centuries, when the island population had been devastated by smallpox, many families were said to have moved from the Shetland mainland to Foula to enable the island to quickly recover. Since then most incomers had come as partners or relations of an islander, settling down within the comfort of an island family. William Beagrie, an Aberdeenshire farm worker, had brought his wife and children in 1946 when the trustees of the island were looking for new tenants for their crofts. But a Beagrie had previously married into one of the island families. At that time the island's population had fallen to 75 and this family had two sons and a daughter, one son attending the Lerwick school, the other two children at the Foula primary school. [57, 38] Their arrival must have provided a great boost to the community. They stayed in the old manse, now referred to as Mornington, taking the name from the nearby croft house that was a ruin, and they attempted to scratch a living from the croft. But Mr Beagrie, soon after arriving in Foula, found that it was not possible to move into an empty, unworked croft and expect it to provide a living for a family of five. He managed to get a job off the island and returned during holidays or when he was able.[38] The Beagrie family had all left by the time we arrived.

Now, with people leaving and the numbers dropping, Foula was rarely considered by outsiders as a viable place. But the world was changing, with large population increases in the towns, partly due to a natural increase but also people leaving the countryside for a better-paid life in the city. This resulted in a few of the town folk searching for a different lifestyle in rural areas. Islands were at the extreme end of this lifestyle change, often lacking good housing and the costs of building being higher as the building materials had to be shipped. But this could be balanced by the free labour undertaken by the incomers who often wanted to build or repair their homes themselves, with the help of available grants.

The work of the Smiths in doing up the house and croft was putting badly needed resources into the island, whether they stayed or left the improved house would be an asset. An initial concern, quickly allayed, was the fear of the new family keeping themselves to themselves, an attitude that would be of little benefit to others. There was a wait and see caution as newcomers could unknowingly make major cultural changes. Customs and traditions would be foreign to the incomers – although they might respect them there was not always a logical reason for embracing them. I remembered when we helped turn the Isbisters' boat round in the same rotation as the sun before launching it – Simon was shaking his head at the needless effort involved in the tradition, but I rather liked it – reminding us all through the superstition that it was dangerous at sea and we had to be careful, as many of these old traditions relied on the threat of bad luck if you did not comply. But perhaps it was just common sense in that everyone involved knew which way the boat had to be turned before it was launched.

Over cups of tea at Ham, every tiny piece of knowledge gleaned about the Smiths was discussed in detail. Simon and Elizabeth were in their element although neither of them had much information. We rarely saw the Smiths and were reluctant to disturb them as they worked hard on improving their home, installing a new generator to provide power for a washing machine and deep freeze. They rarely asked anyone for help, being practical enough to manage most of the improvements themselves. When they discovered their new generator had various parts supplied with it but were not sure of their purpose, I was asked to have a look and realised this was my opportunity to get to know them. Little assistance was needed to complete the assembly and John was relieved when he checked the lights, deep freeze and other appliances to find they all worked. This was a major landmark in changing their lives for the better.

It was not until after they were settled that we regularly saw Sam and Annette. Sam had no income and was looking for any type of work. It was a crucial time for them. The major tasks and pleasure from the challenge of rebuilding their new home was ending and their future now depended on how they were going to generate an income. This was the real test, whether their new life was an improvement on their past. They were now meeting head on the reality of island life, where previously a good job had given them a steady and substantial income. Fortunately for Sam, the council required some help in repairing the roads and he became part of the gang of traditionally hard-working Shetlanders, earning an income for the few weeks they were on the island.

Annette and Sam always appeared happy. Foula, for them, was a challenge and they were young enough to rarely consider it a hardship and committed to being successful. They'd experienced life on the mainland and *chosen* Foula, compared with some of the young islanders who had never, or rarely, worked off the island and tasted another way of life, but in lieu of this the islanders had become expert on island ways and were anchored to it by their ancestral attachment to the land.

Pat – John's wife – was a slight, gentle and kind woman, not used to outdoor work. She had loyally followed her husband's dream but was finding life in Leraback hard. As a soldier's wife she told us she had been used to going off to a hotel with her husband for the occasional weekend and, during the week or when he was away, she could have a busy social life with other soldiers' wives. Now she was being asked to prepare and cook freshly-killed animals while helping to create a vegetable patch, often in wind and driving rain. It had been an enormous leap from her old life and she was working hard to support her family to make sure it worked for them, but to her it appeared to be more of a life sentence than a life style. Unsurprisingly, she had little in common with the island women. Although welcoming, they rarely mixed socially amongst themselves let alone a stranger, but she found Maggie a good friend with experiences in common. In a weak moment she mentioned that she was unhappy and cried many days. It was another case of an island dividing a family. I had seen it in Fair Isle with the shopkeeper, who was also the Methodist preacher, when we were first there. He was in his element on the island and had been there as a boy, but it was obvious that his wife, who was from London, was not – and she didn't have the freshly-killed animals to deal with. Ultimately the preacher left Fair Isle in an attempt to save his marriage.

This difference of interests within families was common everywhere, but in a busy, highly-populated community it rarely mattered as everyone could be catered for. Years later. in Spain, I met a catamaran owner who was using his boat as a home to cruise round the world after building it with redundancy money. His not-so-enthusiastic family crew had complied with his dreams and, when we met them while anchored at Baiona, his wife and two young daughters were beginning to feel the limitations of travelling on a low budget. Seeing they were bored while they waited for spare parts for their wind generator to arrive, Moya asked the mother and two children to our salvage ship for a special tea made by her and the cook. Our ship was not in the tidiest of conditions as she had been working in the Atlantic for several months and bore the rusty, battered look of a vessel that required a good refit. Despite this, the children dressed up for the occasion and were enjoying the visit which finished up in the mess where plates of cakes and scones had been laid out along with fresh fruit. After the meal they became fascinated by our large pile of National Geographic magazines that had been bought in bundles from a second hand book store. When we gave the pile to them, their mother was delighted as they were a good teaching aid and would give them something they enjoyed to focus on. I am sure the father had hoped, with all his best intentions, that this world trip would be a fantastic opportunity for his family. But instead, it was obvious to us, at the moment his family were missing friends and finding it constrictive, their world of travelling experience which on the outside appeared expansive, was in reality very small. I felt Pat had been in the same position – following someone else's dream.

There is a Buddhist proverb applicable to those who come to islands or move to fresh pastures: 'To everyman is given the key to the gates of heaven; the same keys open the gates of hell.'

We had noticed that Dal was taking an interest in fishing and, just when there was a lull on the island, with gossip becoming so trivial that it was hardly worth repeating, Dal, as if on cue, brought us all back to ourselves. His confidence in his ability was not limited to mechanical or electrical issues, it now encompassed boats.

When we first heard from Elizabeth that Maggie and Dal had bought a boat, Simon's immediate reaction was to laugh and predict a disastrous outcome, but later that day we met Dal working at the nurse's peat bank. I asked him about the boat.

'She's a cracker, with a great history,' said Dal. 'She was built by Walter Ratter of Punds [an islander] 50 years ago and the Umphreys at Leraback croft had owned her. She's known as the Leraback boat.'

It was a small yoal, a clinker-built open boat suitable for rowing or sailing. They were common in Shetland and this was a beautiful example.

'What are you going to use it for?' I asked.

'Mackerel fishing in the summer, as well as coarser fish, and catch a few lobster for our own consumption.'

It sounded a great idea and if I had been a nurse's husband I would have been keen; it would be a productive and enjoyable way to spend time.

'I've painted it, and tidied it up for launching into the voe, but I've still to finish fitting a bracket for an outboard,' said Dal. He was a tidy person and I expected the boat to be pristine.

'You'll have a lot of fun with it,' I answered.

'Maggie wants to come out as well,' said Dal. I could see Simon smile; I kept a straight face.

'If you need some help launching it, let us know,' I said. It was a problem getting enough young together to help drag the boats down the beach for launching, not that it would be a heavy boat.

We continued on our way to "the divers' peat bank" and started cutting but, as it was a repetitive job, my mind started to drift through the ramifications of Dal and Maggie's boat. They had what I thought of as an "Italian marriage", where they both could be quite volatile at times but quickly subsided to their normal polite behaviour.


The sea was flat calm and the sun was shining as Simon, John-Andrew and I returned to the voe in the inflatable, passing Maggie and Dal as they left the pier with their small Seagull outboard propelling them seaward. They could not have looked happier. It was a beautiful day. We watched them stop and drift in the calm water. They looked relaxed as they took out their fishing gear and started to cast their lines. It appeared idyllic.

'This could be interesting,' said Simon.

'What do you mean?' I asked.

'You know what he's like with engines,' Simon smiled. 'Remember the times with the generator.'

'It's just an outboard,' I said, but I knew how temperamental old outboards can be. 'At worst they can row back.'

Simon smiled again.

Back at the Haa we ate a modest meal as we were due to go out and work at seven o'clock in the evening. An hour before leaving I was collecting our diving suits from outside to warm them up next to the fire when I heard shouts from the seaward side of the house. I ran round to see what was happening. Off the entrance to the voe I could see Maggie and Dal in their boat. It looked low in the water and Maggie was furiously bailing while Dal stood at the stern trying to start the outboard.

'For God's sake, Maggie. Try and stop the water coming in!' Dal shouted.

'Well, get the outboard going!' replied Maggie in an equally loud voice that would be heard across the island.

Dal gave up on the outboard and returned to the oars. Various other words were unintelligible, but judging by the body language it was not a happy situation. We ran down to the pier, intending to jump in our boat and rescue them, but by the time I slackened off our lines I could see their boat coming round the end of the breakwater. Dal was rowing and Maggie still bailing. I looked into the boat – it was only just floating, the water swishing about just below the seats. As they headed for the steps there was a tense silence, no word was spoken, no eyes met, just the slapping of oars and then the scraping as the boat slid alongside the pier. Maggie, soaked from the waist down, jumped ashore and started running up the track towards her house. Dal abandoned the oars, one sliding into the water and the other being squeezed between the boat and the pier. He climbed onto the steps with arms outstretched, giving an expression of complete despair, and shouted up to us, 'You wouldn't believe it, she bailed the bung over the side!'

It was hard not to laugh as Dal nipped up the steps and handed me the bow rope. 'Look after the boat, Alec,' he said, before turning to run up the pier shouting, 'Mags, Mags, I'm sorry,' the cries tapering off as he sped further away.

'That's the end of their boating,' said Simon. I looked at the boat – the water inside was now level with the outside, the floorboards floating beneath the seats. We took the outboard off and, using a piece of stick as a bung, we emptied out the water before hauling the boat up the beach as far as we could manage, knowing it was unlikely to be used again.

Moya turned out to be an excellent cook and unusual in that she rarely used scales or measuring jugs, being able to estimate most quantities by eye. John-Andrew still brought us wild birds to eat and Moya would cook them, but drew the line at puffins. Not intending to waste the dead birds she had been given, she claimed that if she was given more she would cook the birds in pastry with the beaks and feet sticking out to put us off. We were never supplied with them again.

Fish were plentiful from the fishing boats, and occasionally on the Shaalds we would come across a lobster, usually old and rust-coloured which was caused by the iron dissolved from the wreck being taken in by the lobster. We never sold them – that was the fishermen's livelihood – but if taking one did not interfere with our work we would have it for the pot. At one point we had eaten so many that everyone was fed up with them. 'Not lobster again,' was the cry. It reminded me of my mother who was always reluctant to waste food and, when she had fed the family home-grown rhubarb on a very regular basis, my father had said, 'Oh, rhubarb again, how nice.' My mother got the hint.

Moya was always busy as she often helped on the boat and undertook odd jobs for Elizabeth, as well as cooking for whoever happened to be in the Haa. When we had time on our hands we fenced off part of the Haa yard with driftwood and old netting to give her an area to grow vegetables. It was fertilised with seaweed brought up from the beach, before potatoes, onions, peas, radishes, cabbages and lettuces were all planted. She was not sure what would grow – some rhubarb from Fife had failed – but Edith, from Dykes, who had a beautiful garden, gave Moya a root of her rhubarb which flourished, along with many of the vegetables, apart from the ones taken by the birds. Part of an old trawl net that washed up on the rocks helped to reduce the problem, along with some string with short pieces of tape that flapped in the wind. The vegetable supply was varied, and occasionally supplemented by masses of wild mushrooms which appeared on the croft land at the end of July. It was with relief that Simon and I saw the old days of powdered potatoes, tins and other processed foods being banished forever.

Because of our work and lifestyle we were all incredibly fit. I was able to run along the road and do a somersault without touching the ground and, with our hard, physical work when diving we consumed thousands of calories, being able to eat almost any amount of food, or so we thought. With Moya's cooking often including steamed puddings, in particular syrup sponges to make use of our catering tins of syrup that were the size of petrol cans, we both started to put on weight. When Simon began to have a problem fitting into his diving suit Moya reluctantly made the drastic but necessary decision to cut down to only one pudding a day.

Meals were always a familiar time when we discovered it was not always easy being a threesome. Simon occasionally took the opportunity to tease us, asking questions like, 'Alec, are you a man or a mouse?' in a situation where I was hesitating at fetching the salt when Moya looked to be getting it. But it must have been difficult for Simon, being the single party. Moya also made a major contribution to the business, helping on the boat when John-Andrew had work to do on his croft or if we required an extra hand at sea. She enjoyed her non-domestic role, and was good at it, although this brought up other issues as she was better at operating the winch than Simon. But, whatever difficulties occurred, we all made it work without any arguments. It may have been different if we had not been on an island; the whole project ethos might have changed, lacking the way the island naturally bound us together.

The date of the wedding had been known by the islanders for months, but it was traditional that Simon, as best man, should "bid" everyone to it. He would go to each of the households to formally ask the occupants if they would be kind enough to come. It took him a long time as he enjoyed having a cup of tea and a chat in most of the 16 households. There were also islanders who lived on the mainland, only returning for the summer break, bringing the total number of people from island families up to 39. Kitty Manson, at over 90, was the oldest person on the island and unable to manage a trip to the church. She would have to be visited on the day. The Shetland fishermen who worked around Foula and were regular visitors to the Haa were given a general invitation, the crew of the lobster boat *Juna* intending to come with their families.

'It'll have to be reasonable weather to land at the pier,' said Ian, one of the fisherman.

'We don't want it too good,' replied Simon, 'or Alec'll be wanting to work, you know what he's like.'

Simon had spread the rumour that if it was a diving day we would have to fit the wedding in around our work.

Relations and friends were given a verbal invitation. My mother and some of her relations would come, but it was unlikely that my father would make the trip. He was 69 and did not like to leave his home. Foula, he felt, was a bit too inaccessible and there was limited accommodation on the island.

With no regular organist, we asked Bobby Isbister to play. He was not a church goer but was an able musician. As neither of the two harmoniums in the church worked properly, due to the damp and attacks by mice, Bobby and Eric allowed us to take the one from their house. But the mice had also eaten some of its air pipes, resulting in the tunes played being dictated by what Bobby could play and the notes the mice had left intact.

I was never nervous or concerned about getting married. I had not given it a second thought as I knew I would stay with Moya whether married or not. But I did feel the whole tradition was important to both our families, perhaps mine more than Moya's. It was a mark in time, an occasion we would always remember whether it was a big wedding or a small wedding. It was about commitment, the size of the wedding having little bearing on its significance as it was not the guests making the obligation. On the traditional side, it was like turning the boat round with the sun before launching, the Church still having a major role to play in giving communities a sense of continuity.

With 17 days to go, the minister from Walls – the parish that included Foula – phoned Elizabeth to try and contact us. I called him back, concerned that there might be a problem, but it was a simple request for us to go and see him. He explained that Foula only had a missionary who was primarily the teacher and had no additional religious qualifications. In the three years I had already been in Foula there had been three teacher-missionaries, and my Church attendance was minimal, tapering off to near zero after the first few experiences, and if it was good weather we always worked on Sundays. Moya was not a regular church attender, if at all, and had originally been brought up in the Catholic Church. He therefore had good reason to meet us and we agreed to come across the following day if the weather was suitable. With *Trygg* safe in Tayport harbour for the winter we would have to use the inflatable.

The shipping forecast at 6am the next morning issued gale warnings for our area. This was normal for the time of year, but looking out from the Haa we could see the wind was just a light breeze from the east-north-east with a heavy, glassy swell. As we had become accustomed to the weather patterns we decided the gale was unlikely to come before the evening.

Leaving the pier at 7.25 in the morning, Moya and I were well protected in oilskins and life jackets as we started on the trip to Walls. It was a bumpy crossing, the boat jumping off the top of one wave onto the next, but we did not get a soaking. I was well used to the ride but I could see Moya having to concentrate at hanging on as she sat opposite me on the other pontoon for the 55 minutes it lasted. Feeling exhilarated and confident after the trip, we opened the plastic bags in which we stored dry clothes, tidied ourselves, and walked up to the manse to meet the Church of Scotland minister.

The minister was originally from Iceland and experienced with congregations who worked on the sea, giving us a common interest to discuss before easing the conversation into the subject of the wedding service. It was the first wedding in the Foula Kirk for 29 years as the islanders tended to marry on the mainland. He explained that a qualified minister was required and the weather had to be good enough for the aeroplane to bring him in. As an island wag put it – 'if the minister was any good he could walk across'.

The talk was not intense, but he wanted to feel confident we were doing the right thing, not necessarily from a religious standpoint but from the human side; the marriage must be forever. He was brief, as he understood that we had to return before the weather deteriorated, but the warmth of the manse after the cold, bumpy crossing gave us no reason to hurry. I sat there wondering what he thought of us – the older-looking salvage diver and the young girl who had both come across in a 13½-foot inflatable. We were obviously happy, and maybe not taking it as seriously as we ought.

Leaving the manse with his blessing, and no hint of any complications, I felt we had won his approval. We walked up to A.K. Reid's, the grocers, to pick up our "Waas box", before returning to the pier where the oilskins were donned to replace our smarter clothes. We sped through Vaila Sound and headed back to Foula, seeing it sit proudly on the horizon ahead of us, its rugged, rocky outline looking strong and imposing. It was our home and we looked forward to getting back to it. The boat, as if knowing my thoughts, flew gracefully from one wave top to another and with the tide in our favour it helped us arrive at the entrance to the voe five minutes faster than the outward trip. Tying up at the pier at 10.30am, the weather conditions were beginning to deteriorate. Simon, Jim and Rob helped us lift out the inflatable but the sea conditions were now getting too bad to allow the mailboat a safe trip to Walls and back. The gale was going to hit us within the next few hours.

On the 16th of September, Moya finished making her wedding dress. With only eight days to go much of her time was now spent baking. Pat let us use her deep freeze and, with the continual additions of freshly cooked food, she had to run her generator most of the time to freeze it along with food that Shetland fishing boats had dropped off. Our last day of good weather for working was on the 18th, five days before the wedding date. This free time gave me a chance to catch up with all my dirty washing, repair the exhaust on our pickup and spend time on the phone explaining to people about methods of getting to the island. Unfortunately they were all subject to there being reasonable weather as poor sea conditions would prevent any boats from landing, and fog or high winds would stop the aeroplane. The first to arrive was my cousin from Oban. She had married Charlie who was now a school teacher in one of the Shetland Islands. They managed to cross on a fishing boat and had brought a tent with them.

By the 22nd September the wind was strong from the southeast – a poor direction for any boat trying to get into the voe – but the following day the plane managed in with Moya's parents, my mother and some of my relations. Moya had tidied up the Haa as best she could, but my organising aunt appeared and the first thing she said was, 'I see you haven't had time to clean the house. I'll make a start on it,' leaving Moya open mouthed.

On the 24th September, the day of the wedding, there was only a light north-easterly wind, allowing boats to lie at the pier and the aeroplane to land. Everyone on the island had dressed for the occasion and we all looked like strangers, which was disconcerting. With no idea of the exact numbers coming, it was not surprising that the small Islander plane had to make another unplanned run. It caused a slight delay – not that this was ever a problem in Foula – and the final run brought the minister, not the one we had met, but James Blair from the parish the airport was in.

I sat with Simon in the front of the church. No one was concerned about the delay, least of all me. Moya was already waiting with her father in the small vestry at the back. I looked around. The church was completely full and I wondered when it was last so crowded. We could hear the aircraft arriving with its final load of passengers and I stood on my toes to look out of one of the plain glass windows, but I could only see the sky. The plane revved up as it turned on the runway, moving to the dropping-off point before there was silence as the engines stopped. With only a few minutes' walk to the kirk, the minister, the pilot and a few more guests appeared and Simon gave me a nudge and a smile as Bobby, who had been improvising on the organ to fill in the delay, was extending his repertoire to include *You are my Sunshine*.

The minister came forward and Moya was led down the aisle by her father, with Bobby giving the organ as much volume as it would allow.

'Could you please sit?' said the minister when the music stopped, leaving that total silence you find in the country, only broken by cries from a bird. I moved to sit down when Simon checked me by whispering, 'Not you.'

We had already signed the registration documents as Harry, the island registrar, thought it was easier to sign them first. It was only the minister that was left to sign. After the brief ceremony, *For those in Peril on the Sea* was sung before we left the church. The fresh wind took the confetti up towards Hamnafield as two shotguns went off to scare away the devil.

Simon described it as, 'A delightful, informal wedding. The timing was a bit awry, Foula style, and the bride had to wait at the church for half an hour before the last plane load of guests arrived, but nobody seemed to mind. Pilot Ian Ray parked his plane outside the church and came into the service. As the new Mrs

Foula from Walls showing the sea crossing the mailboat makes to supply the island.

Crawford walked down the aisle she gave her bouquet to old Joann, who was so thrilled she could hardly speak.'[58]

We led the procession down to the school, the steady breeze blowing our clothes at odd angles. John-Andrew followed at the rear with our old pickup, with the elderly and infirm sitting on the back when they found the walk too difficult. There was no designated posing for photographs, people just took snaps when they wanted. Entering the school, the tables were laden with food that Moya and many of the islanders had helped to prepare. After some very short speeches, the cake was cut before I helped Moya into the passenger seat of our Morris 1000 pickup, lifting her legs to avoid getting her dress covered in dirt. We laughed. It seemed so odd, the bride being bundled into an old pickup with holes in its floor and dirt all over it – I had never thought of washing it, not in Foula. We drove to the Isbisters' house at the south end where Kitty, the oldest inhabitant, had been moved from her home in the north to be more easily looked after. Walking the last few yards to the house, we knocked on the door and went in to meet a smiling Kitty sitting on the resting chair. The kettle was already

The Foula wedding. Simon, Moya and Alec.

boiling and we had a quick cup of tea as we shared some wedding cake before returning to the celebrations.

In the school the tables were moved back against the walls as Harry and Jim warmed up their fiddles ready for the dancing. The *Shaalds of Foula* was, appropriately, the first dance. With dancing in full swing, those that were leaving by plane later in the afternoon had no need to be concerned about waiting at the airstrip as the pilot was at the party enjoying himself.

At midnight we left the school, changed into our old clothes at the Haa, then walked up to Loch cottage. Elizabeth had suggested we use it for the night as every spare bed in Foula was to be used, including ours. The walk was pleasant and peaceful after the dancing. Occasionally we heard wild hoots and laughter carrying across the island. It was a dry night with a light breeze and we looked down at the lobster boat *Juna* lying peacefully at the pier. Three miles out from her lay the Shaalds and the wreck that had been instrumental in our meeting. At that moment the world held everything for us. We were happy, we were fit, and we were young – the future could not have looked better.

**Blowburn croft in the north where Kitty Manson lived.** *Lesley Timings*

# Chapter 14
# Fife, Farm and Salvage

The following year we lost *Trygg* during a gale. The mooring chain broke and the wooden boat ended up being washed over the top of the Foula pier and was smashed into thousands of pieces. The islanders had warned us about keeping a boat off Foula, but there were no recriminations. Everyone was sad to see the loss and commiserated with us. Simon had been keen to just ship our recoveries and leave the island with the project unfinished but, with John-Andrew and Moya's encouragement, along with that of most of the islanders, he was persuaded to carry on.

We quickly bought another boat, called *Valorous*, after Tom Clark from Shetland had even offered to loan her to us to avoid any delays in our work.

She was a major improvement on *Trygg*, with a greater lifting capability and carrying capacity, as well as being certified with all the legally required paperwork. But we knew if we lost her we would be unlikely to obtain any insurance again for a vessel kept at Foula. The insurers had allowed us to lose one boat without questioning our ability or the conditions in which she was kept, but they were unlikely to let a second go unnoticed. As a result we had to be more careful, which meant leaving the island in plenty time before the weather deteriorated.

Every trip to the Shetland mainland cost us time away from our work and the decision to leave Foula was often left to the last minute, hoping that the wind direction would change and the boat would be safe on her mooring as none of us really wanted to cross the notorious stretch of water to Shetland. As a result we became used to sudden departures and they became a well rehearsed procedure.

If the weather would allow us, we came alongside the pier to pick up fuel drums to be filled at Scalloway or load parts of our equipment requiring repair, but if we delayed our departure until the weather was too bad the conditions at the pier made it impossible to come alongside and we'd have to leave from the mooring. Simon even ran sheep out in the inflatable to lift aboard *Valorous* in bad weather, not a job he enjoyed, particularly when a large wave came rolling over the parapet, filling the inflatable along with the trailer containing the sheep on the pier. There was a rush to secure the sheep before they floated out of the trailer and a sodden Simon was helped aboard *Valorous* along with the last remaining sheep.

We often had islanders with us, looking forward to a few days on the mainland to see relations or to shop, bringing back anything from a tractor, goats, agricultural machinery or something as small as a packet of Tilley lamp mantles. They all had relations and friends on the mainland and were never short of somewhere to stay, although bunks in the boat were always available.

If we were able to bring *Valorous* into the Foula pier I always followed a routine, first going below to check the bilges and start the engine, before climbing up the steep steps to the wheelhouse where I grabbed my cap that I had usually thrown onto the seat. Unclipping the long, leather strap to open a wheelhouse window I would look out to see the deck being prepared for sea before checking the latest gale forecast and noting whether it was imminent and entering it in the log next to the engine start-up time. Simon and John-Andrew would hammer in the last wooden wedges to secure the hatch cover, while Moya took any urgent letters to be posted from Harry and placed them inside the galley door. After the wedges were driven safely home, anyone coming with us would climb down to the deck, or if it was just Moya coming with me, John-Andrew would leave the boat by jumping from the hatch to the wooden rail, and with another bound he stood safely on the pier beside Harry. It always made me smile as I thought of the time we had watched him taking birds from the island cliffs. But Simon, as relaxed as ever, would walk across the deck to find the easiest route onto the pier.

'All ready then?' I would shout from the wheelhouse, checking to see there were no latecomers.

Moya would look round from her position on deck, nod, and walk towards the stern rope. 'OK,' I would shout, as I put the boat slow ahead with the rudder to starboard and watch as Harry threw the stern rope down to her. She'd catch the end, coil it and tie it to the rail on the side of the wheelhouse, before moving to the bow. John-Andrew would throw down another rope. Finally, after the stern of the boat had swung away from the pier, I'd put her astern with hard left rudder, the spring rope leading from the bow to a bollard on the pier near the boat's stern was then thrown aboard. Waiting until the bow had cleared the pier and the stern was about 20 feet from the rocks, I put her full ahead with full right rudder. She would swing round in a graceful curve, clearing the rocks at the entrance to the voe, and head towards the Shetland mainland.

Looking back, I'd see Harry, Simon and John-Andrew watching us, only their heads visible above the parapet – Harry with his wide-brimmed cap, Simon his bobble hat and John-Andrew with his head of thick, dark hair, and sometimes Jim with his head well above the height of the others. Behind them Elizabeth might be running down the track. She occasionally missed us leaving as she tried to write a quick letter or search for a sheepskin or something she wanted to be taken to the mainland during the short notice she would have before we left. On one occasion she was so desperately waving with a parcel tucked under her arm that I nudged back to the pier to pick it up. Otherwise, if the weather was too bad to come back in, I'd take my cap off and use it to give her a friendly wave. She would stop running and wave back, with old Tom behind her enjoying the spectacle.

Moving away from the shelter of the island, a long swell increased the movement of the boat. Moya took over the wheel while I checked the engine room. The trip would take 3½ hours and, with an imminent gale warning, we could not afford the engine to stop through negligence. With just the two of us it would be harder to cope with any major problems. Returning to the wheelhouse we sat together on the wooden bench, my knee pressed against the wheel to keep a steady course. It was nice to be on our own, the rhythm from the diesel engine sounding steady and reassuring.

It was like breaking a bond when we left the island, being torn away from the Haa, and yet we looked forward to reaching Scalloway in the anticipation of pleasure at the thought of landing there. We could shed the worry of the bad weather and look forward to taking on fuel and fresh stores and enjoy meeting

**The remains of *Trygg* came over the pier after she broke up on the rocks**

everyone at the harbour. We would hear their news, enjoy the bustle of busy lives, buy fresh treats from the bakery and then visit the bookshop and other shops in nearby Lerwick.

Moya stood up after a while, intending to bring some coffee, but stopped to look at my cap. 'We should see about buying you another when we're on the mainland.'

'Mmm,' I said with a smile, with no intention of replacing an old favourite. I'd had it a few years and grown used to it.

We then discussed the long shopping list that detailed our own requirements and also included requests. Beside each item on the list had been written the name of the shop where we could purchase it. I started to look down the list:

Mantles and a cast iron griddle – Stove and Smith.

Two copies of *The Shetland Times* – The Shetland Times Bookshop.

We required a new tide table and I had been told they were published by Harry, the barber, in Lerwick. I wrote it down.

Moya added, 'Cap from the clothing shop.' I looked at her with a look that said *never*, but before I had time to blink the cap had been whipped off my

Moya beside the largest remaining piece of *Trygg* that had been washed up the Ham burn

head and thrown out of the open wheelhouse window. It soared in the air as it caught the wind, then I felt relief as it looked as if it was going to be blown back onto the deck. I cut the throttle and raced out only to see it land on the water, ten feet away from the boat. I watched the oil slick trailing behind it as it drifted astern with two fulmars diving and circling around, checking to see if it was edible. Disappointed, they flew back to join the other birds perched on our foremast.

Moya was smiling as she pushed the throttle forward to increase the speed again. I feigned being cross, then I looked at my jacket that had oil stains on the cuffs, zipping it up firmly and noticeably, secure in the thought that there was no way that it could be thrown over the side.

Our peace was regularly broken by voices on the VHF radio, kept on channel 16 which was the watch channel to listen for anyone in trouble as well as being used to make initial contact with a ship or harbour.

'We're making the right decision,' I said. We looked at each other, the remoteness of the sea, with dark clouds forming all around us as if we were being separated from the rest of the world, conveying an intimate feeling of being the only two people left. An easy silence fell over us, neither of us wanting to speak.

'I expect it'll hit us hard tonight,' said Moya, finally breaking the spell.

'The pier'll be packed with boats.'

'We'll get a berth all right?' she asked.

'There's always been space before.'

Moya went through to the back of the wheelhouse. I could hear her put the kettle on a gas ring and open a cupboard to find a loaf she had cooked in the Haa. Five minutes later she returned carrying two fresh mugs of coffee and a plate with two pieces of bread thickly coated with jam. Steadying herself with her elbows as she came through the door before pushing it shut with her foot, I took the cups and put them on a small shelf with a fiddle that prevented them from slipping off.

The rolling increased and water began to slop over the deck. I could feel the boat being lifted and pushed forward by the increasing swell on our stern. Clearly visible ahead were the small islands we had to weave through on the approach to Scalloway. Today the two of us were enjoying the isolation of the trip; we were in no hurry but the time passed quickly and the entrance to the south channel unexpectedly opened up ahead of us. As the full gale would soon be on us, I lined up "meids" to check that I was not going to go over a shallow reef between the islands, and rechecked the radar to confirm our position. I thought of the Foula mailboat which had no aids other than a compass, not even a radio. Jim was frequently overcautious about leaving on a mailboat trip, but the more that I had seen of the island weather and the condition of the boat, I knew he was often right.

We watched the sheep grazing on the small islands, undeterred by the increasing wind. A small lobster boat with a load of creels on its deck was hurrying to lift a fleet that still lay outwith the shelter of the islands. I wondered if there were any scallops; it would be fun to dive and have a look, maybe get some for a meal.

The pier was soon opening up in front of us. We could see a spare berth at the sheltered side and headed for it. Moya untied the ropes and threw over some fenders, tying bowlines in the end of the mooring ropes with a loop big enough for the Scalloway bollards. I smiled as I watched, so pleased we had met. Ahead of us on the pier lay fresh interests to captivate us in the visible activity of a working port; part of the pleasure, I thought, was the contrast with Foula.

After securing the boat we walked up to visit Bessie and Peter, one of the many Foula families who'd moved off the island. Although living in Scalloway, I always felt their hearts remained in Foula, but I understood why they'd left to give their family all the opportunities the mainland provided. We felt they treated us as family, and yet we were no relation. Their children were in good jobs and had a positive future ahead of them; they were unlikely to return permanently to the island. Apart from the pleasure of being on it, there was nothing for them, and Scalloway was a good place. I would be happy to live there.

When we returned to the harbour late in the evening it was blowing well above gale force. The sky was black with cloud as we ran hand in hand the last hundred yards to the boat, managing to reach the shelter of the galley before the light, wind-blown rain became a downpour. Three vessels had tied outside us – the small harbour still filling up as the wind strengthened – and slipping into one of the bunks we listened to the footfalls of fishermen walking across the deck above us as they tied up their boats and returned home. Left with only the noise of the fenders rubbing as the boats moved in the sheltered motion, we were otherwise at peace for the night, feeling safe and secure as the gale blew itself out above us. This was part and parcel of living in Foula and I loved it.

Next day I bought a new cap – not under duress, but under guidance.

Back on the island, 'Of course we'll do it,' I said to Elizabeth. It was not a difficult decision. Moya and I had realised how important it was for her and the other islanders, but Elizabeth still had to get permission from the relatives and would let us know. Walking to the Haa I was relaxed. I knew Simon would agree, and if he wanted to do something else or stay on the island I could easily get an islander to go with me.

Elizabeth's concern was well meant. It was not as if Tom was a popular person, or even particularly liked, in fact he was rarely spoken to, just acknowledged with a nod or a brief, 'Aye aye, Tom.'

Because he was always on his own, I had asked John-Andrew during our first year on the island, 'Why doesn't he spend some time with Elizabeth as she's his neighbour?'

'He's been trying to get his feet under Elizabeth's table most of his life,' laughed John-Andrew, 'but she'll have nothing to do with the old man.'

But now, she and others thought he should come back to the island. I understood the reason, but was open minded. Apart from him intercepting us at the pier, and as we carried our washing to the burn when the walk was of sufficient length that he had time to recite the news headlines as well as the weather forecast, we'd had no real personal contact with him. Sometimes he made amusing remarks as he renamed names – every time he did it I could see by a slight smile on his old face that it was deliberate – like his sighting of Kohiti's comet which became Kohooter's comet. But he did show himself willing to assist in any way he was able, and when we were in need of an old-fashioned, heavy soldering bolt to repair a copper pipe Tom became excited that he could help. He quickened his pace up the road before disappearing into his blacksmith's workshop, reappearing with a smile and a beautifully-made, wooden-handled, copper soldering bolt which could be heated red hot on our fire. It was perfect for the job.

Each year Rob, Simon and I had cut his peats and later raised them to allow them to dry. As he did not require many we found it an enjoyable task, and so did Tom, who sat on his haunches opposite us with his unlit pipe in his hand giving a recitation on old island habits – like "lug bengie", where you grabbed someone and held them by their ear. Equally keen on attaching himself to visitors, he found them more tolerant than us. We had watched him latch on to two American ladies from Boston who later escaped from him by going across rough ground. The next time I saw him, I asked about the ladies.

'I'll tell thee,' he started, 'yon short een's a fair wife.'

'What about the tall one?' I asked.

'Man, she's that tall she'd ging well we a sail,' he replied, with a big smile.

He sometimes gave us eggs from his few hens. I thought that he could hardly spare them but he insisted we take them. It should have been obvious to us how lonely he was, but my young brain was too busy with my own life and gave little thought to Tom's troubles. During August the previous year the girls had baked him a cake for his birthday and we bought a pouch of tobacco for him. They gave it to him on the road where he was easily found. He shook his head in a sign of grateful thanks, hardly able to speak. Putting the tobacco and pipe in his pocket he carefully cupped the cake with its single candle in both his hands. We watched him walk slowly towards his croft, still shaking his head, with an occasional smile enhanced by the odd tear running down his unshaven cheek.

Over time we became more patient until one day he was finally granted his lifetime wish. Simon and I were walking towards Ham when we found him lying on his back on the road. We bent down to check he was alive. His head moved first, then his mouth. I bent closer to hear what I thought to be his last words. I faintly caught, 'I'll tell thee, I'll tell thee … King Hussein an' yon Arabs, their …' it trailed off, but I knew he was repeating the morning news headlines. We carefully stood him up and with one of us either side carried him to the warmth of Ham and Elizabeth's care while we waited for the nurse. Tom had at last got his feet under the Ham table and along with Joann he remained in Ham to be looked after by Elizabeth.

Recovering sufficiently to occasionally walk out of Elizabeth's earshot, where he continued his recitals, he was restricted in the distance he could travel so would rarely manage the pier. Later, he began to deteriorate and was advised by the nurse to visit the hospital for tests. Elizabeth had washed him, shaved him and cleaned him to the extent that when he left to go on the plane he brandished a stick in one hand and looked as though he was a Highland laird.

It was possibly one of the few times he had been off the island, but definitely the final, as he passed away in the hospital. He was the last of his family on the island, the name Umphray after hundreds of years would be lost to Foula, like two other names we had seen die out in the last few years – the Henrys and Mansons.

Tom's nearest family wished to bury him on the Shetland mainland where they all lived, but many from Foula wanted him buried on the island. I could understand, as the older islanders not only wanted to spend their lives there but also to be assured they would remain for eternity. I wondered if the next elderly person who became ill would refuse to leave the island.

Our offer to Elizabeth to return Tom's body on our boat, at no cost, had been declined. At least Tom didn't have to worry about it.

The population was gradually increasing. John and Isobel, who had lived on the island and had broken marriages, returned during our time there and, with the addition of the Smiths and their family, Annette and Sam along with John-Andrew's two children and Rob's first son, it appeared like a new spring coming. Part of this was balanced by the loss of older folk but it was reassuring that the children would secure the survival of the school, an important part of the island life as it brought a teacher, often with a partner. The noise of children playing, seeing them look for trout in the burn or helping with peats, gave a visible and audible permanence to the population. Although Simon complained there were still too few for a football team.

The islanders encouraged the Smiths to stay, the landlords first offering Sam and Annette the disused shop to repair and live in and, later, Harry showing his usual concern for the island, letting them have Veedal croft on which they could restore the old croft house as Sam had proved himself able to manage practically any type of work.

John-Andrew came and stayed briefly with us in Fife during the winter, before the next season started, in order that we could go on a road trip round various fishing ports to look at the boats advertised for sale. He was looking for an affordable boat small enough to lift out with the Foula crane, but of sufficient size to make an income from lobsters and supply his family with fish. He had saved up for the boat and I knew how valuable the money was to him and how the boat could be the key to his staying on the island – he was looking for more in life than mere survival. We all knew the work on the *Oceanic* would not last much longer and he and his wife Francie had their two young daughters, Amy and Moira, to support. His parents also lived on the island and he had to go down most mornings to help his infirm mother out of bed as she was crippled with arthritis. I remembered her sitting happily but almost tearful at our wedding when she told me how she used to love dancing but now she had come to the stage where she had to be helped out of a chair. Foula was not a good place to have health issues.

John-Andrew chose a nearly new boat that lay in Whitby. Its design was practical with a good beam and a square stern that would increase her carrying capacity. She also had very slight tumblehome, where the top plank sloped in towards the centreline of the boat, as opposed to most boats where it was vertical or sloped out the way. This gave the boat an attractive and distinctive look and, with its modern diesel engine, she was reasonably fast and highly manoeuvrable, making her ideal for working around the rocks and cliffs off Foula. He called her *Lively*. While in Fife he took the opportunity to obtain lorry axles and some steel from a scrapyard in order to construct a trailer. He could then use the existing Foula crane to take out the boat and haul it safely up the pier.

Delivered on a lorry to Tayport Harbour, we lifted *Lively* onto the *Valorous'* deck. With our usual full load of salvage equipment and various bits for Foula, along with several tons of mooring chain for Fair Isle, we set off from Tayport in a thick fog, relying on our radar to guide us safely out the river.

Reaching Fair Isle the following afternoon, after 26 hours at sea, the visibility had become perfect but the wind backed to the north, a bad direction for lying at the North Haven pier as the swell caused the boat to range, making it chew on its ropes as it moved backwards and forwards. We lifted John-Andrew's boat into the water to get access to the chain in the hold for the Fair Isle mooring.

The following morning the weather was good and John-Andrew made a decision. 'I'll just take the boat to Foula myself,' he said, 'it'll give her a good run and I'll see if there's anything wrong.'

'If you set off an hour and a half before us, we'll catch you up if you break down,' I replied, as I handed him some flares from *Valorous*.

'Mind, you're not to pinch any Fair Isle lobsters on the way,' shouted Simon as John-Andrew pulled away from the pier, knowing it would create amusement amongst the Fair Islanders. We waited before leaving and, after clearing the tidal rips around the island, it became a beautiful, calm day.

'Do you think we'll see John-Andrew if he breaks down?' asked Simon

'Easily,' I replied. 'He'll run a good course with the compass he has.'

I made a slight correction to our course after lining up points on the island to check the magnetic compass – its reading had altered noticeably after we unloaded all the chain and laid the steel derrick on the hatch.

'I hope he can make a living. Sam's keen to work with him,' said Simon.

'It'll be like all the islanders, the boat might provide part of his earnings but he'll still need the croft and other work to ensure he can stay on the island.' I thought of the winter where the weather made it almost impossible to work on anything outside for weeks at a time. His boat would have to lie on its trailer, well clear of the sea, for nearly seven months of the year, unable to generate any income.

I turned back to Simon. I always enjoyed chatting on the boat, there was an honesty, almost intimacy in the conversation. 'I hear there's a rumour that the Shetland council may provide a new mailboat. That'd make a difference.'

'It might help the island but there're still no places for people to stay, no shop or other means for the island to generate cash.'

'If a new boat could provide a regular and reliable service John-Andrew might try for work off the island in the winter. He could work for a contractor, even get diving work,' I replied, 'as long as he could guarantee getting time at home.'

I thought of young Davie who had left school at 16. There was no work for him on the island. He would probably get a job on a Shetland fishing boat where the money he earned would give him the opportunity to return to the island at some later stage – or stay on the mainland. It was nearly always determined by the partner he might settle with. Ken, Davie's father, was 40 now. They said he had been given a scholarship to a well-known Scottish private school but declined it in favour of staying on the island. Although the sentiment was good the result was not; he was always bored and restless when on the island and, as a result, spent most of his time on the Shetland mainland.

'What are you thinking about?' asked Simon.

'Ken,' I replied. 'What do you think he would have done if he had taken up the scholarship?'

'He could've done anything, one of his brothers is a teacher.'

'They're probably right when they say if you educate someone they're more likely to leave the island. The only professional jobs on the island are the teacher and the nurse, neither job's particularly suitable when you're related to everyone.'

But recently Ken had seemed more settled. He was changing, perhaps realising he had to get his act together and move away from his childhood ties.

'D'you think the Smiths'll stay?' I asked.

'Surely Sam and Annette will, but I can't see Pat and John staying. Pat seems so unhappy, although grandchildren might keep her there. The winters will be the tipping point.'

We arrived at Foula before John-Andrew. He had been slowed down by a problem with his rudder that in typical fashion he had fixed at sea before following us in. The islanders helped unload our stores and general assortment of goods while Simon used John-Andrew's new boat as a platform for diving to prepare our mooring for *Valorous*.

The following day I left with *Valorous* for Scalloway to pick up Moya who had come north on the ferry. We sailed for Foula the next afternoon, taking Sam with us who had been out on the mainland buying bits and pieces for the island, including some goats. He was looking forward to working with John-Andrew on his new boat.

The days when we had time to walk round the island were diminishing and my dreams of staying were long past. I was a realist – Foula was not for us in the long term, it was time we shaped our own lives. At the end of our final summer we left like the birds, migrating south to a different existence. A job that we originally thought might take a summer or two had kept us on the island for six years. I had no doubt that we carried out the work more thoroughly than was commercially necessary because we had enjoyed the island and wished to remain on it for as long as possible. Meeting Moya had changed my life; both financially and personally we had benefitted from our work.

The island seemed particularly busy that last summer with island relations coming in to help with general work on the crofts, and Jim was building a new shed. Simon had found a girlfriend in Dundee called Alison, who came to Foula to stay with us, enjoying our unusual lifestyle. At the Ham beach the brother of a Shetland photographer had started strengthening the remains of the oldest surviving Foula mailboat, a sixern, in preparation for lifting it onto the council flit boat *Spes Clara*. It was rumoured that he intended to use the hull as a roof on his garage on the Shetland mainland. Many an eyebrow was lifted and knowledgeable tips given about how it should be done, but there was a total disbelief in Foula that someone was going to use it as a garage roof when there were so many good alternative materials available to them. Elizabeth was not shy in putting her pennyworth into the ring, while Simon and I thought

John-Andrew in his newly arrived boat with Sam at the bow. Ken is behind with his yoal *Friendly*.

the boat was more likely to be an exhibit. But did this give the signal that the future of Foula was just a case of preserving the past?

The Smiths appeared settled. Sam and Annette were content, Sam working with John-Andrew on his boat, and there was still talk of a new mailboat and improvements to the pier. Life was definitely looking up.

The only obvious project in Foula would be the building of a hostel, but I'm sure it would have been met with many objections as change is in most places. I'd have enjoyed building it, but running it was not for me and certainly not for Moya. Although our way of life had evolved on the island, and we both felt it was unique, it had relied on us having the challenging work on the wreck. We wanted to achieve something together in salvage and Foula was not the place from which we could do it. With Moya as partner, best friend and soulmate my world had become far more discerning and we were now planning a new base for our salvage business on a small farm in Fife. But I still had twinges of regret every time I saw the ruins of Sloag.

When we started to pack up our equipment I could feel our lives already changing. Simon, too, had started to discuss some of his ideas and ambitions

Moya and Alec in Fife, 2001.

– running a pub in St Andrews was at the top of his list, and an islander was heard to say, 'Simon was only intending to swap one side of the bar for the other.' It was a decision that was enabled by our success on the *Oceanic*. We all knew Simon would be excellent in that role. Later he was to marry the author Alison McLeay in the Roxburgh kirk that was in his late father's parish in the Scottish borders.

As the time to leave approached, talking about life away from the island was becoming exciting as we saw new opportunities opening up. But I still felt sad. I had loved working on the island and knew I would miss it, most of all the people. They were a disparate lot, but so was I.

# Epilogue

Love of a place often becomes less passionate over time as the head gradually overrules the heart and new places and people take their place. But Foula was not lost to us. Young Bobby Gear came south to stay with us to learn and see farming methods, and later John-Andrew and Sam fitted out a steel trawler in our marine salvage workshop while living in a caravan plumbed into our home.

On a return visit to the island I could see that large investments had been made: a mains electricity supply was installed using solar, wind, batteries, water turbine and a stand-by diesel generator. But the wind turbines proved a problem – possibly because of the number of them required – as they said there was a limit on their individual size due to bird kill. There were also issues of having such sophisticated equipment with no immediate access to a person who has the knowledge to repair it.

From my own experience on the island, a state-of-the-art water supply was the most important improvement. The council also constructed a beautiful new school, and extended the pier, benefitting both the new mailboat and the small tenders from cruise ships by giving them sufficient water at all states of the tide to discharge their passengers. Scheduled flights were introduced with the gravel airfield upgraded to comply with the latest regulations. All these works, along with their running and maintenance, generated a number of part-time jobs. The island was gradually moving away from its tradition of producing fish and agricultural produce to becoming a service industry.

I was disappointed by the remains of broken boats, cars and machinery that lay around, particularly down near the pier. In the past those bits and pieces, including old boats, were unusable but whole. To me at the time they were an attraction, but now I felt much of the scrap kept as "spare parts" was just rubbish, of no use or interest to anyone, and would be better removed. The old school and Harry's post office were no longer used and had fallen into disrepair. As these were in the heart of the island, next to the road, they combined with the debris to make the island look unloved and uncared for. Sadly, it was remarked on by other visitors.

The Smiths and Davises had left for the Shetland mainland, but Brian and Marion from Edinburgh replaced them and they had the energy and ability to build some chalets for guests, as well as building a new home from which they could run a boarding house. Jim and Sheila, and John-Andrew's daughter Amy, had built new homes, and one had also been built by Dal who now lived on his own.

John Holbourn and Isobel, who had left just before we arrived, returned to build a new house in the north end and gradually settled back into island life. Isobel devoted most of her time to the island. Apart from writing and broadcasting she was very active in the community as a member of the Foula Heritage Trust, the Foula Airstrip Trust and the Foula Electricity Trust, also being elected to Scottish Natural Heritage north area board.

By 2019 the population was 38, with many enthusiastic young who were mainly the families of my generation, and they in turn had children. It had become a busy place in the summer with an increased number of visitors, brought by the regular flights and cruise ships, now having the choice of being shown round the island to see peat being cut and old crofting ways explained, along with learning the names of plants and birds.

I thought back to the past generation – Harry, Elizabeth, Joann, the Isbisters, Jock Ratter, and old Tom. Some of my generation had also died: the two Holbourn boys – John and Rob, and Ken Gear and Isobel. Unfortunately, a tragic fishing accident had robbed them of one son, Davie.

But life was more comfortable now, conditions were better and the island had moved away from nature's gifts and become more reliant on regular income. Perhaps, like us all who think we are independent and live with an irregular income, it may be inevitable that we become swept into the arms of those who can supply regular wages. It is, after all, survival that counts in the end.

But the kindness of the islanders still blossoms and, on my arrival in 2012 with my daughter Rachel, I was met by Penny, who I remember from her christening. She was driving the fire truck when we landed and immediately asked if Rachel would like to come with her and her family to the Sneck of the Smaalie. Later, on a beautiful Foula evening, a group of the young – Bobby, Kenny, Fran and Magnie – took Rachel round the island in their late father Ken's yoal, *Friendly*, which had been attractively restored in its traditional style. The following day Kevin – Jim and Sheila's son – along with Bobby and Kenny took her out lobster fishing. This was still the old Foula I knew.

Each generation changes and I know I have changed after all those years. But I still love the island and every time I think about it I smile.

# Bibliography

1     *The Shetland Times*, Dr Edward Westermarck, July 29th 1899

2     *Scotsman*, July 31st 1889

3     *The Shetland Times*, August 4th 1900

4     *The Isle of Foula*, Holbourn 1938

5     *The Shetland Times*, July 28th 1883

6     *The Shetland Times*, September 21st 1889

7     *Pride and Prejudice*, Jane Austen

8     *Tales of Foula*, Robert Isbister

9     *The Shetland Times*, Truck laws, October 6th 1883

10    *Peoples Journal*, April 11th 1892

11    *Travels in Shetland 1832-52*, Edward Charlton

12    *The Orkneys and Shetlands*, John R. Tudor 1883

13    *Shetland*, Robert Cowie 1879

14    *The Shetland Times*, May 26th 1888

15  *Log of the Blue Dragon*, 11, Lynam 1909-1910

16  *The Shetland Times*, November 14th 1885

17  *The Shetland Times*, January 21st 1905

18  *The Shetland Times*, September 26th 1907

19  *The Shetland Bus*, David Howarth

20  *Press and Journal*, July 12th 1948

21  The *Scotsman*, November 19th 1931

22  *The Shetland Times*, February 28th 1903

23  The Shetland Isles, Nicolson 1978

24  *Ocean Liners of the Past*, Olympic and Titanic, Patrick Stephens Ltd 1970

25  *Memoirs of the Wernerian Natural History Society*, Vol 4, Part 1, Capt Vetch Royal Engineers, July 1821

26  "The Agriculture of the Shetland Isles", Henry Evershed, Evening Telegraph, February 20th 1892

27  *A tour through the islands of Orkney and Shetland* (Intr. Anderson), George Low 1774

28  *Evening Telegraph*, February 15th 1892

29  *Glasgow Herald*, December 24th 1904

30  *Glasgow Herald*, August 8th 1884

31  *Glasgow Herald*, August 8th 1884

32  *Dundee Advertiser*, November 24th 1883

33  *The Shetland Times*, October 13th 1883

34  *Peoples Journal*, February 13th 1892

35  *Ladies Journal*, October 3rd 1891

36  1st Statistical account 1790's

37  *200,000 feet on Foula*, Powell 1938

38  *Foula the Time of My Life 1954-55*, Chris Milne

39  A brief description of Orkney, Shetland, Pightland Firth and Caithness, John Brand 1700

40  A view of the ancient and present state of the Zetland islands, Arthur Edmondson Vol 2 1809

41  Library of Congress, Emigration and Relocation in U.S. History. Love of Country, Madeleine Bunting

42  *Shield Daily News*, March 20th 1899

43  *Evening Express*, February 18th 1975

44  *St Kilda*, Tom Steel

45    *Description of the Shetland Isles*, Samuel Hibbert 1822

46    *The Shetland Times*, Cliff fall, June 13th 1885

47    Effects of Great Skuas on Arctic Skuas in Shetland, Robert Furness

48    The Great Skua in Foula, Zoologist (1890): 297-301, R.M. Barrington 1890

49    The Arctic Skua project on Fair Isle, J. Davis and P. O'Donald 1973

50    *The Dundee Advertiser*, Monday July 2nd 1894

51    *Peoples Journal*, July 2nd 1894

52    *Press and Journal*, October 1990

53    *The Shetland Times*, October 27th 1888

54    *Press and Journal*, June 5th 1972

55    *The Shetland Times*, "Henrietta rescue", December 29th 1883

56    *The Shetland Times*, July 15th 1899

57    *Press and Journal*, April 20th 1946

58    *The Other Titanic*, Simon Martin 1980


## Other references

2nd Statistical account 1834-1845

*Dundee Advertiser*, September 9th 1898

*The Shetland Isles*, Cluness 1951

*The Shetland Fishing Saga*, C.A. Goodlad 1971

*Island West of the Sun*, Sheila Gear 1983

*Deep Water*, Moya Crawford 1999

The making of the crofting community, James Hunter

Lusitania Resource

*Treasure Islands*, Alec Crawford

# Acknowledgements

I wish to thank 'the Foula folk' and those associated with the island that made it possible for us to have an extraordinary time on the island and who unknowingly contributed to some of the most important decisions in my life.

In writing the book I had the help of Jonathan Miller for his forensic correcting of the manuscript and his help in guiding me in the right direction.

I am also grateful to the National Library of Scotland for the free use of their vast archives for research, and for their permission to reproduce the outline for the map of Foula.

The British Newspaper Archive was a unique asset in providing access to the papers used for research.

BV - #0111 - 151122 - C42 - 240/165/14 - PB - 9600416000086 - Matt Lamination